W9-BFU-789

3 1611 00034 8232

The ABCs of
Learning Disabilities

The ABCs of
Learning Disabilities

Bernice Y. L. Wong

Faculty of Education
Simon Fraser University
Burnaby, British Columbia
Canada

GOVERNORS STATE UNIVERSITY
UNIVERSITY PARK
IL 60466

Academic Press

San Diego   New York   Boston   London   Sydney   Tokyo   Toronto

LC 4704 .W645 1996

Wong, Bernice Y. L.

The ABCs of learning
  disabilities

Cover image © 1996 PhotoDisc Inc.

Find Us on the Web! http://www.apnet.com

This book is printed on acid-free paper. ∞

Copyright © 1996 by ACADEMIC PRESS, INC.

All Rights Reserved.
No part of this publication may be reproduced or transmitted in any form or by any
means, electronic or mechanical, including photocopy, recording, or any information
storage and retrieval system, without permission in writing from the publisher.

Academic Press, Inc.
A Division of Harcourt Brace & Company
525 B Street, Suite 1900, San Diego, California 92101-4495

United Kingdom Edition published by
Academic Press Limited
24-28 Oval Road, London NW1 7DX

Library of Congress Cataloging-in-Publication Data

Wong, Bernice Y. L.
    The ABCs of learning disabilities / by Bernice Y. L. Wong.
        p.   cm.
    Includes bibliographical references and index.
    ISBN 0-12-762545-3 (alk. paper)
    1. Learning disabled children--Education.   2. Learning
disabilities.   3. Learning disabilities--Research.   4. Language
arts.   5. Mathematics--Study and teaching.   I. Title.
LC4704.W645   1996
371.91--dc20   96-33787
                                                      CIP

PRINTED IN THE UNITED STATES OF AMERICA
96 97 98 99   00   01 BC   9 8   7 6   5   4 3 2 1

To my husband, Rod, and daughter, Kristi

Contents

2

Defining Learning Disabilities

3

An Overview on Subtyping Research in Learning Disabilities

4

Research on Memory Processes in Children with Learning Disabilities

5

Social Aspects of Learning Disabilities

6

Metacognition and Learning Disabilities

7

Informal Assessment of Reading Problems

8

Arithmetic and Mathematics and Students with Learning Disabilities

9

Assessment and Instruction of Writing Skills

10

Epilogue

Preface

I never intended to write an entire book on learning disabilities by myself. Hitherto I had been content to produce edited treatises to which my friends and esteemed colleagues had generously donated their time and energy. It was my spouse, R.W., who egged me on in his quiet way to write my own book. I marvel at his unwarranted confidence in me. When I protested behind a shield of genuine self-doubt, Judge Wong (as I dub him) would say jauntily, "You can do it!" So I succumbed to his influence again! Blast!

I'm afraid I cannot say as yet what kind of experience writing this book has been for me. All I know is that I thought perseverance was within my character or personality until writing this book revealed to me that I barely have enough of it to complete my task! The adjective *mortified* does not come close to expressing my feelings with this self-discovery! Well, I shall not indulge in any more self-reflections, even though such a statement sounds inconsistent or blasphemous for someone who writes on metacognition (and learning disabilities)!

In a more serious vein, I did enjoy the actual process of writing: I delighted in trying to find the most felicitous words to express my thoughts. I tried to emulate my friend and esteemed colleague Ruth Garner's writing style: limpid prose sprinkled with excellent choice of words. However, I have a long way to go to perfect my prose. For now, I simply concentrate on enjoying my efforts to reach my goal.

I bring to this book my experience as an undergraduate teacher. I chose to focus equally on imparting knowledge, as well as enabling students to see the big picture, and on thinking about implications of conceptual issues and research data. Often undergraduate students learn details about cited studies without registering the rationales for them. Because of insufficient thought, they cannot draw implications for theory and future research from what they read. Knowing their youthful propensities toward absorbing facts and forgetting that there is life beyond multiple-choice exams, I take care in this book to ensure that they get the big picture and exercise their brain cells.

I have been greatly helped in my writing by consulting some recent books: Janet Lerner's (1994) *Learning Disabilities: Theories, Diagnosers and Teaching Strategies,* Dan Hallahan and Jim Kauffman's (1994) excellent book *Introduction to Special Education,* Don Hammill and Nettie Bartel's (1995) *Teaching Students with Learning and Behavior Problems,* and Richard Conte's (1991) chapter on attention deficit disorder. Richard was most helpful in e-mailing me a list of references on the comorbidity of attention deficit–hyperactivity disorder (ADHD) and learning disabilities (LD).

There are certain individuals to whom I owe a particular "thank-you." I thank my very good friend and much esteemed colleague, J. K. Torgesen for his help and advice, which are always generously given. I cannot thank him enough for his guidance and his critical review of the first draft of the chapter on memory processes in children with LD. I thank my cherished friends Tanis and Jim Bryan for their constant warmth, support, and wonderful hospitality; and Barbara Keogh, whose insight and acumen in conceptual issues and research in learning disabilities have had a profound impact upon me, and whose cordiality I much appreciate. I also thank the staff at Academic Press, in particular, Barbara Curtis, Eileen Favorite, Nikki Fine, and Rebecca Orbegoso.

Last but not least, I thank Mrs. Eileen Mallory for all her help in wordprocessing the 10 chapters in this book. Eileen, thank you so much for working so fast on the chapters and delivering revised chapters so promptly. Above all, thank you for your interest in my book, and your cheerful smiles and encouragement on days when Wong was beginning to think her book a millstone round her neck!

To the Student,

Learning disabilities is a term for a complex phenomenon. In this book, I have tried to (1) explain the meaning of learning disabilities; (2) describe the characteristics of individuals with learning disabilities; (3) review current research on the topic; and (4) teach informal assessment and remediation of academic learning disabilities.

I have not set out to write the perfect text on learning disabilities, but I did try to write about this topic in a more personal manner to better communicate with you. I hope you enjoy reading this book, and at the end of each chapter think a little about what you have read. It is my sincere wish that you enjoy learning about learning disabilities, and that you engage in active thinking about what you've learned.

Cheers!
Bernice Y. L. Wong

P.S. In journals about learning disabilities, the proper way of describing individuals with this cognitive problem is *individuals with learning disabilities*. In my writing, you will find that about 15% of the time, I refer to them as *learning-disabled individuals*. This occurs whenever I consider using the proper way of description, individuals with learning disabilities, produces an awkward or unduly long sentence. Awkward and lengthy sentences impair your reading comprehension. Hence, I choose to avoid them at all costs. In short, I bucked a mainstreamed, sanctioned writing style for pedagogic reasons. So be advised of my occasional inconsistency here.

History of Learning Disabilities

Emergence of the Learning Disabilities Field: Immediate Circumstances

Most of you would be amazed to realize that the learning disabilities field is only thirty-odd years old! Officially, the learning disabilities field became organized only in 1963 and was recognized as a division of the international organization of special education, the International Council for Exceptional Children, in 1965. But within these thirty-odd years, this field literally grew by leaps and bounds. I will elaborate on this rapid growth later on. For now, I shall focus on the immediate circumstances that led to the birth of the learning disabilities field.

Again, you may be amazed to learn about the unexpected, impromptu circumstances of the birth of the learning disabilities field. Picture this scenario. A group of parents held a meeting in a hotel in Chicago in 1963. These were not your ordinary parents. They all shared a rather unique problem and a disturbing concern; namely, they all had a young child who for no apparent reason was failing to learn to read. Most of these children were boys. These parents met to vent their frustrations with two major sources: First, doctors, neurologists, and psychologists were confusing them by providing hard-to-understand information about the reasons for their young children's failure to learn to read. These specialists threw out such terms

1

as *brain-injured* or *minimal brain dysfunction,* terms that these parents naturally found very aversive. Second, the parents could not access appropriate educational services for their children's reading difficulties because the latter's failure to learn to read cannot be readily categorized into existent categories of special education, such as the mentally retarded, the deaf, the blind, multiply handicapped, and so forth. In the United States, a child could not receive government-funded special assistance in school unless he or she fit into one of those established special education categories.

Attending the meeting was Samuel Kirk, a psychologist who had worked with children with language disabilities and with mentally retarded children for many years. He understood the parents' frustrations because he had encountered and worked with children who showed the same characteristics as the children of these parents. Kirk comforted these parents by informing them that their children were not deaf or blind, nor were they mentally retarded. He pointed out an intriguing aspect about them, one that baffles not only parents and teachers, but also specialists such as doctors, neurologists, psychologists, and psychiatrists. This intriguing aspect concerns their inexplicable difficulties in learning to read, in the face of adequate intelligence, intact sensory capacities (in seeing and hearing), supportive homes, and the educational opportunities offered in any traditional classroom.

Simultaneously, Kirk understood the futility of medically oriented terms such as *brain-injured* and *minimal brain dysfunction.* These labels served no useful explanatory functions for parents and educators. To help parents derive a more constructive concept of their children's problems in learning to read, Kirk proposed the term *learning disabilities.* This term extracted the children's problems in learning to read from the web of confusing terminologies that revolve around brain damage. It directed attention to the source of the children's cognitive problems.

Kirk's astuteness in coining the term is obvious. The parents unanimously adopted it and at that meeting immediately formed the parent organization of the Association of Children with Learning Disabilities (ACLD). This organization spearheaded sister chapters all over the United States and eventually Canada. Its goal was to obtain government recognition of this newly discovered cognitive disorder. Such recognition would result in establishing learning disabilities as an additional category within special education. In this way, children with learning disabilities could receive appropriate educational services in the school through government funding.

Predecessors of Learning Disabilities

As you can see, the formal emergence of the learning disabilities field was somewhat fortuitous. But in actual fact, the path of the ultimate emergence of the field had long been paved by others. As early as 1917, Hinshelwood, an ophthalmologist, reported a case of reading disability in a boy who appeared to be functioning normally in other aspects. Then there was Orton, who introduced the term *strephosym-*

bolia, which means twisted symbols. Orton used this term to describe a dominant characteristic that he observed in children who experienced varying degrees of difficulties in learning to read. Specifically, these children reversed letters, especially *b, d, p,* and *q.*

Orton felt that strephosymbolia provided a more plausible explanation for the children's reading disability than the hypothesis proffered by Hinshelwood (1917). Hinshelwood hypothesized that a child's reading disability reflected a congenital developmental defect of the brain area responsible for visual memory of words. Orton rejected such a hypothesis because no such brain center for visual memory of words had been found. In contrast, reversals were widely and readily observed in the sample of 125 reading-disabled children that he studied, and those he encountered in clinical practice. In short, his notion of *strephosymbolia* was empirically based, albeit only in his clinical samples.

Orton (1937) attributed the causation of strephosymbolia to physiological variance in children's establishment of cerebral dominance. He believed that an individual's nondominant cerebral hemisphere contains mirror images of engrams (words) that correspond to those stored in the dominant cerebral hemisphere. According to him, normally, the engrams in the nondominant cerebral hemisphere are suppressed or remain inactive or inoperative. However, if the complete suppression of them in the nondominant cerebral hemisphere was not achieved in the individual, these mirror images of the engrams would persist and cause the individual to reverse letters (e.g., *b* and *d,* confusing *dig* with *big;* and between *was* and *saw*). The same individual would show an interesting facility with mirror reading and mirror writing. This facility underscores the individual's lack of cerebral dominance, because, according to Orton, mirror images of words are stored in the nondominant hemisphere.

Thus for Orton, individual physiological differences in establishing cerebral dominance result in certain children's having difficulties learning to read. It is not a case of pathology or brain defect. Rather, it seems more likely to be developmental delay in the establishment of cerebral dominance.

Characteristics of Children with Strephosymbolia

All children demonstrating *strephosymbolia* reversed letters. There is a *specificity* to their learning problem in that it pertains only to reading acquisition. Moreover, they showed a discrepancy between their measured intelligence (IQ) and their achievement levels in standardized tests in reading, arithmetic, spelling, and writing. Curiously, they showed a facility with mirror reading and mirror writing.

Although the IQs of some of the children and adolescents studied by Orton were in the seventies, he was inclined to think that they were adequate in intelligence. This notion arose from his belief that traditional intelligence tests deflate the performance of such children and adolescents. Orton maintained that they were handicapped by their reading disability to perform well on intelligence tests that tap verbal knowledge and concepts. Because such children and adolescents do not read, they lose out on learning much that is contained in intelligence test items. Hence, Orton left a strong impression that he thought children and adolescents with reading disability have adequate intelligence.

Orton's Opinion on Reading Disability

Orton considered reading disability to be a continuum. Children and adolescents could have a moderate case of reading disability or *strephosymbolia* or a severe case of it. He embraced the centrality of cerebral dominance to explain reversals in reading-disabled children and adolescents. However, he was optimistic about the possibilities of alleviating the problem of reading disability through retraining, in particular, through early and intensive intervention. Orton advocated the use of a multisensory approach to teaching reading to children with reading disability. He reported success with this remedial approach. In contrast, he was against using a sight-word instructional method in teaching reading to these children.

Other Predecessors of Learning Disabilities

Other predecessors of learning disabilities more recent than Orton were Alfred Strauss, William Cruickshank, and Samuel Kirk.

Alfred Strauss

Alfred Strauss was a neuropsychiatrist who, together with his associate, developmental psychologist Heinze Werner, studied mentally retarded children. According to Hallahan and Kauffman (1976), Strauss was an associate professor at the University of Heidelberg, and Werner occupied the same professorial rank at the University of Hamburg. They fled Nazi Germany to come to the United States. In their investigations, Strauss and Werner replicated behavioral findings of a physician by the name of Goldstein. Goldstein studied World War I soldiers who as a result of brain injuries showed behaviors of extreme distractibility, perceptual problems in figure–ground discrimination, and hyperactivity. Additionally, Strauss and Werner discovered evidence of brain injury in the medical records of some of the mentally retarded children. These Strauss called *exogenous* mental retardates. In others, no record or evidence of brain injury was found. Strauss called these children *endogenous* mental retardates (Bryan & Bryan, 1978; Hallahan & Kauffman, 1976; Lerner, 1993).

Although Strauss derived the behavior pattern of extreme distractibility, perceptual problems in figure–ground discrimination, and hyperactivity from observations of mentally retarded children in his research, he generalized the term *brain-injured* to children who demonstrated the same behavior pattern regardless of presence or absence of brain injury. It is this blanket application of the term *brain-injured* to children who failed to learn to read that parents and some professionals found objectionable.

At this point, you may legitimately ask, What does Strauss, who worked exclusively with mentally retarded children, have to do with learning disabilities? Indeed, Strauss dealt with mentally retarded children in his work. His contribution to the learning disabilities field came from making a significant conceptual differentiation and some innovative procedures in teaching mentally retarded children. First, he removed the misconception of homogeneity in the subpopulation of mental retardates. He showed the differentiation between exogenous and endogenous mental retardation, and in his joint research with Kephart, he advocated the need for special educational programs for exogenous retardates. Specifically, in teaching children with exogenous mental retardation, Strauss emphasized making salient important aspects while decreasing salience of nonimportant aspects in the learning materials (Hallahan & Kauffman, 1976). Strauss's achievement here impacts importantly on learning disabilities because it was the differentiation of exogenous and endogenous retardates with learning problems that eventually led to the recognition of the subgroup of learning-disabled children, nonretardates with cognitive problems.

Second, Strauss was the first to attend to the individual profile of cognitive strengths and deficits in a retarded child. Again, this novel approach to understanding intraindividual differences impacts importantly on learning disabilities because it is the basis for making the individualized educational plan (IEP). Third, Together with his associates (e.g., Laura Lechtinen and Kephart), Strauss devised educational methods and programs for mentally retarded children. Subsequent teachers of learning-disabled children capitalized on these educational materials by extrapolating useful parts from them. Finally, Strauss influenced others who worked with children with learning disabilities. One of these individuals was Kephart, who went on to develop his own theory and educational approach in teaching those children. Kephart believed that higher-order cognitive learning builds on a solid foundation of visuomotor learning. Consequently, his educational approach focused heavily on visuomotor coordination and motor learning.

William Cruickshank

Cruickshank was also influenced by Strauss. Cruickshank contributed two major accomplishments: (a) He replicated the findings of Strauss and Werner on perceptual problems in figure–ground discrimination with children with cerebral palsy whose intelligence ranged from being slightly below normal to normal and above normal. (b) He used the remedial methods devised by Strauss and his associates, (e.g., Lechtinen) with children with cerebral palsy of normal intelligence. Cruickshank's work is important because it facilitated a transfer from the focus on mentally retarded children to those with normal intelligence who showed extreme distractibility, perceptual problems in figure–ground discrimination, and hyperactivity (Hallahan & Kauffman, 1976).

In educational recommendations for such children, Cruickshank advocated structuring the learning environment to reduce their distractibility. His book on educating the brain-injured is well known (Cruickshank, Bantzen, Ratzeburg, & Tannhauser, 1961). His key contribution to learning disabilities was the establishment of the International Academy of Research in Learning Disabilities, which promotes rigorous research. Throughout his life, Cruickshank maintained that children and individuals with learning disabilities should be considered along a continuum of intelligence as one of the diagnostic criteria for learning disabilities. One may not agree with Cruickshank's perspectives, but in examining his lifetime achievements and his experiential background, one can readily understand his insistence that learning disabilities occur across the entire IQ spectrum, and the importance of perceptual problems in learning disabilities.

Samuel Kirk

Kirk has been called father of the learning disabilities field because of his historic role in organizing the field in 1963. But he has contributed much more to the learning disabilities field than his spontaneously catalystic role in that historical meeting in Chicago in 1963. Specifically, he brought to the field an emphasis on language problems. This is important because it provided a healthy balance to the predominant emphasis on visuoperceptual and visuomotor processes and functions that was generated by Strauss, and shared by Kephart, Frostig, and Cruickshank. Moreover, Kirk was the first to attempt to develop a test to measure processing problems in children with learning disabilities. The goal was ambitious; Kirk wanted his test to have a dual function. It should diagnose the processing problems that underlie a child's learning disabilities, and subsequently, the test data should enable ready formulation of an appropriate remedial program for that child. This test is the Illinois Test of Psycholinguistic Abilities (ITPA) (Kirk, McCarthy, & Kirk, 1968).

Initially, the ITPA had a lot of promise. It was timely for the learning disabilities field to have such a test because the field badly needed assessment tools then. For professionals in learning disabilities, having an assessment tool that could diagnose process problems and yield results that led immediately to remedial planning and treatment was like having their prayers answered! It was believed that by pinpointing the child's problems on the ITPA and proceeding with remediation of those underlying processing problems, the learning-disabled child should be able to learn to read. Thus process training came into vogue. Children with learning disabilities were trained in visual and auditory discrimination, visual and auditory memory, visuomotor coordination, and so on, and expected to proceed to read after successful process training.

Unfortunately, to be able to read, learning-disabled children appeared to need more than process training (Hammill & Larsen, 1974a,b). They needed additional training on phonological processing skills and phonics. Recent research findings collaborate the need for phonological processing training (Blachman, Ball, Black, & Tangel, 1994), and direct and explicit phonics training for at-risk or learning disabled children to learn to read (Williams, 1980). The findings of Hammill and Larsen (1974a,b) discredit the ITPA's second goal of facilitating remedial planning and promoting reading acquisition among learning-disabled children. Construct validity problems discredit the first diagnostic goal of this test. Apparently, some subtests of the ITPA do not test what they were supposed to test. For example, the nonverbal items were supposed to involve no verbal processes. This was refuted because verbal processes are involved in the nonverbal items of the ITPA. Although the ITPA has been revised many times since its debut, it has not been in wide use because it could not redress the problems shown in Hammill and Larsen (1974a,b). However, occasional use of subtests in specific studies (e.g., the Grammatical Closure subtest) has been reported.

Even though the ITPA is flawed in its theoretical premises and some of the item construction, it served as a model for test development in learning disabilities. Some of the subsequent assessment tests developed basically modeled the assessment concept in the ITPA, namely, pinpointing cognitive strengths and deficits in children and adolescents with learning disabilities.

Another contribution of Kirk to learning disabilities is his claim that children and adolescents with learning disabilities need specially designed education techniques (Kirk, 1986). By implication, traditional ways of teaching are not sufficient or effective with learning disabled individuals. Kirk's claim has cardinal significance. First and foremost, it buttresses the demand for special educational services by parents for their learning-disabled children. Second, it may create problems 30 years down the road if little empirical research shows learning-disabled students need instructional techniques specially designed for them! But Kirk's major contribution to the learning disabilities field was moving it from a medical to an educational model. He did this by focusing attention on the cognitive nature of children's failures to learn to read. His leadership here freed such children from instructionally futile diagnostic labels, such as minimal brain dysfunction.

Minimal Brain Dysfunction

What is "minimal brain dysfunction"? This term was used by medical professionals to describe the problems that underlie children's failure to learn to read. They believed that such children sustain some form of brain damage. However, the damage is not so substantial as to cause general cognitive deficits, as is the case with mental retardation. Nevertheless, it suffices to impede the child's capacity to learn to read.

Hence, they devised the term "minimal brain dysfunction" as a diagnosis of those particular children. This diagnosis rests on a neurologist's detection via soft neurological signs of brain damage. What this means is that the neurologist cannot identify hard neurological signs of dysfunction in the child. Soft neurological signs involve an awkward gait, minimal tremors, and visuomotor coordination problems. The detection of these soft signs depends on the skills and subjectivity of the neurologist, because they are subtle neurological abnormalities.

As you could imagine, parents of children who encounter serious difficulties in learning to read did not and still do not respond to that term favorably. One may ask: How *minimal* is minimal brain dysfunction? More important, what instructional use does it have in attaching such a diagnostic label to any child? Clearly, the term "minimal brain dysfunction" has limited relevance in the learning disabilities field!

Prevalence

In 1975 the prevalence of learning disabilities was estimated to be about 1–3% of the school population (Lerner, 1993). But at present, it is 4–5% of students aged 6–17 years (Hallahan & Kauffman, 1994). What are we to make of such a jump in learning disabilities?

There are professionals and researchers both within and outside of the learning disabilities field who think the increased prevalence means the concept of learning disabilities has been overgeneralized, and that overidentification of learning disabilities has occurred (Stanovitch, 1986; Torgesen, 1991). The practice of overidentification is reflected in the kinds of students served in the learning assistance centers in the schools. Typically, you can find students with learning disabilities, low achievers, English as a Second Language (ESL) students, and, depending on the school, even educable mentally retarded (EMR) students. Basically, such overidentification reflects teachers' noble goal of teaching as many problem learners as possible, and not restricting instructional help only to students with learning disabilities (Wong, 1986).

However, this is not to say that the increase reflects entirely overidentification of learning disabilities! There are substantial reasons why the prevalence rate in learning disabilities soared. Lerner (1993) provides some sound reasons. First, she points out the public's increased awareness of learning disabilities. Parent groups, professionals, and nascent research in learning disabilities result in people becoming much better informed about learning disabilities. Second, assessment techniques improved across the years, and continue to improve. This resulted in more reliable diagnoses of learning disabilities. Third, as the public became increasingly more informed about learning disabilities, misconceptions were shed, and general tolerance and acceptance of the phenomenon results. These are the major reasons that may well have led to an increased prevalence rate in learning disabilities.

On the Myth That Learning Disabilities Mean Reading Disability

Some people, especially the lay public, equate learning disabilities with reading disability. As seen in Figure 1, reading problems form one major type of academic learning disability, along with other academic learning disabilities, such as in mathematics, writing, and spelling. But there are nonacademic learning disabilities. These include perceptual problems, language problems, memory problems (auditory and visual), and visuomotor problems.

Why do people equate learning disabilities with reading disability? How did such a misconception develop? Well, it arose probably because about 60% of learning disabled individuals have a reading disability in addition to whatever areas of learning disabilities they may have. Hence, it is understandable why people tend to think that someone with learning disabilities is simply a person with a reading disability. If you should meet someone with that misconception, it is important for you to remove it, with suitable diplomatic sensitivity.

Etiology

Throughout the history of the learning disabilities field, involved professionals assumed that this cognitive disorder was neurologically based. Initially, it was assumed

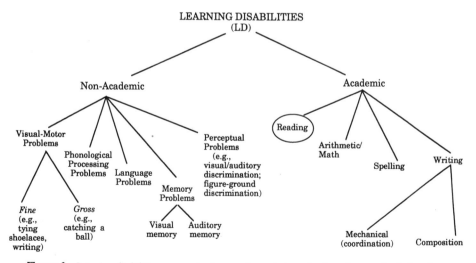

Figure 1   Learning disabilities as an umbrella term for various academic and nonacademic learning disabilities.

that brain damage underlay children's unusual difficulties in learning to read. However, overt signs of brain damage could not be found in these children, for example, they showed a consistent absence of definitive (hard) neurological signs of brain damage. Consequently, the assumption of brain damage gave way to the notion of minimal brain damage. This meant that children with learning disabilities sustained slight brain damage that affected the way they learn (Silver, 1990).

This notion of minimal brain damage was formally stated in an early 1963 document of the cognitive disorder that we now call learning disabilities. At that time, however, professionals who characterized this disorder did not differentiate among characteristics that more aptly describe attention-deficits disorder (ADD) (e.g., attentional problems, hyperactivity, and impulsivity), and those that pertain to learning disabilities (e.g., academic problems in reading, mathematics, writing, visuomotor coordination), or those that concern emotional problems (Silver, 1990). Subsequently and gradually, informed by research, our notions of the characteristics of individuals with learning disabilities became clearer, and we began to make more precise differentiations among those with learning disabilities, those with ADD, and those with emotional and/or behavioral disturbance.

Returning to the issue of etiology, in the late 1980s and now the 1990s, with the advent of technology in positron emission tomography (PET) scans, magnetic resonance imaging (MRI), and blood flow techniques, it is possible to obtain closer examinations of the nature of structural abnormalities and differences in functional efficiency in the brains of adults with reading disabilities. Below, I shall summarize data from autopsy research, MRI, then data from PET scans, and finally, data from blood flow studies.

Autopsy Studies

In autopsy studies of six male and three female dyslexics, Galaburda and his associates found symmetry of the planum temporale, which is located in the left hemisphere. The left hemisphere is the area implicated in language functions. Normal adults typically show asymmetry, with the left being larger than the right planum temporale. What is the meaning of Galaburda and his associates' findings? Well, cutting through technical jargon on brain anatomy, it means these dyslexics showed a larger right hemisphere than nondyslexics (Galaburda, 1991).

In five of the male and two of the female dyslexics, Galaburda and associates found cortical abnormalities. Specifically, in these dyslexics, they found clusters (nests) of neurons where they normally did not occur in nondyslexic adults. In the dyslexic brains, clusters of neurons were found in the most superficial (top) layer of the cortex. Moreover, there was loss of the well-arranged, tidy patterned lamination of the neighboring cortex.

The abnormal location of cell clusters is rare in the brains of nondyslexic adults under autopsy examinations. However, they have been found in a large number of congenital brain abnormalities. Again, what is the meaning of such abnormal location of neurons? The meaning lies in Galaburda's hypothesis: "The neurons in question are not only misplaced, but the affected cortex is different in terms of its cellular and connectional architecture, hence its functional architecture as well" (Galaburda, 1991, p. 127).

Magnetic Resonance Imaging

This is a noninvasive means of obtaining structural images of the brain in vivo. Moreover, when the individual is given a task or tasks before or after the MRI scan, one can correlate structures ("structural indices") in the brain activated by the individual's cognitive processing with functional indices (measures of the tasks) (Berninger, 1994, p. 41).

To obtain an MRI scan of the brain, the individual lies inside a narrow tunnel in the center of the magnet, wearing a helmet-like headgear which has an opening in front of the face. The headgear descends over his or her head to about the top of the shoulders. For technical details and principles underlying MRI, interested readers should read Filipek and Kennedy (1991, pp. 135–138).

Currently, MRI has not yet been proven useful in diagnoses of developmental disorders such as dyslexia and severe reading disability. One reason appears to be that subtle structural abnormalities do not show up reliably in MRI (Filipek & Kennedy, 1991, p. 142). But MRI shows much promise as a research tool, in particular, with the use of morphometry, which measures volume, shape, and geometric configuration of the brain (Filipek & Kennedy, 1991).

To illustrate the research role of MRI in highlighting associations between neuroanatomical constraints and developmental dyslexia (reading disability in young children), the following study of Semrud-Clikeman, Hynd, Novey, and Eliopulos (1991) is briefly summarized. They investigated the relationships between structure and function in three groups of children. One group had ADD, another had dyslexia, and the last was a control group devoid of either disorder. All children received reading and language measures. Semrud-Clikeman et al. found that only in the group of dyslexic children was small right frontal width significantly related statistically to poor performance in reading comprehension. Moreover, these dyslexic children showed reversed asymmetry (left larger than right) or symmetry of the right frontal region; neither of these findings was in turn significantly related to poorer word attack skills. In general, children in all three groups showed reversed asymmetry (right larger than left) or symmetry of the planum, and these findings were related to substantially lower scores on the verbal comprehension factor of the Wechsler Intelligence Scale for Children (WISC-R). These latter results point to the planum as a structure that concerns language processing. Clearly, MRI holds much promise as a research tool that may shed light on how particular brain structures correlate to particular cognitive processing functions.

Positron Emission Tomography Scan

This technique is invasive and expensive. However, it gives good resolution (imaging precision), and the subject can be scanned while processing a task. Specifically, PET and blood flow techniques yield functional images of those parts of the brain that are activated as the subjects perform a given or specific task. Whereas PET yields better temporal and spatial resolution (imaging precision), blood flow techniques yield clearer demarcations between gray and white matter of the brain (Berninger, 1994).

Both techniques are invasive in that a radioactive substance is either injected or inhaled by the subject. Once this substance enters the subject's bloodstream, it travels to the brain and acts as an index or marker of the location of neural activity at a specific moment in time. This is why PET and blood flow techniques are not used with children, but only with adults.

Using blood flow techniques, Wood and his colleagues investigated normal nondyslexic adults and adults who were diagnosed as dyslexic in childhood. The task they gave the subjects involved having them listen to words and indicate whether the words were precisely four letters long. Flowers, Wood, and Naylor (in press) found adults with a childhood diagnosis of dyslexia had reduced blood flow (activity) in Wernicke's area in the left temporal lobe (Wernicke and Broca's regions are involved in language functions). Nondyslexic adults showed no such reduction. Moreover, the dyslexic adults showed higher blood flow in the angular gyrus than did the nondyslexic adults.

In another study involving the technique of blood flow, Wood, Flowers, Buchsbaum, and Tallal (1991) gave normal and reading-disabled adults a phoneme task. They found that in reading-disabled adults, high task accuracy was accompanied by an increase in blood flow in the left temporal region, but in normal adults, it was accompanied by a reduction in blood flow in the same region! Importantly, Wood et al. (1991) replicated these findings.

At the start of this section on etiology, I pointed out that throughout the history of the learning disabilities field, a tacit assumption exists that the cause of learning disabilities is neurologically based. Current research using advance techniques of PET, MRI, and blood flow attempts to map out the biological or neurological bases of learning disabilities. These studies are essentially exploratory attempts to link brain and behavior in dyslexic and nondyslexic individuals as they engage in given cognitive tasks. Moreover, structural abnormalities should not be viewed as direct causes of dyslexia (severe reading disability). Rather, they pose risks in the development of dyslexia, and obviously, risk increases as the number of structural abnormalities increases (Semrud-Clikeman et al., 1991).

Genetic Factors

There is cumulative evidence that genetic factors may cause learning disabilities. Studies of identical twins show a higher chance of reading disability in the remaining twin if the other has it than in fraternal twins. Other researchers have also found that learning disabilities appear to run in families. (Hallahan & Kauffman, 1994).

Environmental Factors

These are conceivable causes, but they appear hard to substantiate. They include malnutrition and poor instruction.

Rapid Growth of the Learning Disabilities Field

When the learning disabilities field started in 1963, it struggled for recognition and separate status from existing categories of special education. Yet within thirty-odd years, it has grown enormously. Today, the Division of Learning Disabilities (DLD) within the Council for Exceptional Children (CEC) is the biggest division regarding membership (Hallahan & Kauffman, 1994).

The expansion of the field can also be seen in the number of professional journals devoted to the subject of learning disabilities. These include *The Journal of Learning Disabilities, Learning Disability Quarterly, Learning Disabilities Research & Practice, Exceptionality.* There are also a number of organizations that hold regular conferences to disseminate research and practical information in learning disabilities. These include the DLD in the CEC, the Council for Learning Disabilities (CLD), the International Academy of Research in Learning Disabilities (IARLD), and the Learning Disabilities Association of America (LDA). Additionally, local associations of learning disabilities in each American state and Canadian province have their own annual conferences.

How Has the Learning Disabilities Field Changed?

Since its inception in the 1960s, the learning disabilities field has undergone some quite dramatic changes in its conceptual viewpoints. Specifically, it has forsaken the so-called perceptual deficits hypothesis of learning disabilities, and it has taken a life span approach to understanding learning disabilities. What is this perceptual deficits hypothesis? Let us first define perceptual deficits, then explain its origin and role in the history of learning disabilities.

The Perceptual Deficits Hypothesis of Learning Disabilities

Perceptual deficits or perceptual handicaps refer to an individual's deficits in interpreting or making sense out of visual information despite intact vision and visual system. Examples of such visual deficits include difficulties in accurate form perception or shape discrimination, perception of letters or figures in certain spatial orientation (problems here result in reversals of letters or numbers), visual closure, figure–ground discrimination (Hallahan & Kauffman, 1976). Also, there may well be problems in a related area: fine or gross visual–motor coordination.

In the early days of the learning disabilities field, there was widespread speculation that such perceptual deficits caused learning disabilities that were then manifested in the child's enormous difficulties in learning to read. This speculation became known as the perceptual deficits hypothesis. Those who were favorably inclined towards it included Cruickshank, Frostig, and Kephart, although Kephart emphasized perceptual-motor match (visuomotor coordination). One reason for the prominent role given to perceptual deficits comes from the influence of Werner and Strauss, whose work with retardates focused much on visual perceptual problems. In turn, they influenced William Cruickshank, who was one of the pioneers of the learning disabilities field. The support for this causal view of learning disabilities naturally generated a wave of perceptual process training and perceptual-motor training in which children with learning disabilities were given exercises in areas such as visual discrimination and in eye–hand coordination. For a detailed description on perceptual process training and visuomotor training, see Hallahan and Kauffman (1976, pp. 94–99; 131–139). These training programs, however, did not advance reading acquisition in children with learning disabilities. Hammill and Larsen's evaluative studies (1974a,b) convincingly demonstrated the futility of perceptual process training in helping children with learning disabilities to learn to read. An earlier review by Hallahan and Cruickshank (1973) found only 7 out of 42 such training studies to be free of methodological confounds. And in these, Hallahan and Cruickshank could not find consistent trends of efficacy! Little wonder then that the perceptual deficits hypothesis went into demise.

At present, within the learning disabilities field, based on ample research findings, we support a language-oriented view of learning disabilities. Specifically, we think phonological processing problems underlie the child's development of reading disability (Mann, 1991). However, this does not exclude specific cases in which some children's difficulties in learning to read are compounded and exacerbated by visual perceptual problems, or by their slow processing of visual information (Willows, 1991).

A Life Span Approach to Learning Disabilities

When the learning disabilities field began in the 1960s, and children whose inexplicable difficulties in learning to read were finally acknowledged, no one considered whether the condition would be overcome in time with due remediation. Now, through cumulated research findings, we realize that learning disabilities constitute a lifelong condition, and appropriately, we adopt a life span approach toward understanding, learning about, and dealing with this phenomenon.

Framed in this life span perspective, we may profitably ask, What characteristic distinguishes the child, the adolescent, and the adult with learning disabilities? Specifically, what is one indisputable characteristic about the child, the adolescent, and the adult with learning disabilities that research findings have converged on and highlighted? By indisputable, I mean this characteristic has been consistently found by numerous and independent researchers. In short, we have *convergent validity* on the characteristic, and consequently, wide consensus among researchers on it. Let us first direct the question to research on children with learning disabilities.

A Distinct, Indisputable, Research-Based Characteristic of Individuals with Learning Disabilities

Children

Currently, a vast empirical base clearly indicates that problems in phonological processing underlie a young child's enormous difficulties learning to read. This finding boasts of convergent validity, which means numerous independent researchers had obtained, and continue to obtain, the same finding that children devoid of phonological processing skills are impaired in their attempts in learning to read. Research pointing to this unmistakable observation spans two decades (see studies by Fox & Routh, 1975, 1976, 1980; Snowling, 1980, and more recent ones by Blachman, Ball, Black, & Tangel, 1994; Mann, 1991; Torgesen, Wagner, & Rashotte, 1994). To date, the empirical base justifies the theory that phonological processing problems cause reading disability in a sizable portion of reading-disabled children, adolescents, and adults (Mann, 1991; Stanovich, 1988; Torgesen, 1993).

What are phonological processing skills? How are they measured? Why are they important in young children's learning to read? Phonological processing skills refer to skills in using "information about the sound structure of our language in processing written and oral language" (Wagner, 1988, p. 623). Researchers have found three kinds of phonological processing skills that are positively correlated to early reading skills: (a) phonological (phoneme) awareness, (b) phonological memory (short-term memory as measured on span tasks), and (c) rate of access for phonological information (rapid naming of letters, digits either in isolation or in a series; colors, objects). Of the three kinds of phonological processes, the causal role of the first, phonological (phoneme) awareness, in early reading seems better understood. At least phoneme awareness seems to lend itself better to intervention research. It is difficult to think or conceive of ways to increase a reading-disabled or at-risk child's capacity in phonological memory, whereas researchers have been most creative in devising numerous motivating games and activities to enhance phoneme awareness in normally achieving kindergarten, at-risk, and young reading-disabled children. Intervention attempts with at-risk children that combined phonological (phoneme) awareness plus phonics (or some form of reading instruction) had been effective (e.g., Blachman et al., 1994). For these reasons, I focus only on phonological (phoneme) awareness.

Phonological (phoneme) awareness is "one's sensitivity to, or explicit awareness of, the phonological [sound] structure of words in one's language" (Torgesen et al., 1994, p. 276). Segmentation and synthesis tasks are typical tasks given to assess a child's phoneme awareness skills. Examples of segmentation tasks include asking children to segment words into syllables, (e.g., the child is asked to clap the number of sounds in, *hamburger*). Or the child is asked to segment a word into phonemes (e.g., saying a little bit of the word *Pete,* which results in the *p* sound) (Fox & Routh, 1975). The same skill in segmenting a word into phonemes is measured in a task that asks the child to locate a word out of three or four with the same initial or final sound as a given word (e.g., given the word *leg,* a child has to identify a picture of the word beginning with the same sound as *leg* from a choice of three pictures: *lamp, hand, fish*). Alternately, a child has to identify a picture of a word that contains a different initial sound than the given word. For example, given four pictures, *fork, fan, foot, shirt,* the child has to choose the one that begins with a sound different from the rest (*shirt*). These examples are taken from Torgesen and Bryant's Test of Phonological Awareness (Torgesen & Bryant, 1994). A variant form of segmentation task is the deletion task. Here the child is asked to say a word with a particular sound deleted. For example, say *dog* without *d*.

Synthesis is the reverse of segmentation. The child is given a series of sounds and asked to provide the word. For example, given *m-a-t,* she or he is expected to say *mat*. Although you may find different versions of segmentation and blending tasks in the research literature on phonological processing, they all involve the same principles in the examples that I have given. The principles underlying segmentation and blending tasks is to discover whether or not the child has what we refer to technically as phoneme awareness. It is this specific aspect of phonological processing skills that is critical to a young child's learning to read.

Why is phoneme awareness so critical in a child's reading acquisition? Children aged 6 show an astounding grasp of language and its use. For them, language is a communicative tool. But in first grade, when formal instruction in reading begins, they will learn a more abstract aspect of language. Specifically, they will learn to attend to various sounds in words, to learn to tease out individual sounds in words, either at the initial or final positions. Witness first-grade teachers getting children to pay attention to a particular sound at the start of a string of four words, *b* in *ball, boy, bat, boat,* and the way they draw out emphatically the target sound for the benefit of the children. Through various instructional activities, including the preceding auditory discrimination exercise, rhyming activities, and so on, teachers instill in first-grade children a more explicit awareness of component sounds in words. This explicit awareness leads children to realize (a) that a word is composed of sounds, and (b) they can break a word down into its component sounds, most of the time at least, and blend them back into the original word. At the same time, they learn that each sound has its own representative in the 26 letters of the English alphabet. When children develop this explicit awareness that (a) words are composed of sounds strung up in a particular order, and (b) each sound is represented by a particular letter in the English alphabet, they have attained that very abstract aspect of language that researchers technically refer to as "phoneme awareness" (Mann, 1991).

Why is phoneme awareness so important to children's learning to read? You can answer this question now. Think for a moment what reading involves. Yes, yes, reading involves meaning construction or comprehension. Of course. But before you can construct meaning or understand what you are reading, what lower level skill must you possess in abundance? Clearly, you have to be able to decode each word that your eyes fix on! What does decoding involve? Attaching the right sound to the right letter! Indeed. If you fail to decode each word in a sentence that you are reading, your meaning construction would be naught. If you fail to decode some of the words in a sentence that you are reading, your comprehension would not be precise.

Decoding involves actualizing phoneme awareness. In the process of decoding, the child must attach the right sound to the right letter in the word as she or he sequentially processes the word from left to right. To engage her- or himself thusly, the child has already attained the understanding that a word is composed of separable sounds (as much as is possible in separating the sounds), and that each isolated or segmented sound has its own alphabetical representative. This is why phoneme awareness is so critical for children learning to read.

In light of the above, it comes as no surprise to find that there is ample research data attesting to the importance of phoneme awareness in children's learning to read (Mann, 1991). Children who did not develop phoneme awareness were found to have reading disabilities later on. This finding had been reported by various researchers (see Stanovich, 1986; Mann, 1991, for reviews). More importantly, interventions comprising phoneme awareness *and* phonics have been successful with at-risk and reading-disabled children (Williams, 1980; Blachman et al., 1994; Torgesen et al., 1994).

Thus, a prominent portrayal by current research findings of the child with learning disabilities is his or her phonological processing problems. The prominence of this portrayal in part comes from the amount of convergent research findings that span two decades, and in part from major, vanguard theorizing, as contained, for example, in Keith Stanovich's (1988) seminal paper.

Recently, the causal role of phonological processes in children's reading acquisition has been modified. Schooling apparently impacts on children's development of phonological processes. Reading instruction apparently promotes fuller development of their phonological processes and phoneme awareness. Hence, phonological processes and reading instruction have a reciprocal relationship in that each impacts on and promotes development in the other (Wagner, Torgesen, & Rashotte, in press). Ehri (1979) had long voiced the influence of print in children's development of phonological processes and awareness.

Adolescents

The most prominent empirical picture of adolescents with learning disabilities is that they profit most from strategy instructions. This is the recognized modus operandi for producing successful learning in them. In fact, the recognition given to this instructional approach with learning-disabled adolescents is so ensconced that it appears to be taken for granted! Yet it is important to revisit the rationale and origin of this instructional approach with these adolescents to see why it meets their needs so marvelously well.

The notion of strategy instruction with adolescents with learning disabilities came from Alley and Deshler (1979). Strategy instruction refers to teaching learning-disabled adolescents how to learn, specifically, teaching them cognitive and metacognitive strategies that greatly facilitate their learning. It is a credit to Alley and Deshler's remarkable insight and acumen that teaching such adolescents how to learn should be our instructional goal rather than tutoring them to pass immediate tests or complete assignments in high school. In the long run, learning to learn, or learning to approach tasks in a planful and strategic manner, would avail much for adolescents with learning disabilities in postsecondary learning and living, because they need to continue to learn new skills, assimilate new information, and adapt to changing environments. More immediately, strategic instruction benefits them importantly in at least two ways: (a) It enables them to manage the vast amount of curricular information in high school. They can learn strategies to enhance their comprehension, organization, and retention of textual materials. (b) Cumulative and integrative learning of various cognitive and metacognitive strategies would not only expand their repertoires of effective strategies, but also make them increasingly more active, autonomous, and self-regulating (Schumaker & Deshler, 1992).

Together with their research associate, Dr. Jean Schumaker, and generations of very able graduate students under their training, to name but a few, Keith Lenz, Ed Ellis, Fran Carke, and Jan Bulgren, Alley and Deshler began many years of programmatic research that produced numerous valuable learning strategies that enhance academic and nonacademic (social skills) learning in adolescents and young adults with learning disabilities. They set up the Institute for Research in Learning Disabilities at the University of Kansas (KU-IRLD), which was funded by one of the funding agencies of the American federal government.

KU–IRLD has produced and continues to produce innumerable useful cognitive and metacognitive strategies that enhance learning and social skills in adolescents and young adults with learning disabilities. Past graduate students have long come into their own and contributed importantly in new conceptual frameworks and strategies for enhancing content learning in adolescents with learning disabilities (e.g., Ellis, 1993; Ellis & Friend, 1991; Lenz, Bulgren, & Hudson, 1990). Two of the most widely used cognitive strategies in current practice of learning disabilities teachers include COPS for teaching mechanical skills in writing such as punctuation and spelling; and Multipass (Schumaker, Deshler, Alley, Warner, & Denton, 1982) for enhancing reading comprehension.

The strategy instructional approach conceptualized and researched by the KU–IRLD has had a tremendous impact on contemporary intervention research in reading comprehension, writing, and mathematics, with intermediate and high school students with learning disabilities. Clear examples of this impact are seen in the research of Steve Graham and Karen Harris, Marjorie Montague, and Bernice Wong.

Adults

Unfortunately, at present, we cannot identify a characteristic among adults with learning disabilities through convergent research findings. This is mainly due to methodological problems, especially in longitudinal studies that result in the inconsistency of data on these adults where one researcher's findings may be contradicted by another (Horn, O'Donnell, & Vitulano, 1984). Consequently, in many research areas, such as educational attainment, rate and success of employment, and social relationships, we do not have definitive data. In light of this empirical state, in examining adequate research studies, a more appropriate and reasonable question would be, How does research inform us about the adult with learning disabilities?

In educational attainments, some research indicated higher dropout rates among adults with learning disabilities (Adelman & Vogel, 1991). Other research indicated college degrees to be within reach of adults with learning disabilities (Rawson, 1968). Such discrepant findings appear to be resolved when we consider level of intelligence and socioeconomic status (SES). In Rawson's (1968) study, the adults with learning disabilities who successfully completed college had high IQs and came from wealthy families.

The important role of SES is highlighted in a study of O'Connor and Spreen (1988). These investigators found that a father's SES and educational level predicted astonishingly well education level attained, future job, and earnings of their sons and daughters with learning disabilities. Fathers who were well educated and in the high-income bracket would have high SES. O'Connor and Spreen (1988) suggested that high SES implies that (a) well educated parents might encourage their children with learning disabilities to continue to value academic learning; (b) the parents could afford private tutoring to ameliorate academic difficulties; (c) being articulate, these parents would demand and get assessment and remedial services for their children from schools; and (d) with their good connections in their profession (e.g., in business), with corporate network, they could more easily place their children in jobs or apprenticeship after high school or college with a phone call or two.

However, employment of adults with learning disabilities appears to be affected by general economic climate. In times of economic growth, employment prospects of these adults appear to be good. But in recession, adults with learning disabilities appear to be among the first to be let go by their employers (Spreen, 1988).

On the social relations scene, adults with learning disabilities have lower self-concept and problems making and keeping friends. Female adults with learning disabilities apparently experience more social relational problems. The severity of these social relational problems sometimes result in health problems (Barr, 1990). Because of these problems, some adults with learning disabilities rely on their families for social support. Relatedly, many of the adults with learning disabilities still live at home because they are not financially independent (Adelman & Vogel, 1991).

Information from More Recent Research

In general, the picture from the summary of research findings by Adelman and Vogel (1991) on adults with learning disabilities is quite pessimistic. More important, although we know there are adults with learning disabilities that do well, for example, those reported in Rawson's (1968) study, we cannot explain why they succeeded where so many failed. More recent research by Werner (1993) and Spekman, Goldberg, and Herman (1992) sheds some light on factors that differentiate between successful and unsuccessful adults with learning disabilities.

Recently Werner (1993) reported interesting and more positive findings. In her longitudinal study of at-risk children who were subsequently diagnosed with learning disabilities, she found that as adults, they turned out to be doing quite well. Specifically, now in their thirties, they have settled down, and lead satisfactory lives. They are self-supporting (none on welfare), and they enjoy the same rate of marital success as non-learning disabled peers. However, it is important to note that they still hold low-ranking jobs. All are employed in semi-skilled labor, and none holds a four-year university degree.

Werner calls these at-risk children "vulnerable but invincible" because they had survived all odds to become self-supporting and maritally happy citizens. She explained the success of these adults with learning disabilities by tracing it to what she termed five protective clusters.

Cluster 1 refers to the person's positive temperament that draws positive reactions from caregivers, peers, teachers, and spouses. Cluster 2 refers to values and skills that make the person put to good use whatever natural talents she or he possesses. The person also thinks that he or she can overcome problems. As well, he or she sets realistic learning and career plans. At home, he or she shows responsibility and self-regulation towards household chores and responsibilities. Cluster 3 refers to parents who have effective parenting skills, who provide structure and stability at home, and who foster self-esteem in the child. In these homes, the mothers are well educated, they had education beyond high school, and held good jobs. They provided a good model for their daughters. Cluster 4 refers to the presence of a mentor who acted as "gatekeeper" for the future. This person could be a grandparent, a youth leader, or church member. The mentor showed steadfast confidence in the individual with learning disabilities. Cluster 5 refers to timely opportunities for individuals with learning disabilities at crucial life transition points, for example, from high school to job setting, that charted the course of such individuals to adulthood (Werner, 1993, pp. 31–32).

Echoing Werner's protective clusters, Spekman et al. (1992) found successful and unsuccessful adults with learning disabilities can be differentiated on several factors. These include self-awareness, persistence, and the ability to accept one's learning disability, to establish and plan realistically one's career goals, join in social activities, and deal with stress and frustrations.

Studies by Werner and by Spekman et al. pave the way for more focused research on factors that differentiate between successful and unsuccessful adults with learning disabilities. More information about the differences would provide clearer understanding of the sources impeding successful attainments in education, job, and social relations in adults with learning disabilities. In turn, better understanding would lead to better interventions and preventions.

Why is it that we can find one undisputed piece of empirical information or knowledge that characterizes respectively the child and the adolescent, but not the adult with learning disabilities? One plausible reason is that the prominence of the characteristic of phonological processing problems in learning-disabled children, and that of the suitability of strategy instruction of the learning-disabled adolescent have the facilitation of two very favorable factors in research: (a) A cumulative research base of 20 years or more in one case, and 15 in the other; and (b) timely and influential theoretical papers that gave the ample research base conceptual shape and direction (Alley & Deshler, 1979; Ellis, 1993; Stanovich, 1988).

In contrast, research that is devoid of methodological problems appears to be only on the rise currently in the area of adults with learning disabilities. To obtain an undisputed, research-based characteristic of the adult with learning disabilities, we need to build up a rich database. Only from ample research data that have convergent validity from numerous, independent researchers, can we hope to distill an undisputed characteristic of the adult, as is found with the child and the adolescent with learning disabilities.

However, in all fairness to researchers in the area of learning-disabled adults, we should acknowledge the obstacles they encounter that are not encountered to the same extent by those researching children or adolescents with learning disabilities.

Conducting research in adults with learning disabilities is a very difficult task (see Horn et al., 1984, for details). One major problem is recruiting subjects. Adults with learning disabilities who are successful in their work tend to be reluctant to participate as research subjects. Those who respond to researchers' quest for subjects tend to be most in need for academic and social skills remediation (Barr, 1990). Consequently, researchers may not be able to obtain a representative sample of adults with learning disabilities in their studies.

Changing Focus of the Learning Disabilities Field

Clearly, the learning disabilities field is thriving. More important, there is a discernible shift in focus. The field began as a service-oriented field. There is now tacit consensus that the learning disabilities field is striving towards becoming a scientific discipline. In the past 15 years, the learning disabilities field evidenced a significant increase in research activities, both basic and applied. And research activities continue in multiple directions and scope. Moreover, closer attention to subject selection and more rigor in research methodology and sophistication in data analyses have yielded more quality research. This change in focus may signal the coming of age in the learning disabilities field.

REFLECTIONS

Why do we need to study the history of learning disabilities? To some university students, the history of any field is boring. So let's consider the question and answer it. There are at least two reasons why you should learn about the history of the learning disabilities field.

First, as Bryan and Bryan (1978) aptly pointed out, learning about the history of learning disabilities informs us on the origin of assessment and remedial approaches in our field. History informs us which related disciplines as well as what key figures shaped our initial conceptual outlooks and practical procedures in learning disabilities. Consequently, we understand what drove contemporary conceptualizations of learning disabilities and practices in assessments and remediations. We also understand the origin of specific issues in conceptual disagreements (e.g., Cruickshank's insistence of the irrelevance of IQ, in diagnosis of learning disabilities). To date, this conceptual disagreement still prevails (see Chapter 2).

A second reason for learning about the history of learning disabilities is that those very characteristics observed by parents, educators, psychologists, and medical professionals about children with learning disabilities in 1963 are the very same characteristics that we see today in children, adolescents, and adults with learning disabilities! These characteristics are an enormous difficulty in learning to read despite adequate intelligence, intact sensory capacities, and sufficient opportunities to learn in any regular classroom. These salient characteristics define both the individuals with such cognitive disorder and the field itself. Studying the history of learning disabilities enables us to trace this important thread from the past to the present, and anchors the conceptual significance of the term *learning disabilities* for us.

References

Adelman, P. B., & Vogel, S. A. (1991). The learning-disabled adult. In B. Y. L. Wong (Ed.), Learning about learning disabilities (pp. 563–594). San Diego: Academic Press.

Alley, G., & Deshler, D. (1979). Teaching the learning-disabled adolescent: Strategies and methods. Denver: Love Publishing Company.

Barr, P. M. (1990). The adaptation of adults with learning disabilities in four life domains. Unpublished doctoral dissertation, University of Calgary, Calgary, Alberta.

Berninger, V. W. (1994). *Reading and writing acquisition: A developmental neuropsychological perspective.* Madison, WI: Brown & Benchmark.

Blachman, B. A., Ball, E. W., Black, R. S., & Tangel, D. M. (1994). Kindergarten teachers develop phoneme awareness in low-income, inner-city classrooms. *Reading and Writing: An Interdisciplinary Journal, 6,* 1–18.

Bryan, T. H., & Bryan, J. H. (1978). *Understanding learning disabilities* (2nd ed.). Sherman Oaks, CA: Alfred Publishing Co.

Cruickshank, W. M., Bentzen, F. A., Ratzeburg, F. H., & Tannhauser, M. T. (1961). A teaching method for brain-injured and hyperactive children. Syracuse, NY: Syracuse University Press.

Ehri, L. C. (1979). Linguistic insight: Threshold of reading acquisition. In T. G. Waller & G. E. MacKinnon (Eds.), *Reading research: Advances in theory and practice* (Vol. 1, pp. 63–114). New York: Academic Press.

Ellis, E. S. (1993). Integrative strategy instruction: A potential model for teaching content area subjects to adolescents with learning disabilities. *Journal of Learning Disabilities, 26*(6), 358–383, 398.

Ellis, E. S., & Friend, P. (1991). Adolescents with learning disabilities. In B. Y. L. Wong (Ed.), *Learning about learning disabilities* (pp. 505–561). San Diego: Academic Press.

Filipek, P., & Kennedy, D. (1991). Magnetic resonance imaging: Its role in the developmental disorders. In D. D. Duane & D. B. Gray (Eds.), *The reading brain: The biological basis of dyslexia* (pp. 133–160). Parkton, MD: York Press.

Flowers, D. L., Wood, F. B., & Naylor, C. E. (in press). Regional cerebral blood flow correlate of language processes in adult dyslexics. *Archives of Neurology.*

Fox, B., & Routh, D. K. (1975). Analyzing spoken language into words, syllables and phonemes: A developmental study. *Journal of Psycholinguistic Research, 4,* 331–342.

Fox, B., & Routh, D. K. (1976). Phonemic analysis and synthesis as word-attack skills. *Journal of Educational Psychology, 68*(1), 70–74.

Fox, B., & Routh, D. K. (1980). Phonemic analysis and severe reading disability in children. *Journal of Psycholinguistic Research, 9,* 115–119.

Galaburda, A. (1991). Anatomy of dyslexia: Argument against phrenology. In D. D. Duane & D. B. Gray (Eds.), The reading brain (pp. 119–131). Pankton, MD: York Press.

Hallahan, D. P., & Cruickshank, W. M. (1973). *Psychoeducational foundations of learning disabilities.* Englewood Cliffs, NJ: Prentice-Hall.

Hallahan, D. P., & Kauffman, J. M. (1976). Introduction to learning disabilities: A psycho-behavioral approach (1st ed.). Englewood Cliffs, NJ: Prentice-Hall.

Hallahan, D. P., & Kauffman, J. M. (1994). *Exceptional children: Introduction to special education* (6th ed.). Boston: Allyn and Bacon.

Hammill, D. D., & Larsen, S. C. (1974a). The relationship of selected auditory perceptual skills and reading ability. *Journal of Learning Disabilities, 7*(7), 429–435.

Hammill, D. D., & Larsen, S. C. (1974b, September). The effectiveness of psycholinguistic training. *Exceptional Children, 5*–15.

Hinshelwood, J. (1917). *Congenital word blindness.* London: Lewis.

Horn, W. F., O'Donnell, J. P., & Vitulano, L. A. (1984). Long-term follow-up studies of learning-disabled persons. *Annual Review of Learning Disabilities, 2,* 77–90.

Kirk, S. (1986). *On interventions with learning-disabled students.* Address given at the conference on Future Directions in Learning Disabilities Research, Salt Lake City, Utah, January 1986.

Kirk, S. A., McCarthy, J. J., & Kirk, W. D. (1968). *Illinois Test of Psycholinguistic Ability.* Urbana, IL: University of Chicago Press.

Lenz, K. B. K., Bulgren, J., & Hudson, P. (1990). Content enhancement: A model for promoting the acquisition of content by individuals with learning disabilities. In T. E. Scruggs & B. Y. L. Wong (Eds.), *Intervention research in learning disabilities* (pp. 122–165). New York: Springer-Verlag.

Lerner, J. (1993). *Learning disabilities: Theories, diagnosis and teaching strategies* (6th ed.). Princeton, NJ: Houghton Mifflin.

Mann, V. (1991). Language problems: A key to early reading problems. In B. Y. L. Wong (Ed.), *Learning about learning disabilities* (pp. 29–162). San Diego: Academic Press.

O'Conner, S. C., & Spreen, O. (1988). The relationship between parent's socioeconomic status and education level, and adult occupational and educational achievement of children with learning disabilities. *Journal of Learning Disabilities, 21*(3), 148–153.

Orton, S. T. (1937). *Reading, writing and speech problems in children.* New York: Norton.

Rawson, M. (1968). *Developmental language disability: Adult accomplishment of dyslexic boys.* Baltimore: Johns Hopkins University Press.

Schumaker, J. B., & Deshler, D. D. (1992). Validation of learning strategy interventions for students with LD: Results of a programmatic research effort. In B. Y .L. Wong (Ed.), *Contemporary intervention research in learning disabilities: An international perspective* (pp. 22–46). New York: Springer-Verlag.

Schumaker, J. B., Deshler, D. D., Alley, G. R., Warner, M. M., & Denton, P. H. (1982). Multipass: A learning strategy for improving reading comprehension. *Learning Disability Quarterly, 5,* 295–304.

Semrud-Clikeman, M., Hynd, G., Novey, E., & Eliopulos, D. (1991). Dyslexia and brain morphology: Relationships between neuroanatomical variation and neurolinguistic tasks. *Learning and Individual Differences, 3,* 225–242.

Silver, L. B. (1990). Attention deficit-hyperactivity disorder: Is it a learning disability or a related disorder? *Journal of Learning Disabilities, 23*(7), 394–398.

Snowling M. J. (1980). The development of grapheme-phoneme correspondence in normal and dyslexic readers. *Journal of Experimental Child Psychology, 29,* 294–305.

Spekman, N., Goldberg, R. J., & Herman, K. L. (1992). Learning disabled children grow up: A search for factors related to success in the young adult years. *Learning Disabilities Research & Practice, 7,* 161–170.

Spreen, O. (1988). *Learning-disabled children growing up: A follow-up into adulthood.* Oxford, NY: Oxford University Press.

Stanovich, K. E. (1986). Cognitive processes and the reading problems of learning disabled children: Evaluating the assumption of specificity. In J. K. Torgesen & B. Y. L. Wong (Eds.), *Psychological and educational perspectives in learning disabilities* (pp. 110–131). New York: Academic Press.

Stanovich, K. E. (1988). Explaining the differences between the dyslexic and the garden-variety poor reader: The phonological—core variable—difference model. *Journal of Learning Disabilities, 21,* 590–604.

Torgesen, J. K. (1991). Learning disabilities: Historical and conceptual issues. In B. Y. L. Wong (Ed.), *Learning about learning disabilities* (pp. 3–37). San Diego: Academic Press.

Torgesen, J. K. (1993). Variations on theory in learning disabilities. In G. Reid Lyon, D. B. Gray, J. F. Kavanagh, & N. A. Krasnegor (Eds.), *Better understanding learning disabilities: New views from research and their implications for education and public policies* (pp. 153–170). Baltimore, MD: Paul H. Brookes Publishing Co., Inc.

Torgesen, J. K., & Bryant, B. R. (1994). *Test of Phonological Awareness* (TOPA). Austin, TX: Pro-Ed.

Torgesen, J. K., Wagner, R. K., & Rashotte, C. A. (1994). Longitudinal studies of phonological processing and reading. *Journal of Learning Disabilities, 27*(5), 276–286.

Wagner, R. K. (1988). Phonological processing abilities and reading: Implications for disabled readers. *Journal of Learning Disabilities, 19*(10), 623–630.

Wagner, R. K., Torgesen, J. K., & Rashotte, C. (in press). The development of reading-related phonological processing abilities: New evidence of bi-directional causality from a latent variable longitudinal study. *Developmental Psychology.*

Werner, E. E. (1993). Risk and resilience in individuals with learning disabilities: Lessons learned from the Kauai longitudinal study. *Learning Disabilities Research & Practice, 8*(1), 28–34.

Williams, J. P. (1980). Teaching decoding with emphasis on phoneme analysis and phoneme blending. *Journal of Educational Psychology, 72*, 1–15.

Willows, D. M. (1991). Visual process in learning disabilities. In B. Y. L. Wong (Ed.), *Learning about learning disabilities* (pp. 164–193). San Diego, CA: Academic Press.

Wong, B. Y. L. (1986). Problems and issues in the definition of learning disabilities. In J. K. Torgesen & B. Y. L. Wong (Eds.), *Psychological and educational perspectives on learning disabilities* (pp. 1–26). New York: Academic Press.

Wood, F., Flowers, L. Buchsbaum, M., & Tallal, P. (1991). Investigation of abnormal left temporal functioning in dyslexia through CBF, auditory evoked potentials, and positron emission topography. *Reading and writing: An interdisciplinary journal, 3*, 379–393.

2

Defining Learning Disabilities

Sources of Confusion Surrounding the Definition of Learning Disabilities

The concept of learning disabilities literally defies definition. Achieving a consensus on its definition among all those in the field may amount to a miracle! The interesting thing is that if you were to gather together professionals in learning disabilities known to disagree strongly with one another on how to define learning disabilities, you would find that they agree totally on the characteristics of an individual with learning disabilities! Isn't that ironic? Why is that so? The reason appears to be that they disagree on specific components in the definition of learning disabilities. Specifically, they disagree on the respective places for the notion of processing problems and intelligence (IQ) in the definition of learning disabilities. Below, I elaborate on these disagreements.

The Enigma of Processing Problems

You will recall from Chapter 1 that parents were distressed to find their young children unable to learn to read despite having adequate intelligence and hearing and

26

seeing capacities. Similarly, educators, psychologists, and medical professionals (doctors, psychiatrists, neurologists) were concerned and intrigued by the youngsters' failure to learn to read. These professionals thought that some deep-seated problems impeded the children's ability to process what they were attempting to learn. Depending on their theoretical orientations, various individuals emphasized various processing mechanisms underlying learning disabilities. For example, Kirk emphasized language-processing problems, whereas Kephart and Frostig leaned on visuo-motor processing problems. The long and short of it was that processing problems were considered to cause learning disabilities. We can see how this notion was articulated in the 1969 official formulation of the definition of learning disabilities (see later section on definitions).

But the problem with psychological processing problems is that there are no standardized tests to measure them as there are tests of intelligence, reading, mathematics, spelling, and writing. We can conceptualize psychological processing problems but we haven't been able to operationalize them, and this is the crux of the matter! Again, if we gather together several experienced and effective teachers of children, adolescents, or adults with learning disabilities and ask them about psychological-processing problems in those students, they would be able to describe them and detail how they accommodated those students' processing problems in their teaching. Yet they would all agree that there isn't a ready test to measure those psychological-processing problems, the very problems that they can describe and accommodate successfully in their teaching! This is the problem in trying to keep the notion of psychological-processing problems in the definition of learning disabilities.

How shall we deal with it? Shall we throw it out of the definition of learning disabilities? This way, we can extricate ourselves from an awkward situation, namely, that skilled teachers of learning disabled students can tell you about the nature of psychological processing problems but unfortunately, they haven't produced any test for measuring them yet. Certainly, there are professionals in the learning disabilities field who support deleting "psychological processing problems" from the definition of learning disabilities. But wait, let's consider the opposing viewpoint.

Those in favor of retaining the notion of psychological processing problems in defining learning disabilities argue that as we advance in our understanding of component skills in reading, and in the sophistication of measuring cognitive processes, we would be able to measure psychological processing problems in individuals with learning disabilities (Torgesen, 1991; Wong, 1986). Already, we are making headway in designing tests for component skills in early reading development. Specifically, Torgesen and Bryant (1994) have recently produced the Test of Phonological Awareness (TOPA), which focuses on testing young children's ability to tease out constituent phonemes in spoken words. For example, first- and second-grade children are given a stimulus word, such as *web,* and asked to mark in their answer books one of three words that ends with the same sound as the stimulus word: *tub, bowl, pet.* (The correct answer is *tub* and not *bowl* because *bowl* contains the *b* sound in the initial position.) All the words were presented to the children in the form of pictures in their respective answer booklets. The examiner reads the words to them. As well, children's on-task attention is carefully elicited by various pictures at the top of the page, for example, a picture of a clock. This is a clever device in that it allows for the probability that some children may not be sufficiently familiar with numbers as indices of different pages. Testing children's ability to identify similar end sounds of words is followed by testing their ability to identify different end sounds of words, and it follows the same format. TOPA contains two versions, one for testing children in kindergarten, the other for children in grades 1 and 2.

Because psychological processing problems are basically information-processing problems, to ignore them would be like an ostrich burying its head in the sand. We cannot afford to ignore them because undertaking any cognitive task involves information processing on our part. For example, reading involves information processing (Wong, 1986).

The Debate over the Place for Intelligence (IQ) in the Definition of Learning Disabilities and as a Diagnostic Criterion

Context of the Debate

A major diagnostic criterion in learning disabilities is the reliance on demonstrated discrepancy between the individual's measured intelligence and his or her achievement in, say, reading, mathematics, or writing. Essentially the child, adolescent, or adult with learning disabilities is a person whose academic or cognitive performance is out of line with his or her measured intelligence.

This discrepancy was observed, reported, and graphically presented by Orton (1937), and by others who first reported the phenomenon (e.g., Hinshelwood, Morgan) and reaffirmed more recently by Kirk in the 1950s. Additionally, these pioneers in learning disabilities observed that those children's reading disability was very specific in that the child did not experience the same degree of learning difficulty in other areas. Indeed, the individual had often been found to excel in some other areas of learning, skill, or performance.

You will recall from the preceding section that there is no standardized test for measuring processing problems in learning-disabled individuals. Consequently, researchers and practitioners in learning disabilities have come to use and rely increasingly on the discrepancy formula in diagnosing learning disabilities. However, this use of the discrepancy formula is not universally embraced. In particular, Siegel (1989) voiced strong opposition to it.

Siegel's Objections to the Discrepancy Model or Formula

Why does Siegel (1989) so strongly oppose the use of the discrepancy formula in diagnosing learning disabilities? Of the arguments marshalled by Siegel against the use of the discrepancy formula, I shall examine the two that are directly relevant to the topic here.

First, based on her prior research findings in 1988, Siegel (1989) argued that IQ levels do not differentiate between reading-disabled children. Second, based on her own research data, Siegel argued that low IQ children too can perform adequately in word recognition. Hence, according to her, IQ and reading (word recognition/decoding) are independent (i.e., no relationship between the two). I will elaborate on her arguments.

IQ Levels Do Not Differentiate between Reading-Disabled Children

Siegel (1989) pointed out that the discrepancy formula or model implies that children of different IQ levels should show differential performances in a wide range of reading, spelling, language, memory, and arithmetic tests. However, she failed to find such expected performance differences in children of varying IQ levels. The children that she compared had IQs falling in four categories: Less than 80, 80–90, 91–109, 110, and above.

Although Siegel presented persuasive data as well as supportive data from other researchers on this point, Torgesen (1989) gave some well-considered rebuttals. First, he disagreed with her on the lack of relationship between IQ and reading and language skills. In support of his counter-argument, he cited data in the manuals of the Wide Range Achievement Test (WRAT), the Woodcock-Johnson Psycho-Educational Battery, and the Peabody Individual Achievement Test. These manuals provide data on the robust relationship between IQ and word-reading skill. Second, and more important, from Siegel's (1989) data, Torgesen calculated a significant relationship between IQ and reading ability (see Torgesen, 1989, p. 484). He suggested that Siegel's failure to obtain a relationship between IQ and reading levels in her 1989 data comes from faulty research design. He reasoned thus because in the same study, Siegel failed to obtain a relationship between comprehension skill and IQ in her reading-disabled subjects. Robust relationships between IQ and reading comprehension have long been recognized in the research literatures in reading and intelligence. Even Siegel (1989) acknowledged that comprehension and IQ tests measure similar processes. Similarly, Stanovich pointed out that in Siegel's (1989) data, her subjects showed "some mild trends" that are congruent with the idea of differential cognitive processing as a function of IQ.

It is evident that Siegel's first major argument is provocative, but that it does not rest on terra firma. I turn now to her second argument.

Low IQ Children Can Learn to Read as Well

Siegel argued that there are cases of children or individuals with a low IQ who can decode words and nonwords (pseudowords). She cited a case study in her (1989) paper to support her argument that IQ bears no relationship to reading ability.

Again, Torgesen disagreed with her. He said that Siegel's argument means that low IQ or IQ, in the range used by Siegel (below 80), is an insufficient cause for a child's poor reading or development of reading disability. To explain how the low IQ children in Siegel's (1989) study could adequately decode single words and pseudowords, Torgesen suggested compensatory factors, such as, an extremely strong motivation to learn to read, supportive home, or an exceptionally effective teacher:

> What the broad correlations between IQ and word reading skill reported earlier suggest is that IQ may be causally related to reading acquisition given that all other factors associated with reading skill are held constant. The correlations do not mean that some children with low IQ might not be able to learn to read well. (Torgesen, 1989, p. 485)

Clearly, Siegel's second argument against the use of the discrepancy formula does not stand up to close scrutiny.

On the other hand, like others (Tanis Bryan), I am sympathetic to Siegel's efforts. Basically, she argues for the centrality of phonological processing problems as a key to understanding reading disability. On this issue I agree with her wholeheartedly. From this perspective, and reasoning that phonological processing bears zero relationship to intelligence, Siegel considers IQ irrelevant to defining and diagnosing reading disability. But IQ and phonological processing have more than a zero relationship. Stanovich (1986) calculated a .31 correlation between the two. Moreover, one needs to remember that not all reading disabilities are caused by phonological processing problems (Torgesen, 1989), and learning disabilities may not mean reading disability (Lyon, 1989).

Nevertheless, what Siegel advocates is sound; namely, using nonword reading as a diagnostic task, we can effectively screen children who are at risk or have reading disability, and provide early intervention or suitable remediation. We can thus cut through unnecessary testing and get to the heart of the matter of remediation. Her approach would ensure those who need remediation in reading receive it. In the final analysis, that is the ideal, especially in an inclusive learning environment.

You have seen how the definition of learning disabilities is confounded by controversies over the issues of psychological processing problems and IQ. Now you will see two additional sources of confusion. These include the relationship between attention deficit–hyperactivity disorder (ADHD) and the concept of learning disabilities, and the myth that learning disabilities equal reading disability. These two issues, however, are not as contentious as the first two.

The Relationship between ADHD and the Concept of Learning Disabilities

The disorder of ADHD[1] adds to the confusion surrounding the definition of learning disabilities, mainly because some children are diagnosed with both kinds of disorders: they have ADHD and learning disabilities. Put differently, the confusion comes from the overlap of ADHD with learning disabilities. The point to remember is that the majority of children with learning disabilities does not have the simultaneous diagnosis of ADHD. Similarly, there are children diagnosed with the ADHD who do not have learning disabilities.

What Do We Know about ADHD?

Knowledge about ADHD comes from research and clinical observations of professionals (doctors, psychiatrists, psychologists, educators, and parents). Although we still lack definitive answers in many areas (e.g., causation of ADHD, as seen in the categorized information below), we have made substantial progress in unraveling the mysteries of ADHD.

Age of Onset or Manifestation

Although some mothers claim that they knew their children were "difficult" from birth, most parents would agree that deviant behaviors are in place by age 3 or 4 (e.g., pronounced overactivity). These behavioral problems, associated with attentional problems, become more pronounced when the child begins school. The attentional demands and the presence of rules and structure in school likely compound or exacerbate the child's problem of short attention span.

With increasing age, hyperactivity subsides in the ADHD child. However, other problems come to the fore, such as problems in completing assignments and possibly, problems in social relations. Adherence to the unspoken social rules (etiquette) and accurate readings or perceptions of social cues that underlie successful social relationships may pose serious problems for the teen with ADHD (Conte, 1991).

Sex Distribution of ADHD and Characteristics

Recent prevalence estimates of ADHD is between 4–6% of the school population, with the disorder being three times more common in males than in females. Children age 6–8 are more marked by attention disorders (ADD) than

---

[1] With the exception of the subsection on Comorbidity of ADHD and Learning Disabilities, the original sources of the information on ADHD in this section are Conte (1991) and Pelham (1986).

overactivity. This is because, as in normal non–ADHD children, activity declines with age.

The chief symptoms of ADHD are *short attention span, impulsivity, and overactivity.* These symptoms adversely affect academic learning in ADHD children. Hence, it is not surprising that ADHD children do poorly at school or have learning problems (Conte, 1991).

ADHD and Learning Disabilities: Comorbidity

Prevalence

ADHD does co-occur with learning disabilities in a portion of children diagnosed with ADHD. The technical term for the co-occurrence is comorbidity. The rate of learning disabilities found in children diagnosed to have ADHD varies, ranging from 7 to 92%. Such variability likely arises from differential subject selection criteria, procedures in sampling and measurements, and in the use of inconsistent definitional criteria of learning disabilities in studies reporting prevalence rates of comorbidity (Semrud-Clikeman et al., 1992). Semrud-Clikeman et al. were able to demonstrate that using a psychometrically reliable method to identify learning disabilities in children with ADHD, a more modest prevalence rate was obtained. Specifically, they found a looser or more liberal definition of learning disabilities led to substantially higher rates of identified learning disabilities in 60 clinically referred children with ADHD (38%) versus the rates obtained using two more stringent definitions (23%; 15%). Clearly, their results highlight how using liberal definitions of learning disabilities can inflate the rates of learning disabilities in ADHD children, thereby exaggerating the rate of comorbidity of these disorders. Not surprisingly, a liberal definition of learning disabilities even overidentifies learning disabilities in normally achieving children! (Semrud-Clikeman et al., 1992).

Children who are diagnosed to have both ADHD and learning disabilities have been reported to have more severe attentional and cognitive problems than those with only one disorder (Korkman & Personen, 1994). This is understandable. They would show problems associated with distractibility, impulsivity, and restlessness, which are symptoms of the ADHD disorder, as pertaining to the diagnostic criteria of *Diagnostic and Statistical Manual of Mental Disorders (DSM-III-R)*. Moreover, they would show processing problems and the manifest academic problems in reading, mathematics, and so on, as pertaining to the definition of learning disabilities (Silver, 1990).

One issue that attracts empirical attention concerns the genetic base for the comorbidity. Faraone et al. (1993) gathered family genetic data with the purpose of clarifying the relationship between ADHD and learning disabilities. They examined the rates of learning disabilities in relatives of diagnosed ADHD children with and without learning disabilities.

They found relatives of children with ADHD with and without learning disabilities to have substantially higher risks of ADHD than the relatives of normally achieving, non-ADHD children. However, the risk of learning disabilities was found to be higher only among relatives of children who have both ADHD and learning disabilities. The two disorders, ADHD and learning disabilities were found to be independently transmitted in the families of children with both ADHD and learning disabilities. This means the presence of ADHD in the relatives does not increase their risk of learning disabilities. Lastly, the investigators found nonrandom mating between spouses with ADHD and learning disabilities. Specifically, in the 13 mothers with ADHD, 15% had husbands with a reading disability. In contrast, in mothers without ADHD, 1% of their husbands had a reading disability. Regarding fathers, in 16 of those with ADHD, 13% had wives with a reading disability, whereas it was 0% in wives of fathers without ADHD.

Faraone et al. (1993) concluded that their findings indicate that ADHD and learning disabilities are etiologically independent, and that one source of co-occurrence (comorbidity) appears to be nonrandom mating in the parents. They view their results to corroborate those of Gilger, Pennington, and DeFries (1992).

Using identical and fraternal twin pairs, Gilger et al. (1992) investigated the etiology of comorbidity of ADHD and learning disabilities. They were interested in whether or not the two disorders shared a common, genetic etiology. Towards this end, they selected identical and fraternal twin pairs, in which one twin had received the diagnosis of reading disability. They then focused on examining the rates of ADHD in the cotwin of the identical and fraternal twin pairs. If the rate of ADHD in the cotwin of identical twin pairs was higher than that in the cotwin of fraternal twin pairs, then a common genetic etiology would be indicated.

The results indicated that when one twin was identified as reading disabled, the rate of ADHD in the cotwin of identical twin pairs was 44%; the rate in the cotwin of fraternal twin pairs was 30%. Clearly, the rate of ADHD is higher in cotwins of identical twin pairs than in the cotwins of fraternal twin pairs. However, the difference failed to reach statistical significance. Consequently, it is not justified to conclude that the results point to a common, genetic etiological base for the two disorders. However, one study by no means settles the provocative issue of genetic etiology for the comorbidity of ADHD and learning disabilities. It is sure to attract more research. We should expect interesting and perhaps conflicting data in future studies as researchers test their own biases.

In their follow-up study of children with speech and language impairment, Cantwell and Baker (1991) found sizable prevalence of learning disabilities and ADHD. Specifically, at the start of their study, 19% of the 600 children with speech and language impairment were diagnosed according to the criteria of *DMS-III-R* to have ADHD, and 7% of them to have learning disabilities. Of the 7% learning-disabled children (42 of them), 40% (17) had ADHD also. That is, 17 of these children had comorbidity of learning disabilities and ADHD. At the start of the study, the mean age of the children was 5.6 years, with a range of 1–16 years.

Cantwell and Baker's follow-up study occurred 4–5 years later when the mean age of the children was 9.1 years. Also, the sample was reduced to 300 children, possibly due to attrition of the subject pool, for example, family relocation. The investigators now found that 37% of them had ADHD, and 30% (91 children out of 300) of them had learning disabilities. Moreover, 53% (48) of them had comorbidity of learning disabilities and ADHD, compared to 17 cases of comorbidity at the start of the study.

Clearly, these percentages of ADHD, learning disabilities and comorbidity of ADHD and learning disabilities were substantially higher at follow-up. The data thus suggest that in a specific sample of children with speech and language impairment, there appears to be a very substantial probability or risk of developing ADHD, learning disabilities, and comorbidity of ADHD and learning disabilities. The implications are clear for replication study, and for further research to clarify the relationships between speech and language impairment and children's subsequent development of ADHD, learning disabilities, and ADHD and learning disabilities.

Pointers on ADHD

Undoubtedly and unfortunately, ADHD and learning disabilities co-occur in a portion of children. The technical term is *comorbidity* of the two disorders. We have seen how the prevalence rate of comorbidity varies depending on whether the researchers use a liberal or more conservative definition of learning disabilities in their search for learning disabilities among diagnosed ADHD children. Suffice it to say that it is *not* 92%!

We have also examined important research on the genetic base of the comorbidity of ADHD and learning disabilities. Gilger et al.'s (1992) study is very important because it is the first study involving twins to answer the question of genetic base of the co-occurrence of ADHD and learning disabilities. Their data and those of Faraone et al. (1993) converge on the conclusion that a genetic base for comorbidity is not justified, at least not currently. However, this conclusion appears to apply at a global or general level, but not at a more specific level of subtypes of problem children, such as children with speech and language impairment (Cantwell & Baker, 1991). You will recall that Cantwell and Baker (1991) followed 300 of these children and found substantially high rates of ADHD, learning disabilities, and ADHD and learning disabilities. The possibility exists that for specific subtypes of problem children, comorbidity of ADHD and learning disabilities may spring from a common genetic base. In short, the issue of genetic base continues to provoke empirical interest and is far from settled. The verdict on it will be a long time coming!

Much as we are attracted to issues of rate and genetic base of comorbidity of ADHD and learning disabilities, we must not forget the essential issues of accurate assessment, diagnosis, and appropriate treatment! Ultimately, these children need to be taught academic skills, to learn to sustain attention when necessary, to self-regulate impulsivity and restlessness, and their parents must be given professional help and guidance in rearing them. Children with both disorders may well profit from a combined program that attends to their problems ensuing from ADHD as well as from learning disabilities. Thus in addition to the academic remediation attendant to learning disabilities, regular classroom teachers and learning disabilities teachers may add behavioral management, and even, with the help of doctors, the use of medication.

Overlap with Conduct Disorder

According to Pelham (1986), 30–65% of children diagnosed with ADHD also meet criteria for conduct disorder (CD). Although ADHD is characterized primarily by inattention and impulsivity, CD is characterized by "a lack of respect for the basic rights of others" (Conte, 1991, p. 68). The huge degree of overlap between ADHD and CD can lead one to think that these two disorders may be the same thing. But empirical findings indicate family dysfunction is more likely to occur in cases where ADHD and CD co-occur, but not with ADHD alone. These data suggest different causes for the two disorders. Hence we should not consider ADHD and CD to be the same (Conte, 1991).

Not Caused by Specific Brain Damage

At present, research findings favor biological variables as causes of ADHD. Thus, developmental and chronic health problems appear to play a causal role in a child's ADHD. The developmental problems refer to speech problems, clumsiness, slowness in reaching milestones in talking and walking, and low birth weight. But neurotransmitter abnormalities do not appear to have firm empirical support as the causal factors of ADHD. On the other hand, allergies appear to be quite closely associated with ADHD. However, association or correlation does not equate causation (Conte, 1991).

Not Caused by Family Dysfunction

Family dysfunction appears to be more closely associated with CD than with ADHD. Hence, there is no substance to the notion that ADHD is caused by family dysfunction (Conte, 1991).

How Is ADHD Diagnosed?

ADHD is diagnosed according to the criteria listed in *DMS-III-R*. This manual includes the results of surveys of practicing psychiatrists who were asked to report patient symptoms used in their formulation of a diagnosis of ADHD. These symptoms are primary and dependable. The survey results were tabulated, and the most frequently cited symptoms formed definitions and diagnostic criteria for psychiatric disorders such as ADHD and CD.

Before its revision, *DSM-III* listed two definitions of ADD: ADD *with* hyperactivity and ADD *without* hyperactivity. The attentional component of the disorder included two classes of symptoms: inattention and impulsivity. However, as stated above, when *DSM-III* was revised, the distinguishing characteristic of presence or absence of hyperactivity between the two kinds of attentional disorder was eliminated. Consequently there is only one unitary construct or single entity of ADHD. As explained previously, this treatment of ADD as a unitary entity does not have universal acceptance. It is highly likely that future revisions of *DMS-III-R* will see a reversal to restoring the distinction of hyperactivity as co-occurring in some cases of ADD but not in others.

Meanwhile, a diagnosis of ADHD in a child must meet at least eight of the stated 14 symptoms in *DMS-III-R*. Moreover, the observed disorder should be pervasive (i.e., the behavioral symptoms of the child should prevail at home and at school). As well, they should persist for at least 6 months (i.e., the observed behavioral problems should not be episodic).

Apart from the diagnostic criteria in *DMS-III-R,* parents and teachers can use the Connors Parent–Teacher Questionnaire to assess ADD. This scale is reputable and has been widely used. It serves well in discriminating between children with and without ADD. However, it does have its detractors. For example, it has been criticized to be overly sensitive to the hyperactivity component and less so to the attentional component of ADHD (Conte, 1991).

Treatment

Various ways of treating ADHD have been attempted. In general, these treatments have not shown desirable maintenance effects. Behavior modification (BM), cognitive behavior modification (CBM), and behavior modification combined with medication or drug treatment are some of the approaches used. Apparently, short-term gains have been often noted in BM and drug treatment. For example, Pelham (1986) reported that ADHD children using medication had improved math performance. The children completed more items and scored higher in number of correct items. But long-term benefits of BM and drug treatment are unknown. Pelham also stated that even under treatment, normalization of behavior in ADHD children did not occur.

Conceptually, CBM appeared to be very promising in treating children with ADHD. Sadly, this promise was not borne out. In my view, the attentional problems in ADHD children would greatly impede their learning the steps in any CBM strategy. Not only do they need to sustain attention to understand thoroughly the individual component steps in the strategy, but they also need to rehearse them to mastery. Then they need to self-check accuracy in strategy implementation. For ADHD children with and without hyperactivity, the demands of CBM may be exorbitant. In short, I do not think CBM is suitable for treatment with ADHD children because of the poor match between learner and strategy characteristics.

At present, another approach is to encourage the training of parents as therapists for their ADHD children. The impetus comes from the success with parent interventions with children with CD. It also makes sense to train parents to treat their children with ADHD, because as caregivers they provide a continuous presence with their children. Hence, when properly trained, they could induce, maintain, and enable generalization of appropriate behaviors in their ADHD children (Conte, 1991).

Making Sense of All the Definitions of Learning Disabilities

The student may be overwhelmed by the different definitions of learning disabilities that occur as the field evolves. One way to avoid being confused and overwhelmed is to try to understand the shaping forces, motives, and goals of each of those definitions. Let's turn to the first definition of learning disabilities.

Shortly after the historic meeting in 1963 and the establishment of the division of learning disabilities in 1965 within the International Council for Exceptional children, the first attempt at defining learning disabilities was made by Task Force I, which was sponsored by the National Society for Crippled Children and Adults as well as by the National Institutes of Neurological Diseases and Blindness of the National Institutes of Health. It reads as follows:

> The term "minimal brain dysfunction syndrome" refers in this paper to children of near average, average to above average general intelligence with certain learning or behavioral disabilities ranging from mild to severe, which are associated with deviations of function of the central nervous system. These deviations may manifest themselves by various combinations of impairment in perceptions, conceptualization, language, memory, and control of attention, impulse, or motor function (1966, pp. 9–10).

This definition suggests the influence of medical professionals because of the focus on the relationship between minimal brain dysfunction (MBO) and learning problems. With the emphasis on brain dysfunction, it relegates diagnosis to medical professionals because educators cannot make such a diagnosis. However, the nature of the brain dysfunction is supposedly minimal, which would suggest the need for more education-oriented assessments. Clearly, this definition does not lead to useful diagnosis and educational programming. It therefore comes as no surprise that it was replaced by another. This one was formulated by the National Advisory Committee on Handicapped Children (1967). It says

Children with special learning disabilities exhibit a disorder in one or more of the basic psychological processes involved in understanding or in using spoken or written language. These may be manifested in disorders of listening, thinking, talking, reading, writing, spelling, or arithmetic. They include conditions which have been referred to as perceptual handicaps, brain injury, minimal brain dysfunction, dyslexia, developmental aphasia, etc. They do not include learning problems which are due primarily to visual, hearing, or motor handicaps, to mental retardation, emotional disturbance, or to environmental disadvantage.

This definition was later used for the U.S. federal legislation regarding funding for services of children with learning disabilities. The particular piece of legislation was the 1969 Children with Specific Learning Disabilities Act, Pl 21-230, The Elementary and Secondary Amendments of 1969 (Bryan & Bryan, 1978).

This second attempt at defining learning disabilities contains some key points: (a) Disorders in psychological processes are assumed to be the mechanisms underlying learning disabilities. (b) Learning disabilities constitute a distinct cognitive disorder that is not aligned with learning problems caused by other kinds of sensory or physical handicaps, nor emotional or environmental handicaps.

In contrast to the exclusionary sentence making the second key point is an inclusive one in the definition: "They include conditions which have been referred to as perceptual handicaps, brain injury, minimal brain dysfunction, dyslexia, developmental aphasia, etc." What is the purpose of this all-inclusive sentence? Basically it simply served to accommodate the interests of all the professionals who have a finger in the pie called learning disabilities at that time! "Perceptual handicaps" refer to the group of professionals who emphasized the importance of perceptual problems (e.g., figure–ground discriminations in learning disabilities). Brain injury refers to those who were partial to the importance of the Strauss syndrome (extreme distractibility, hyperactivity). Minimal brain dysfunction and developmental aphasia refer to interests of medical professionals who emphasized the role of MBD in development of learning disabilities and brain abnormalities (e.g., tumor) in a child's loss of speech. (A child may lose speech despite normal understanding of speech because of the presence of a tumor in a specific part of the brain).

However, this 1969 definition of learning disabilities too has its drawbacks. In particular, there is the problem of assessing psychological process problems. As indicated previously, there are no standardized tests for assessing psychological-processing problems. Again, to make the definition of learning disabilities operational for assessment purposes, expansions or amendments to it became necessary. This expansion came in 1977 in the definition of a specific learning disability proposed by the U.S. Office of Education, and it provides regulations and guidelines in operationalizing the definition of learning disabilities. It says:

A specific learning disability occurs in a student if (1) s/he does not achieve commensurate with his/her age and ability in one or more of several specific areas when s/he has been given with suitable instructional experiences, and (2) the student shows a severe discrepancy between achievement and intellectual ability in one or more of seven areas: (a) oral expression, (b) listening comprehension, (c) written expression, (d) basic reading skill, (e) reading comprehension, (f) mathematics calculation and (g) mathematics reasoning.

The above operationalization of learning disabilities became the second part of a two-part definition of learning disabilities. The first part is identical to the 1969 definition, which had been subsequently incorporated in the U.S. federal Public Law 94-142, Education for All Handicapped Children Act (1975). In 1990, this two-part definition was incorporated into U.S. federal Public Law 101-476, the Individuals with Learning Disabilities Education Act (IDEA) (1990). (See Lerner, 1993, pp. 8–12).

The motives and goal of this two-part definition of learning disabilities are to enable educators in their assessments and educational planning for individuals with learning disabilities. The original 1969 definition was kept intact as the first part of the 1975 definition because it was still considered adequate and that research had not shed sufficient new light to warrant changes in it.

Nevertheless, there was discontent with the original 1969 definition. Some learning disabilities professionals felt the inclusive clause of "perceptual handicaps, brain injury, minimal brain dysfunction, dyslexia, developmental aphasia" and the term "basic psychological processes" confounded their understanding of the nature of learning disabilities. Consequently, they wanted to remove these elements from this definition. Also important was distinguishing between learning disabilities and learning problems, and acknowledging the coexistence of learning disabilities with other handicaps (e.g., deafness).

In an attempt to streamline the definition of learning disabilities and to improve its clarity, in 1981 the National Joint Committee on Learning Disabilities (NJCLD) formulated a definition of learning disabilities. It reads as follows:

> Learning disabilities is a generic term that refers to a heterogeneous group of disorders manifested by significant difficulties in the acquisition and use of listening, speaking, reading, writing, reasoning or mathematical abilities. These disorders are intrinsic to the individual and presumed to be due to central nervous system dysfunction. Even though learning disability may occur concomitantly with other handicapping conditions (e.g., sensory impairment, mental retardation, social and emotional disturbance) or environmental influences (e.g., cultural differences, insufficient/inappropriate instruction, psychogenic factors), it is not the direct result of those conditions or influences.

It is important to note that the NJCLD comprised representatives of the following national organizations in the United States: the American Speech-Language-Hearing Association (ASHA), the Association for Children with Learning Disabilities (ACLD), the Council of Learning Disabilities (CLD), the Division of Children with Communication Disorders (DCCD), the International Reading Association (IRA), and the Orton Dyslexic Society. The only organization that adopted a neutral stance toward it was the Division of Learning Disabilities (DLD) within the Council for Exceptional Children (CEC).

In 1988, NJCLD felt that the definition should acknowledge recent advances in research. Specifically, it was necessary to acknowledge input from research on social and self-regulatory problems in individuals with learning disabilities. These problems could characterize some learning-disabled children, adolescents, or adults. However, they may not be assumed to be primary causes of learning disabilities. Also, a definition of learning disabilities needs to acknowledge explicitly that this cognitive disorder is a lifelong disorder. The revised definition of learning disabilities reads as follows:

> Learning disabilities is a general term that refers to a heterogeneous group of disorders manifested by significant difficulties in the acquisition and use of listening, speaking, reading, writing, reasoning, or mathematical abilities. These disorders are intrinsic to the individual, presumed to be due to central nervous system dysfunction and may occur across the life span. Problems in self-regulatory behaviors, social perception, and social interaction may exist with learning disabilities but do not by themselves constitute a learning disability. Although learning disabilities may occur concomitantly with other handicapping conditions (for example, sensory impairment, mental retardation, serious emotional disturbance) or with extrinsic influences such as cultural differences, insufficient or inappropriate instruction, they are not the result of these conditions or influences. (Hammill, 1993, p. 4).

Hammill (1993) states that the above 1988 NJCLD definition and the 1977 U.S. Office of Education definition have the broadest acceptance. Earlier he argued that the NJCLD definition has the broadest consensus in the learning disabilities field at present (Hammill, 1990).

What about Canada? Does Canada have its own definition of learning disabilities? Yes, it does. The Canadian definition models the 1981 NJCLD definition. However, it differs from the American definition in giving social and emotional problems more prominence. The Canadian definition of learning disabilities is as follows:

> *LEARNING DISABILITIES* is a generic term that refers to a heterogeneous group of disorders due to identifiable or inferred central nervous system dysfunction. Such disorders may be manifested by delays in early development and/or difficulties in any of the following areas: attention, memory, reasoning, coordination, communicating, reading, writing, spelling, calculation, social competence, and emotional maturation.
>
> *LEARNING DISABILITIES* are intrinsic to the individual, and may affect learning and behaviour in any individual, including those with potentially average, average, or above average intelligence.
>
> *LEARNING DISABILITIES* are not due primarily to visual, hearing, or motor handicaps; to mental retardation, emotional disturbance, or environmental disadvantage; al-

though they may occur concurrently with any of these. Learning disabilities may arise from genetic variation, bio-chemical factors, events in the pre- to post-natal period, or any other subsequent events resulting in neurological impairment. (Learning Disabilities Association of Canada Definition, 1987)

Including social problems in the definition of learning disabilities obscures the differentiation between primary (causal) and secondary (by-product) characteristics. More important, it may produce the misconception that social problems are ubiquitous in individuals with learning disabilities. In due time, revision of the Canadian definition of learning disabilities will surely attend to the observed problems.

As the learning disabilities field evolved, successive attempts were made to draft and revise the definition. Each of these was crafted with specific goals in view. Thus the initial 1967 definition was concerned with specifying the underlying mechanisms of learning disabilities, and the goal of establishing this cognitive disorder as a new division within International CEC. These motives and goals explain the particular wording of that definition.

In turn, the second definition came into existence because of the need to improve on the first. The improvement lay in the provisions in the 1975 definition, operational guidelines and regulations that enable educators to assess learning disabilities and produce educational programs based on assessment data.

The final rounds of reformulations by NJCLD aimed to clarify or eliminate unnecessary terminologies, and thus streamline the definition and update it in light of current research findings. The resulting 1988 NJCLD definition appears to be widely accepted in the learning disabilities field. The Canadian version incorporates elements from the American versions.

Finally, one may ask, What is the current status of the definition of learning disabilities? As Hammill (1993) insightfully says, NJCLD has not written the perfect definition. But it has produced one to which professionals can subscribe. And this unifying function is vital not only for practical reasons, but also for the survival of the field (Hammill, 1993). Funding for services for the learning disabled may be cut or reduced if we lack a consensual definition of learning disabilities. It is therefore comforting that NJCLD has provided a very usable definition.

The Meaning of Learning Disabilities

What does the term *learning disabilities* mean? It really refers to a heterogeneous bunch of academic and nonacademic problems that reside in certain children, adolescents, and adults. Figure 1 in Chapter 1 distinguishes academic and nonacademic learning disabilities. Academic learning disabilities include problems in familiar areas of reading, arithmetic and mathematics, writing and spelling; and nonacademic problems, such as those in phonological processing, language, visual and auditory discrimination, memory processes, and visuomotor coordination.

An individual with learning disabilities can have any combination of academic and nonacademic problems. It is uncommon that two such individuals would have identical sets of problems in severity or instructional needs. You may, for example, encounter two eighth-grade students with learning disabilities who both have reading disabilities. But it would be very unlikely that they would both have exactly the same error patterns in their oral reading or the same degree or complexity of reading comprehension problems, or require identical instructional accommodations. In short, students with learning disabilities are very heterogeneous in the kinds of problems they have and in their instructional needs.

When we meet children and adolescents with learning disabilities in school, we find ourselves struck by some consistent characteristics. Specifically, in examining their academic work, we find clear demonstrations of academic retardation or underachievement. In their test files, we find records of adequate performance on standardized intelligence tests.

Against the backdrop of such information, their academic underachievement may surprise us because we do not expect any discrepancy between their measured intelligence and academic achievement. Also, individuals with learning disabilities have no sensory deficits (i.e., no deafness or blindness). Because of their intact sensory capacities, we are puzzled by learning disabled students' singular difficulty in learning to read.

These consistent and salient characteristics of individuals with learning disabilities describe them well, and help define them for our purposes of identification and diagnosis. Indeed, as we have seen, they are contained in definitions of learning disabilities. But it is pertinent to note that these are descriptive characteristics, not explanatory or primary characteristics.

Primary characteristics of learning disabilities are explanatory ones. Which characteristics then are primary? They are processing problems. And in what way are they explanatory? Processing problems with linguistic materials impair the child's ability in learning to read, and underlie his or her substantial problems in reading, and/or arithmetic, writing, and spelling. Hence, they constitute the primary or causal characteristics of learning disabilities.

There is an important implication from the discussion on processing problems as the primary characteristics of learning disabilities. It is the need to have information-processing models. The reason is this: We need to analyze the processing demands of to-be-learned tasks by learning-disabled students so that we can anticipate where they may have difficulties and generate solutions to help them. To do so, we need information-processing models that would guide us to perform a good cognitive task analysis. The latter informs us on the necessary and sufficient cognitive processes that must be activated in the learning-disabled student for him or her to learn the given task.

Secondary characteristics are those that the individual with learning disabilities develops as a result of prolonged academic failures. These pertain to motivation, self-esteem, and self-efficacy (in short the self-system), and metacognition.

Prolonged academic failures erode motivation to learn in learning-disabled students. Consequently, they lose persistence at learning; for example, they would refuse to continue with a task upon the first sign of difficulty or initial failure, and they are reluctant to invest effort at new learning. They simply will not try new tasks. These motivational problems have both short-term and long-term effects. The immediate consequences are that the learning-disabled student does not learn or master new tasks. The more long-term consequences are (a) that they do not learn the importance of effort in successful learning, and (b) that they rob themselves of the opportunities to develop new strategies and approaches to various tasks.

Prolonged academic failures have additional negative effects on the self-esteem and self-efficacy of students with learning disabilities. Over time, they develop poor self-esteem; they have poor self-perceptions in academic achievements. They also become increasingly entrenched in the belief that they are unable to succeed in academic work; their sense of self-efficacy is extremely low.

All these negative affect, motivation, and self-perceptions with a concomitant lack of effort at learning ensure that learning-disabled students would continue to do poorly at school. You see then, that they are in a vicious cycle of academic failures leading to negative motivation and self-system (self-concept and self-efficacy), which in turn, increases their chances of more academic failures. The effects of this vicious cycle are very real. Witness the widespread academic failures of these students once they move beyond the primary grades. From an initially specific problem in decoding, they show problems across various academic areas as they move into the upper grades. The snowballing effects of this vicious cycle are clearly discernible in students with learning disabilities. Stanovich (1986) referred to them as the "Mathews Effects."

Another secondary characteristic concerns learning-disabled students' insufficient self-regulation (one aspect of metacognition). Successful students typically show effective strategies in self-regulation and time management in completing assignments and preparing for tests. They have developed these strategies spontaneously in the context of learning and performance in which they persist at trying and using different ways to tackle difficult tasks. More important, they approach tasks with the view of understanding and mastering them. This view ensures focused and sustained efforts at learning. In contrast, the students with learning disabilities typically show a passive approach to tasks, with little attempt at self-initiated learning or sustained attempts at learning.

Secondary characteristics of learning disabilities greatly enhance our understanding of students with learning disabilities. But it is important to realize and remember that these characteristics are by-products of their academic problems, and not the cause of them. Remember, it is processing problems that cause their academic problems.

Differentiations between Learning Disabilities and Learning Problems Associated with Other Nonsensory Handicapping Conditions

It is important to realize that learning problems or disabilities may occur in sensory-intact children, adolescents, and adults who are not diagnosed as learning-disabled. Specifically, learning problems or disabilities can be found in those with mental retardation, emotional disturbance, behavior disorder, and low achievers. How do we differentiate them from those with learning disabilities?

Differentiating between Learning-Disabled and Mentally Retarded Individuals

Children, adolescents, and adults with learning disabilities have adequate intelligence as measured in traditional intelligence tests, such as the Wechsler Intelligence Scale for Children (WISC-R, 1976) and the Wechsler Adult Intelligence Scale (WAIS). Moreover, they typically tend to show an erratic pattern or scatter in the subtests performance. That is, on some items they would do poorly (e.g., digit span subtest), but on other items, they may do much better than average. Hence, in any test, someone with learning disabilities tends to show peaks and troughs in the performance profile.

In contrast, mentally retarded individuals tend to show a very flat performance profile on a given test, with performance in the subtests consistently falling well below average. By definition, such individuals do not have adequate intelligence as measured by traditional intelligence tests.

But intelligence as measured on standard intelligence test is only one of two criteria in the diagnosis of mental retardation. The second and equally important criterion is adaptive skills, which refer to an individual's abilities to cope with his or her environment. One source of adaptive skills is self-help skills, such as the ability to perform household chores.

The current formal definition of mental retardation endorsed by the American Association on Mental Retardation (AAMR) states:

> Mental retardation refers to substantial limitations in present functioning. It is characterized by significantly subaverage intellectual functioning, existing concurrently with related limitations in two or more of the following applicable adaptive skill areas: communication, self-care, home living, social skills, community use, self-direction, health and safety, functional academics, leisure, and work. Mental retardation manifests before age 18. (American Association on Mental Retardation Ad Hoc Committee on Terminology and Classification, 1992, p. 5)

The above definition is sufficiently clear. However, there is one aspect of it that bears elaboration and emphasis: the reference of subaverage intellectual functioning. The above AAMR definition endorses a cutoff score of IQ 70–75 to indicate mental retardation. Traditionally, the range of severity of mental retardation was conveyed by specific ranges of IQs. Thus, approximately, IQ 55–69 indicates mild retardation; IQ 40–55 moderate retardation; IQ 25–40 severe retardation, and IQ below 25 profound retardation. However, in 1992, the AAMR Ad Hoc Committee on Terminology and Classification suggested a rather dramatic change in classification means. Instead of using IQ ranges to classify mentally retarded individuals, it was suggested to base classification on degrees or levels of support. To replace those former retardation categories based on IQ (mild, moderate, severe, and profound), the following categories are used based on degrees or levels of support needed: intermittent, limited, extensive, and pervasive. For example, intermittent support means the retardate simply needs help or support episodically. She or he may need help on specific occasions (e.g., in a sudden medical crisis). In contrast, a retardate that needs pervasive help or support is one who needs constant and much help or support in all of life's settings. At this moment, we do not know if professionals in the field will use the suggested system in mental retardation (Hallahan & Kauffman, 1994).

Differentiating between Learning-Disabled Individuals and Those with Emotional Disturbance

Individuals with learning disabilities have emotional problems that are associated with their histories of academic failure. But these emotional problems can be ameliorated and appear to subside as the learning-disabled person achieves academic success or improvement.

In 1990, the National Mental Health and Special Education Coalition in the United States proposed to replace the old term *serious emotional disturbance* with *emotional or behavioral disorder.* This organization represents over 30 professional and advocacy groups. Hallahan and Kauffman (1994) think that this new terminology may become ubiquitously accepted in the field of emotional and behavior problems.

Although definitional problems plague emotional and behavior disorders, Hallahan and Kauffman (1994) suggest we focus on some central or common themes in the various definitions of this special educational category. These commonalities include extremeness of the behavior, chronic nature of the problem, and behavior that is intolerable because of social or cultural expectations.

Children and adolescents with emotional and behavioral disorders have impaired learning performance. However, we can differentiate between them and those with learning disabilities by the extremeness of their behavioral problems, and their persistent inability to make or sustain satisfactory relationships with others. Their difficulties in relating to peers or adults mainly lie in their reactions to friendly approaches. Either they react aggressively or with hostility, or they withdraw out of fear, nonchalance, or disinterest (Hallahan and Kauffman, 1994).

One may venture to predict progress in academic learning in students with learning disabilities, but not in those who are emotionally disturbed. Given a moderately learning-disabled student who is bright, match him or her with an appropriate educational program and effective learning strategies, she or he may make rapid progress in learning. Appropriate educational programming and strategies may not suffice to induce learning progress in an emotionally disturbed student because she or he must first receive successful therapy to eliminate his or her emotional disturbance.

Differentiating between Learning-Disabled Students and Low Achievers

Who are these low achievers? They appear to be students who hover above the failing grade, whose best grade may be a C−. They tend to share many attributes of students with learning disabilities. Specifically, they are unmotivated in academic learning; they are passive in class and in learning style; they do not persist in difficult tasks; and they lack efficient learning strategies. Unlike students with learning disabilities whose efforts at learning have been crushed by continual failure, low achievers rarely apply themselves.

How do they differ from students with learning disabilities? They differ from the latter in at least two important ways: (a) In all likelihood, they would not have the discrepancy between ability and performance as found in those with learning disabilities. (b) They do not have processing problems as found in those with learning disabilities (e.g., memory problems).

REFLECTIONS

Why is defining learning disabilities so difficult? you may ask. And you may moan to yourself thus: "Haven't you told us ad nauseum that a person with learning disabilities has a discrepancy between his or her measured intelligence and achievements. She or he has processing problems but no sensory deficits?!"

Well, our task in defining learning disabilities would be much more straightforward if there weren't the ever-present and everlasting debates on the respective roles of IQ (intelligence) and processing problems in the definition of learning disabilities! The debates over these conceptual problems take the front stage so often that they distract us from remembering the functions of a definition of learning disabilities. These functions are

1. To enable universal recognition of the phenomenon called learning disabilities. This would include ready recognition of the salient characteristics of it.

2. To enable clear diagnosis. This means the definition could be translated into operational guidelines and regulations by professionals so that they can perform the diagnosis without any hindrance.

3. To enable professionals to embark on a proper course for treatment of the individual diagnosed with learning disabilities.

At present, the 1988 NJCLD definition proffers an adequate definition of learning disabilities. It has shed the cumbersome language and ambiguous terminology (e.g., developmental aphasia) of the original 1967–1969 version of the definition of learning disabilities, which was repeated verbatim in the first part of the 1975 version of the definition. Additionally, the 1988 NJCLD definition incorporates new information from recent advances in learning disabilities research. Regarding operational guidelines, professionals can use the second part of the 1975 definition.

How do we deal with the perpetual debates over the respective roles of IQ (intelligence) and processing problems in the definition of learning disabilities? Basically, we wait to be informed by current and future research on how to resolve the controversies. It may be that 5 years from now, methodological advances in measuring cognitive processes would permit us to measure some of the processing problems that are found in learning-disabled students. Already, we have made some progress in measuring specific components in phonological processing, such as segmentation. For now, we keep our minds tuned in to these debates while we use the 1988 NJCLD definition of learning disabilities. Who knows, in the next revised definition of learning disabilities, intelligence and processing problems may occupy substantially clearer positions!

References

Bryan, T. H., & Bryan, J. H. (1978). *Understanding Learning Disabilities* (2nd ed.). Sherman Oaks, CA: Alfred Publishing Co.

Cantwell, D. P., & Baker, L. (1991). Association between attention-deficit hyperactivity disorder and learning disorders. *Journal of Learning Disabilities, 24*(2), 88–95.

Conte, R. (1991). Attention disorders. In B. Y. L. Wong (Ed.), *Learning about Learning Disabilities* (pp. 60–101). San Diego, Academic Press.

Faraone, S. V., Biederman, J., Lehman, B. K., Keenan, K., Norman, D., Seidman, L., Kolodny, R., Kraus, I., Perrin, J., and Chen, W. J. 1993). Evidence for the independent familial transmission of attention-deficit hyperactivity disorder and learning disabilities: Results from a family genetic study. *American Journal of Psychiatry, 150*(6), 891–895.

Gilger, J., Pennington, B. F., & DeFries, J. C. (1992). A twin study of the etiology of comorbidity: Attention-deficit hyperactivity disorder and dyslexia. *Journal of American Academy of Child & Adolescent Psychiatry, 31*(2), 343–348.

Hallahan, D. P., & Kauffman, J. M. (1994). *Exceptional Children: Introduction to special education* (6th ed.). Boston: Allyn & Bacon.

Hammill, D. D. (1990). On defining learning disabilities: An emerging consensus. *Journal of Learning Disabilities, 23,* 74–84.

Hammill, D. D. (1993). A timely definition of learning disabilities. *Family Community Health, 16*(3), 1–8.

Korkman, M., & Personen, A. (1994). A comparison of neuropsychological test profiles of children with attention-deficit hyperactivity disorder and/or learning disorder. *Journal of Learning Disabilities, 27*(6), 383–392.

GOVERNORS STATE UNIVERSITY
UNIVERSITY PARK
IL 60466

Lerner, J. (1993). *Learning disabilities: Theories, diagnosis & teaching strategies* (6th ed.). Dallas: Houghton Mifflin.

Lyon, R. G. (1989). IQ is irrelevant to the definition of learning disabilities: A position in search of logic and data. *Journal of Learning Disabilities, 22*(8), 504–512.

Orton, S. T. (1937). *Reading, writing and speech problems in children.* New York: Norton.

Pelham, Jr., W. E. (1986). The effects of psychostimulant drugs on learning and academic achievement in children with attention-deficit disorders and learning disabilities. In J. K. Torgesen & B. Y. L. Wong (Eds.), *Psychological and educational perspectives on learning disabilities* (pp. 257–295). New York: Academic Press.

Semrud-Clikeman, M., Biederman, J., Sprich-Buckminster, S., Lehman, B. K., Faraone, S., & Norman, D. (1992). Comorbidity between ADDH and learning disability: A review and report in a clinically referred sample. *Journal of American Academy of Child & Adolescent Psychiatry, 31*(3), 439–448.

Siegel, L. S. (1989). I.Q. is irrelevant to the definition of learning disabilities. *Journal of Learning Disabilities, 22,* 469–479.

Silver, L. B. (1990). Attention-deficit hyperactivity disorder: Is it a learning disability or a related disorder? *Journal of Learning Disabilities, 23*(7), 394–398.

Stanovich, K. (1986). Matthew effects in reading: Some consequences of individual differences in the acquisition of literacy. *Reading Research Quarterly, 21,* 360–407.

Torgesen, J. K. (1989). Why IQ is relevant to the definition of learning disabilities. *Journal of Learning Disabilities, 22*(8), 484–486.

Torgesen, J. K. (1991). Learning Disabilities: Historical and conceptual issues. In B. Y. L. Wong (Ed.), *Learning about Learning Disabilities* (pp. 3–37). San Diego: Academic Press.

Torgesen, J. K., & Bryant, B. R. (1994). *Test of phonological awareness (TOPA).* Austin, TX: PRO-ED, Inc.

Wong, B. Y. L. (1986). Problems and issues in the definition of learning disabilities. In J. K. Torgesen & B. Y. L. Wong (Eds.), *Psychological and educational perspectives on learning disabilities* (pp. 1–26). New York: Academic Press.

3

An Overview on Subtyping Research in Learning Disabilities

In any group of about 30 children with learning disabilities, we may find that they share one problem; for example, if they were in grades 4 and 5, they may all have a reading problem of varying degrees. But apart from this common problem, they may have very different additional problems. Among these fourth and fifth graders with learning disabilities, some of them may have more severe arithmetic problems; others may have relatively moderate or mild arithmetic problems. Moreover, a few of them may have a memory problem and find it hard to learn multiplication tables, as well as a moderate writing problem. For fourth and fifth graders with a serious reading problem but a relatively mild or moderate arithmetic problem, we may consider them as one subtype of learning disabilities, namely, reading disability. Conversely, we may consider those with a more severe arithmetic problem but relatively milder or moderate reading problem, as constituting another subtype of learning disabilities, namely, children with arithmetic problems.

In this chapter, I discuss the topic of subtypes of learning disabilities. These subtypes are formed for research and instructional purposes.

On Subtypes of Learning Disabilities

We all recognize the heterogeneity of learning disabilities, and that within this heterogeneity, there are numerous types of learning disabilities. This recognition quite naturally leads to the desire among educators and researchers to map out as many types of learning disabilities as possible. Delineating them should enable a clearer understanding of the characteristics of various kinds of learning disabilities which would in turn initiate more suitable and more effective treatment, as well as stimulate more basic and applied research. With the goal of differentiating various types of learning disabilities in mind, researchers engage in subtype research.

What is meant by subtype research and what purposes does it serve? Subtyping individuals with learning disabilities is basically a way to create more homogeneous groups of such persons so that we can (a) better understand their characteristics, (b) make focused attempts at unraveling causes of their manifest academic and nonacademic learning disabilities, and (c) examine systematically the efficacy of various interventions. In short, researchers hope that through subtyping of learning-disabled children, adolescents, and adults, we would reach a more thorough understanding of the phenomenon.

As a result of subtype research, we now recognize subtypes such as learning-disabled children with severe reading problems, attention deficit-hyperactivity disorder (ADHD), memory processing problems, language disorders, and arithmetic-disabled children. Clearly these do not encompass all the subtypes in learning disabilities, but they represent those that have sufficient empirical substantiation.

Approaches in Subtype Research

Clinical and Inferential Subtypes

This subtyping approach originated in the 1950s and 1960s when it was a popular way of conceptualizing a child with learning disabilities as someone with an uneven performance profile in given tests. The unevenness in performance refers to the child's scoring adequately or well on some subtests and poorly on others. A child presenting such an uneven performance profile was said to have a developmental imbalance (Gallagher, 1966). Usually, this developmental imbalance was deduced from the child's uneven performance in the Wechsler Intelligence Scale for Children (WISC-R, 1976).

Subtest Scatter

Some professionals focus on the subtest scatter within the WISC-R, whereas others on the gap between the child's Verbal and Performance IQs. A discrepancy of 15–20 points is taken to be a significant index of imbalance in the child's cognitive functions and to imply presence of learning disabilities.

However, the diagnostic use of the WISC-R does not have empirical validation. Specifically, in studies that compared WISC-R discrepancy between Verbal and Performance IQ between normally achieving and children with learning disabilities, no notable differences were found (Feagans & McKinney, 1981, 1991; Kaufman, 1981; 1976). Hence, it is invalid to use the discrepancy between Verbal and Performance IQ as a diagnostic base for learning disabilities (Kavale & Forness, 1984). Nevertheless, in clinical settings (hospitals), this diagnostic use of the WISC-R still prevails (see the work of Byron Rourke, 1989).

IQ–Achievement Discrepancy

Because professionals in learning disabilities have yet to develop valid measures of psychological processing problems that supposedly cause academic learning problems for individuals with learning disabilities, they have come to rely on the IQ–achievement discrepancy as a means to identify and diagnose learning disabilities. But this formula has its own problems. It could result in overidentifying bright children to have learning disabilities, and overidentifying normally-achieving children in upper grades to be learning disabled (Ysseldyke & Algozzine, 1983).

Academic Subtypes

In this approach, learning disabilities subtypes are formed based on academic performance. Examining children's reading error patterns, Ingram, Mann, and Blackburn (1970) found three subgroups: auditory dyslexia, visuospatial dyslexia, and a mixed group. Johnson and Myklebust (1967) independently suggested two reading subtypes: visual and auditory dyslexia. Myklebust (1978) subsequently expanded them to include additional subtypes of crossmodal dyslexia.

A good illustrative case of subtyping involving this clinical inferential approach is Boder's (1970; 1973) studies. She analyzed reading and spelling errors of over 100 children with reading disability ranging in age from 8–16. From these analyses, she sorted 93% of them into three subtypes: dysphonetic, dyseidetic, and alexic (mixed). Dysphonetic children had difficulties in phonics attack skills and hence, resort to using a visual, whole-word analysis approach in word recognition. Dyseidetic children were said to behave as though they had word blindness (i.e., showing little word recognition) and to labor at it. The alexic group had mixed problems and had the most severe reading disability. Although Boder's subtyping approach is intuitively appealing, empirical attempts to validate her three subgroups have been unsuccessful (Feagans & McKinney, 1991).

Neuropsychological Classification

Researchers who use a neuropsychological approach to subtyping are interested in brain–behavior relationships. They are interested in both explicit and more subtle impairments in visual, auditory, cognitive and motor areas, and cross-modalities caused by malfunctions in the brain (e.g., delayed or abnormal developments, lesions, and injuries to the brain). Through the use of neuropsychological tests, supplemented sometimes with electroencephalograms (EEGs), they aim to measure such impairments in children, adolescents, and adults.

Subtyping attempts using a neuropsychological approach have not yielded replicable or consistent subtypes. One obvious problem with studies using this approach lies in the use of clinical samples, which suggests that the subject pools might not have been representative of children with learning disabilities.

Rationally Defined Subgroups

This subgroup approach was devised and advocated by J. K. Torgesen (1982). Essentially, in this approach the researcher focuses on a single, target characteristic in learning disabilities that she or he is interested in researching and recruits subjects with learning disabilities that unequivocally demonstrate this characteristic (e.g., memory processing problems). The researcher takes great care to screen the subjects with learning disabilities on this target variable. When she or he finds sufficient children with learning disabilities matched on this target variable, and comparison groups of learning disabilities and normally achieving children with adequate performances on the same (target) variable, she or he begins the experiment. It is important to remember that although subjects in a rationally defined subgroup of children with learning disabilities are matched on the target variable or characteristic, they may well vary on other unmatched characteristics.

Using rationally defined subgroups, Torgesen and his associates (Torgesen & Houck, 1980) conducted research on memory processing problems in children with learning disabilities. They had three groups of children in the study: learning-disabled children with severe short-term memory (STM) problems, learning-disabled children without STM problems, and normally achieving children. Torgesen and Houck had very interesting results. Specifically, they were able to increase recall in learning-disabled children without STM memory problems with monetary incentive. In striking contrast, use of monetary incentive failed to improve recall in learning-disabled children with severe STM problems. In short, although the latter children wanted to recall more digits in order to earn money, they were unable to recall the requisite amount of digits for the monetary reward. Thus they demonstrated clearly structural constraints of severe STM deficits on recall capacity or performance.

Clearly, rationally formed and defined subgroups of children with learning disabilities have a very definite place in subtype research. It enables researchers to address pertinent questions regarding learning-disabled children with one specific characteristic or processing problem of particular interest to them. Although the above studies are basic research studies, intervention studies have also used rationally defined subgroups, for example, writing interventions of Graham and Harris (1991), Englert (1990), and Wong et al. (1994).

Multivariate Empirical Classification

In this subtyping approach, researchers use sophisticated statistical procedures (e.g., cluster analysis) to form more homogeneous subgroups of children with learning disabilities out of huge heterogeneous samples of such children. Formation of these subgroups of children with learning disabilities come from their performances across a range of tests and tasks, and within a particular subgroup, children share similar performance profiles. The statistical procedure (e.g., cluster analysis) functions on the principal of increasing homogeneity in members within each subgroup while decreasing the overlap between subgroups (increasing the distance among subgroups formed) (Feagans & McKinney, 1991).

This subtyping approach has enabled researchers to find clusters of children with learning disabilities who have problems in auditory-linguistic and visual-perceptual domains as well as children with learning disabilities who performed in the average range. Although cluster analysis has advanced our understanding of the heterogeneous nature of types of learning disabilities, it has raised concerns in such atheoretical or empirical approach to subtyping. It seems that the kinds of subtypes one may find may relate to the range of tests or tasks used. Because different researchers used different test batteries, replications of subtypes can be difficult (Morrison & Siegel, 1990). Despite these concerns, cluster analysis as a means towards subtyping learning disabilities can untangle the various kinds of learning disabilities within any huge sample of diverse learning-disabled children.

Types of Learning Disabilities Found through Multivariate Empirical Classification (via Cluster Analysis or Q-Factor Research)

At present, subtypes obtained from research using this multivariate empirical classification approach reflect more the kinds of tests and measures used. Hence, we cannot draw definite conclusions about their existence, the exact number of subtypes of learning disabilities, and the number of children each subtype roughly represents. Nevertheless, we should note that from this subtyping research approach, certain subtypes had been found. These include specific-deficit subtypes in either the visuoperceptual (visuomotor) or the auditory-linguistic deficits, and mixed deficit subtypes (Feagans & McKinney, 1991).

The presence of specific deficit subtypes (e.g., visuoperceptual, visuomotor vs. auditory-linguistic deficits) explains the feasibility of early single-deficit theories in learning disabilities that highlighted perceptual processes in reading (Hallahan &

Cruickshank, 1973). But the presence of mixed-deficit subtypes in addition to specific deficit subtypes in one area or domain but not another reminds us that we cannot pigeonhole all children with learning disabilities neatly into one subtype or another. Clearly, they do not fall neatly into the larger confines of perceptual and linguistic processing deficits.

REFLECTIONS

What have we learned from subtyping research in learning disabilities? First and foremost, the answer is that from an essentially heterogeneous subpopulation of children, adolescents, and adults with learning disabilities, we can form more homogeneous groupings of individuals with learning disabilities for the purpose of more in-depth study or research. In turn, such in-depth study enables a deeper understanding of the core elements and essence of specific types of learning disabilities, which should lead to more efficacious treatment.

Second, at present, researchers appear to embrace two approaches in subtype research in learning disabilities: the rationally defined subgroups approach (e.g., Torgesen, Siegel), and the multivariate empirical classification approach. Compared to the latter approach, subtype research proceeding from the rationally defined subgroups approach is substantially smaller in scope. Nevertheless, research using it has provided valuable insights into memory processing problems, and arithmetic problems of children with learning disabilities. Subtyping research using the multivariate empirical classification approach is necessarily larger in scope, involving huge samples. Findings from this approach have shed light on specific-deficit and mixed-deficit subtypes, as well as attention deficit disorder (ADD) and ADHD.

Subtyping research remains an important area for research in learning disabilities, and we should expect to be informed of the nature of other types of learning disabilities as such research continues.

Subtype Classification Scheme

Certain researchers have devoted many years to subtype research, for example, in the United States Paul Satz has been engaged in such work since the 1970s; in Canada, Byron Rourke at Windsor University and more recently, Linda Siegel at the Ontario Institute for the Study of Education (OISE).

In discussing subtypes of learning disabilities, I shall focus on the research of Linda Siegel and Byron Rourke. I discuss Rourke's subtyping research because it involves nonverbal learning disabilities. I focus on Siegel's subtyping research, for three reasons:

1. Siegel's subtype classification scheme is based on academic deficits in reading and arithmetic. As such, learning disabilities researchers, teachers, and univer-

sity students can relate to it easily. Moreover, because it involves measurable academic deficits, the classification scheme can readily be implemented (i.e., it is operational).

2. Siegel's subtype classification has sufficient empirical base. This point is important because some other equally appealing classification schemes (such as Boder's classification scheme, which is based on spelling patterns) fail to obtain reliable or replicable data.

3. Siegel's classification scheme has been shown to apply to adolescents and adults. This extension strengthens its reliability (Shafrir & Siegel, 1994), and befits a life-span approach to studying learning disabilities.

Siegel's subtype classification scheme essentially contains three subtypes of learning disabilities and an additional one of ADD. I will address the former three.[1] The first subtype is Reading-Disabled (RD), which is defined as a child reading on the Wide Range Achievement Test (WRAT-R) (Jastak & Wilkinson, 1984) at or below 25th percentile and on the arithmetic subtest, to be performing at or more than 30th percentile. The second subtype is Arithmetic-Disabled (AD) in which the child performs at or below 25th percentile on the arithmetic subtest in the WRAT, and at or above 30th percentile in reading (word recognition) in the WRAT. The third subtype is the child who is both reading-disabled and arithmetic-disabled (RAD). The RAD child reads at or below 25th percentile in the WRAT word-recognition subtest and is also at or below 25th percentile in the arithmetic subtest on the WRAT.

To flesh out Siegel's subtype classification scheme, examine Table 1. Look at the performance patterns of normally achieving NA children. Apart from the slightly below-average (50th percentile) performance in arithmetic in the older groups, they perform adequately in both reading and arithmetic. Now look at the AD children. Compare their reading levels to their arithmetic levels. What do you see? Yes, they do much poorer in arithmetic than in reading. Now look at the RD children, concentrate first on the age groups of 7–8 and 9–10. Their performance patterns in reading and arithmetic are the opposite to those of AD children: RD children show better performance in arithmetic than in reading, even though they are poor in both. Now look at the performances in arithmetic and reading in the age groups of 11–12 and 13–14 RD children. As they age, RD children develop arithmetic problems as well. There are at least two possible factors that interfere with RD children's performance in arithmetic word problems: their decoding problems and working memory problems.

Now turn to Table 2, in which the classification applies to adolescents and adults with learning disabilities. Examine the performance patterns of AD and RD indi-

---

[1]ADD is a disorder in its own right (see Chapter 1). It can be considered a subtype of learning disability when it overlaps with a learning disability. Such a subtype comprises children with both learning disability and ADD.

Table 1 Percentiles for Ages 7–14[a]

Age		Arithmetic	WRAT percentiles reading	Spelling	Nonword reading (Mean % correct)
Normally achieving					
7–8	(n = 48)	64.9	73.4	71.2	44.5
9–10	(n = 46)	52.7	72.6	64.8	67.2
11–12	(n = 33)	46.3	73.8	71.3	80.9
13–14	(n = 11)	42.6	69.1	64.4	80.0
Arithmetic-disabled					
7–8	(n = 4)	22.3	57.8	39.3	18.9
9–10	(n = 8)	17.0	50.8	37.0	53.4
11–12	(n = 33)	11.9	62.1	41.5	65.6
13–14	(n = 28)	11.1	64.0	50.6	76.5
Reading-disabled					
7–8	(n = 10)	30.5	13.1	27.2	5.8
9–10	(n = 16)	20.1	12.8	9.5	17.1
11–12	(n = 22)	9.3	14.9	10.1	34.0
13–14	(n = 17)	7.2	13.4	11.5	44.4

[a]Reproduced with permission from Siegel & Ryan (1988). Copyright © (1988) by the American Psychological Association. Reprinted with permission.

viduals. The ADs perform much better in the WRAT reading (word recognition) than in arithmetic, and the RDs perform much better in arithmetic than in word recognition in the WRAT. Also, in both Tables 1 and 2, word attack skills as assessed by pseudowords (nonword) reading are very poor in RD persons but adequate in AD persons, except in 7–8-year-olds.

Table 2 Percentiles for Adolescents and Adults[a,b]

Sample (N = 331)[c]	Arithmetic	WRAT percentiles reading	Spelling	Woodcock Word Attack (pseudowords/nonwords)
Normally achieving				
(n = 130)	58.3 (19.1)	70.3 (17.7)	59.9 (23.0)	62.7 (23.6)
Arithmetic-disabled				
(n = 88)	14.5 (7.3)	61.9 (18.2)	45.2 (24.2)	57.7 (25.0)
Reading-disabled				
(n = 32)	54.6 (17.6)	15.2 (6.1)	25.7 (16.7)	22.6 (16.8)
Reading-disabled & arithmetic-disabled				
(n = 81)	8.9 (7.3)	6.8 (6.9)	7.3 (9.7)	14.2 (15.6)

[a]16–72 yr 9 mos.; $\bar{X}$ = 27.7 yrs (10.0) SD.
[b]From Shafrir & Siegel (1994). Tables 1 and 2. Copyright © (1994) by PRO-ED, Inc. Reprinted by permission.
[c]<20 years: 76 students; 20–30 years: 149 students; 30–40 years: 62 students; over 40: 44 students.

Characteristics of Subtypes of Learning-Disabled Children

Understandably, the children in the three subtypes of Siegel's classification show different characteristics. Specifically, RD children consistently have much difficulty with such phonological tasks as nonword reading and grammar. They also have working memory problems that interfere with their reading and reading comprehension. On the other hand, until they get older, they are relatively adequate in arithmetic.

In contrast, AD children have adequate word recognition and decoding skills but have problems with arithmetic and working memory. Finally, RAD children are the most disabled because they have both reading and arithmetic problems.

Research Data on Differential Characteristics of RD and AD Children

In Siegel and Linder (1984), the researchers were interested in whether or not children with reading-disability and those with arithmetic learning disability would show acoustic confusability with rhyming stimuli in their recall. They had three groups of children in the study: the aforementioned children and a normally achieving (NA) group. Three short-term memory tasks were used: visual-written (VW), visual-oral (VO), and auditory-written (AW). There were two versions of each task, a five-letter per trial version and a six-letter per trial version. Each child was given the tasks individually, and the five-letter versions always preceded the six-letter versions. Scoring was very strict, in that only letters recalled in the right serial order were considered correct.

In the VW task, children were presented with cards that contained either 5 or 6 letters on them. Half of these sets contained rhyming letters (e.g., B, C, D, G, P, T, V) and the others nonrhyming letters (e.g., H, K, L, Q, R, S, W). These letters were shown for 3 seconds only. After the card containing the letters was removed, the child had to write the letters on the card.

In the VO task, the children were shown cards containing the letters as in VW, but they had to repeat the letters shown. In the AW task, children heard the stimuli on a tape recorder and then had to write the letters down.

The results showed that young reading-disabled children in the age range of 7–8 recalled as many rhyming as nonrhyming letters, which suggests that they were insensitive to the acoustic confusability in the stimuli. However, older reading-disabled children from 9–13 showed the same pattern of recall as the normally achieving children: they recalled more nonrhyming letters than rhyming ones. Even though they showed the same trends in recall, older reading-disabled children still had poorer recall than the normally achieving children.

Regarding children with arithmetic disability, the findings showed that at the younger age range of 8–9, no differences in recall between rhyming and non-rhyming letters were found. However, at the older age ranges, 10–11, 12–13, they recalled more nonrhyming letters than rhyming ones. These data paralleled data found with the reading-disabled children.

Siegel and Linder (1984) interpreted their findings to reflect a developmental delay in the development of sensitivity to intralist phonemic similarity in reading-disabled and arithmetic-disabled children. Put differently, they suggested their data show such children are slower in developing sensitivity to phonological aspects of the stimuli used in their short-term memory tasks. Unlike young (7–9-year-olds) normally achieving children, reading-disabled and arithmetic-disabled children in those age ranges recalled as many rhyming as nonrhyming letters. If they were sensitive to the rhyming aspect of the string of rhyming letters, they would be acoustically confused by them and recall them poorer than the string of nonrhyming letters.

However, reading-disabled and arithmetic-disabled children eventually do develop such sensitivity. This is shown in their recall patterns as they got older (10–11, 12–13). In light of such data, Siegel and Linder proposed a plausible interpretation of developmental delay.

Siegel and Ryan (1989) investigated working memory in children with reading and arithmetic disabilities and normally achieving children. They used two working memory tasks, one involving sentences and the other counting. The first task was modeled on one originally developed by Daneman and Carpenter (1980), in which the child was given a sentence aurally with the last word missing. The child's task was to supply this missing word. Such sentences with the last word missing in each were grouped into sets of 2, 3, 4, and 5 sentences. Within each set, when a child had finished supplying missing words to all the sentences in the set, she or he must recall the missing words that she or he had supplied in the same order as the sentences. Care was taken to minimize word-finding problems in the children.

The working memory counting task was from a study by Case, Kurland, and Goldberg (1982). It consisted of having the child count yellow dots from a field of yellow and blue dots that were arranged in a randomly designated irregular pattern. These patterns were on 5 × 8-inch index cards. Again the cards came in sets of 2, 3, 4, or 5 cards. After counting dots on cards in each set, the child had to recall the number counted in the same order as the cards were presented.

The results of the working memory sentence task showed that arithmetic-disabled children performed comparably to the normally achieving children, whereas the reading-disabled children performed very poorly compared to the normally achieving children.

Interestingly, the results of the working memory counting task showed that both reading-disabled and arithmetic-disabled children performed significantly poorer than normally achieving children. Moreover, although both normally achieving and arithmetic-disabled children did better as they aged (from 9–10 to 11–13), no significant age-related improvement in this working memory counting task was observed in the reading-disabled children. However, it is important to remember that arithmetic-disabled children still performed poorer than the normally achieving children.

Siegel and Ryan then examined data from a group of 7–8-year-old children with a specific reading disability whom they set aside as a follow-up comparison group in the same study. Of pertinent note is that unlike the above reading-disabled group, this specific reading disability group had no arithmetic problems. They had normal WRAT arithmetic scores, whereas the reading-disabled group, whose working memory performances are described above, had arithmetic problems in addition to their reading disability. Siegel and Ryan found that children with a specific reading disability performed substantially poorer than the normally achieving children in the two working memory tasks.

In sum, Siegal and Ryan's (1989) findings indicate that reading-disabled children, with or without an arithmetic disability, had problems with both working memory tasks (sentence and counting). In contrast, they found children with an arithmetic disability had problems only with the working memory counting task. Consequently, they interpreted their findings to show a generalized deficit in working memory in reading-disabled children, and a specific working memory problem involving numerical elements in arithmetic-disabled children.

Siegel and Ryan cautioned that more research involving 7–8-year-old arithmetic-disabled children and older reading-disabled children without arithmetic problems is necessary. Such research is needed to confirm their findings of specific working memory deficits in arithmetic-disabled children.

Siegel and Ryan (1988) investigated grammatical sensitivity, phonological, and short-term memory skills in normally achieving, reading-disabled, arithmetic-disabled and ADD children. As above, I will focus only on comparisons between the first three groups because this is our major interest.

To test grammatical sensitivity, the researchers used the following tasks: First, the grammatical closure subtest of the Illinois Test of Psycholinguistic Abilities (ITPA) (Kirk et al., 1968), in which the child had to supply a missing grammatical part in a sentence. Siegel and Ryan divided this subtest into 15 regular and 18 irregular sentences. Regular sentences have grammatical parts missing that follow regular grammatical rules (e.g., the past tense of a verb being formed by adding *ed,* and the plural of a noun by *s*). Irregular grammatical parts will be verbs that change from present to past tenses (e.g., steal, stolen). Second, the second grammatical task was a sentence-repetition task in which the child had to repeat 10 sentences. Third was an error-correction task in which the child was to correct errors in 21 sentences she or he heard. This task was originally designed by Willows and Ryan (1986). Fourth, the grammatical sensitivity task was an oral-cloze task (Willows & Ryan, 1986) in which the child listened to 15 sentences consecutively, in each of these sentences there was a missing word. The child was to supply the missing word, which varied in class (e.g., verbs, nouns, conjunctions, etc.).

Phonological and reading-skills tasks consisted of reading and spelling of non-words, one subtest from the Gates-McKillop, the Visual Form of Sounds subtest. In this subtest, children have to select a word that matches one that they have heard, a nonword (e.g., *whiskate,* and choose from *iskate, wiskay, wiskate,* and *whestit*). Additionally, the child was to read a list of 36 regular words, such as *cut, gave, few, nice,* and 36 exception words, such as *sew, put, have, police* (Baron, 1979). Finally, children were given the reading comprehension subtest from the Gilmore Oral Reading Test.

Short-term memory tasks contained rhyming and nonrhyming letters, presented for either 3 or 6 seconds. The child was shown cards with five letters on them and had to write the letters seen when the card was removed. Each child was given seven trials per letter type (rhyming or nonrhyming), with the presentation order randomized.

Results of the grammatical sensitivity tasks showed that reading-disabled children performed more poorly on error correction, oral cloze, and the ITPA (irregular) tasks than normally achieving and arithmetic-disabled children. At the older age ranges (13–14), no differences between these groups were found because of performance ceiling effects. For the ITPA regular items and the sentence-repetition task, differences between reading-disabled and normally achieving children occurred only in 7–8-year-olds.

Arithmetic-disabled children performed similarly to normally achieving children, except for the performance of the youngest 7–8-year-olds on sentence repetition, where they scored much more poorly than the normally achieving children. Siegel and Ryan (1988) interpreted the findings to suggest that arithmetic-disabled children in their study did not have a language deficit as was the case with the reading-disabled children, but they more likely had a short-term memory problem.

Regarding phonological skills, reading-disabled children performed consistently more poorly than normally achieving children on all the tasks, nonword reading, spelling, and so on. Interestingly, in the phonemic tasks, there were no significant differences between normally achieving and arithmetic-disabled children in the older age ranges from 9–14. But at the youngest age ranges (7–8-years-old), arithmetic-disabled children did very poorly in nonword reading and spelling compared to normally achieving children.

In the reading-comprehension subtest of the Gilmore Oral Reading Test, reading-disabled children did more poorly than the normally achieving children. But arithmetic-disabled children did not differ from the normally achieving children. However, both types of learning-disabled children read more slowly than the normally achieving children.

In phonological coding in the short-term memory tasks, both reading-disabled and arithmetic-disabled children showed no sensitivity to phonetic confusability at the younger age range of 7–8, especially at the 3-second presentation rate.

Siegel and Ryan (1988) interpreted their data to show that reading-disabled children are delayed in developing sensitivity to basic grammatical structures of language. Such delay appears to be specific to reading-disabled children, because arithmetic-disabled and ADD children did not show similar difficulties with grammar. Of importance is their note that the problem in grammatical sensitivity in reading-disabled children cannot be attributed to a problem in short-term memory of the sentences because they found no differences in the sentence recall task except at the youngest age range. The researchers thus argue that their data support Vellutino's (1979) notion that reading disability represents a language disorder. Their data clearly showed that reading-disabled children's problems in phonological skills occur at all ages and grade levels.

Caveats about Siegel's Subtype Classification Scheme

The main assets of Siegel's subtype classification scheme were stated at the start of this section. What are the concerns about it? As Siegel admits, it is very hard to identify arithmetic-disabled (AD) children at the younger age ranges of 7–8. You will notice that in Table 1, she had only four AD subjects aged 7–8. Similarly, Siegel pointed out that as reading-disabled (RD) children get older, they develop arithmetic problems as well so that eventually there is a possibility for the RD children to become RAD. For these reasons, more research to ascertain the reliability and generalizability of her classification scheme is needed. Nevertheless, it seems to be the most usable and viable one to date.

I turn now to discuss briefly Byron Rourke's subtyping research. It is of interest because he focuses on nonverbal learning disabilities.

Byron Rourke's Research on Nonverbal Learning Disabilities

Rourke and his associates ran a series of eight studies, the data from which led to his developing the concept of nonverbal learning disabilities (NLD). Rourke's interest initially centered on two groups of children, both of which showed poor arithmetic performances but contrasting performance in word recognition and spelling in the WRAT. Specifically, one group of children, (referred to as Group 2 in Strang and Rourke, 1983, and Group R-S—Reading and Spelling—in Rourke, 1989), had arithmetic performance higher than word recognition and spelling in the WRAT (see Strang & Rourke, 1983, Table 1, p. 36). However, their arithmetic performance was still subnormal. The other group of children (Group 3 in Strang & Rourke, 1983; and Group A in Rourke, 1989) showed a reverse pattern in the WRAT: adequate word recognition and spelling but abysmal arithmetic performance.

Analyses of arithmetic errors of Group 2 children indicated that they involved problems in remembering multiplication tables and particular steps in computational procedures. Moreover, they showed a tendency to avoid math problems that required reading. Thus, Rourke and his associates sum up the arithmetic problems of Group 2 children to involve difficulties in reading and insufficient experience and knowledge with arithmetic.

Analyses of arithmetic errors of Group 3 children indicated that they made a much wider range of errors and a greater number of errors. Rourke (1989) detailed these in seven overlapping categories (pp. 31–32):

1. Spatial organization: errors involve incorrect alignment of numbers in the columns.
2. Visual detail (e.g., misreading a mathematical sign).
3. Procedural errors.
4. Failure to shift psychological set (e.g., after a series of addition problems, when child comes to a subtraction problem, she or he continues to add).
5. Graphomotor skills: problems in writing numbers clearly.
6. Memory problems: problems in accessing the correct rule or procedure at the appropriate moment, rather than problems remembering a specific fact (as with Group 2 children). Group 3 children have the math facts in memory but just fail to retrieve it when needed. (Implied: do not know or recognize clues that indicate need of specific math fact or rule).
7. Judgment and reasoning (e.g., failure to generalize learned math skill).

Clearly, the nature of arithmetic errors differs between Groups 2 and 3 children.

Additionally, Rourke and his associates showed that these two groups of arithmetic-disabled children had vastly different performance strengths and deficits in neuropsychological tests. Specifically, Group 3 children do very poorly in visuo-spatial organization, psychomotor, tactile-perceptual tasks, complex visual-motor tasks, nonverbal problem solving, concept-formation, and adapting to novel tasks. In contrast, Group 2 children show adequate performances in those areas, but do poorly in sentence recall and auditory analysis of common words. Group 3 children have strong performances in auditory-perceptual areas. Last, Group 2 children are said to be more adaptive in social settings than Group 3 children.

Rourke later expanded the NLD syndrome to include more than children with learning disabilities. He reasoned that in his work, he found other kinds of children who also show behaviors and neuropsychological test performance profiles that fit the syndrome of NLD. These children include children with moderate to severe head injuries; children with hydrocephalic condition who unfortunately did not receive prompt or successful treatment; children with childhood cancer such as acute lymphocytic leukemia who were treated with huge dosages of x-irradiation over a long time; children born without the corpus callosum; and children with substantial amount of tissue removed from the right hemisphere (Rourke, 1989, pp. 108–110).

When Rourke and his associates analyzed the performances in neuropsycholog-ical tests, they found children with the NLD syndrome to be deficient in functions and skills for which the right hemisphere is responsible. This led Rourke (1989) to theorize that deficient white matter in the right hemisphere accounts for children's developing the NLD syndrome. In particular, he theorized that lesions and de-struction of white matter involving intermodal connections in the right hemisphere results in NLD in the child.

Rourke's NLD syndrome has clinical and heuristic value. Like all theories, his theory of how NLD develops in a child needs empirical substantiation.

Reflections on Arithmetic Subtype of Learning Disabilities

What have we learned from Siegel and Rourke's research?

1. We learn certainly that children with learning disabilities comprise a hetero-geneous and diverse group; that reading disability though dominant in this group, may not be the exclusive kind of learning disability.

2. We learn that Siegel and Rourke both converge on the need to differentiate among the subtypes of learning disabilities in the heterogeneous groupings of learn-ing-disabled children. Their respective research findings point to the need to extract more homogeneous groups of learning-disabled children from such heterogeneous groupings.

Specifically, Siegel argues that if you use nonword tests or the WRAT word-recognition subtest, you will be able to find children who have reading disability with or without concomitant arithmetic problems. The older the child, the more likely she or he will have concomitant arithmetic problems. This group of reading-disabled children would show phonological processing problems and likely their reading comprehension problems reflect decoding deficits. Thus, using nonword tests, you will net a much more homogeneous group of learning-disabled children with reading disability. In turn, such a group would greatly facilitate research and remediation.

Similarly, arguing from a neuropsychological perspective, Rourke says that you need to supplement academic assessment of learning disabilities with a neuropsy-chological assessment. This way you will find a valid means to differentiate between the two types of arithmetic-disabled children, because these children have distinct-ly different performance profiles in neuropsychological tests.

3. Siegel's arithmetic-disabled children are the same as Rourke's Group 3 chil-dren.

4. They differ in this way: Siegel pursues investigations of psychological pro-cessing of reading-disabled versus arithmetic-disabled children. Thus, she and her associates researched short-term memory and working memory processing in those

children. Rourke, on the other hand, pursues investigations of neuropsychological functions and processes in Group 3 children (Group A in his 1989 book). He is more interested in linking neuropsychological commonalities in Group 3 children with other types of children who evidenced or suffer some form of brain damage. His interests led him to develop the broader concept of NLD and eventually his theory of what caused the development of NLD.

References

Baron, J. (1979). Orthographic and word specific mechanism in children's reading of words. *Child Development, 50,* 60–72.

Boder, E. (1970). Developmental dyslexia: A new diagnostic approach based on the identification of three subtypes. *The Journal of School Health, 40,* 289–290.

Boder, E. (1973). Developmental dyslexia: A diagnostic approach based on three atypical reading-spelling patterns. *Developmental Medicine and Child Neurology, 15,* 663–687.

Case, R., Kurland, D. M., & Goldberg, J. (1982). Operational efficiency of short-term memory span. *Journal of Experimental Psychology, 33,* 386–404.

Cruickshank, W. M. (1967). *Brain-injured child in home, school and community.* Syracuse, N.Y.: Syracuse University Press.

Daneman, M., & Carpenter, P. A. (1980). Individual differences in working memory and reading. *Journal of Verbal Learning and Verbal Behavior, 19,* 450–460.

Englert, C. S. (1990). Unraveling the mysteries of writing through strategy instruction. In T. E. Scruggs & B.Y.L. Wong (Eds.), *Intervention research in learning disabilities* (pp. 186–223). New York: Springer Verlag.

Feagans, L., & McKinney, J. D. (1981). Pattern of exceptionality across domains in learning disabled children. *Journal of Applied Developmental Psychology, 1*(4), 313–328.

Feagans, L. V., & McKinney, J. D. (1991). Subtypes of learning disabilities: A review. In L. V. Feagans, E. J. Short & L. J. Meltzer (Eds.), *Subtypes of learning disabilities: Theoretical perspectives and research* (pp. 3–31).

Gallagher, J. J. (1966). Children with developmental imbalances: A psycho-educational definition. In W. M. Cruickshank (Ed.), *The teaching of brain-injured children.* Syracuse, NY: Syracuse University Press.

Graham, S., & Harris, K. R. (1991). Self-instructional strategy development: Programmatic research in writing. In B. Y. L. Wong (Ed.), *Contemporary intervention research in learning disabilities: An international perspective* (pp. 47–64). New York: Springer-Verlag.

Hallahan, D. P., & Cruickshank, W. M. (1973). *Psychoeducational foundations of learning disabilities.* Englewood-Cliffs, NJ: Prentice-Hall.

Ingram, T. T. S., Mann, A. W., & Blackburn, I. (1970). A retrospective study of 82 children with reading disability. *Developmental Medicine and Child Neurology, 12,* 271–282.

Jastak, S., & Wilkinson, G. S. (1984). *The wide range achievement test-Revised.* Wilmington, DE: Jastak Associates.

Johnson, D., & Myklebust, H. (1967). *Learning disabilities: Educational principles and practices.* New York: Grune & Stratton.

Kavale, K. A., & Forness, S. R. (1984). A meta-analysis of the validity of Wechsler Scale profiles and recategorizations: Patterns of parodies? *Learning Disability Quarterly, 7,* 136–156.

Kaufman, A. S. (1981). The Wechsler Scales and learning disabilities. *Journal of Learning Disabilities, 14*(7), 397–398.

Kirk, I. A., McCarthy, J. J., & Kirk, W. D. (1968). *Illinois Test of Psycholinguistic Ability.* Urbana, IL: University of Chicago Press.

Morrison, S. R., & Siegel, L. S. (1990). Arithmetic disability: Theoretical considerations and empirical evidence for this subtype. In L. V. Feagans, E. J. Short, & L. J. Meltzer (Eds.), Subtypes of learning disabilities: *Theoretical perspectives and research* (pp. 189–208). Hillsdale, NJ: Erlbaum.

Myklebust, H. R. (1978). Toward a science of dyslexiology. In H. R. Myklebust (Ed.), *Progress in learning disabilities* (Vol. 4, pp. 1–39). New York: Grune & Stratton.

Rourke, B. P. (1989). *Nonverbal learning disabilities: The syndrome and the model.* New York: Guilford Press.

Shafrir, U., & Siegel, L. S. (1994). Subtypes of learning disabilities in adolescents and adults. *Journal of Learning Disabilities, 27,* 123–134.

Siegel, L. S., & Linder, B. A. (1984). Short-term memory processes in children with reading and arithmetic learning disabilities. *Developmental Psychology, 20*(2), 200–207.

Siegel, L. S., & Ryan, E. B. (1988). Development of grammatical sensitivity, phonological, and short-term memory skills in normally achieving and learning disabled children. *Developmental Psychology, 24*(1), 28–37.

Siegel, L. S., & Ryan, E. B. (1989). The development of working memory in normally achieving and subtypes of learning-disabled children. *Child Development, 60,* 973–980.

Strang, J. D., & Rourke, B. P. (1983). Concept-formation/non-verbal reasoning abilities of children who exhibit specific academic problems with arithmetic. *Journal of Clinical Child Psychology, 12*(1), 33–39.

Torgesen, J. (1982). The use of rationally defined subgroups in research on learning disabilities. In J. P. Das, R. F. Mulcahy, & T. E. Wall (Eds.), *Theory and research in learning disabilities* (pp. 111–132). New York: Plenum.

Torgesen, J. K., & Houck, G. (1980). Processing deficiencies in learning-disabled children who perform poorly on the digit span task. *Journal of Educational Psychology, 72,* 141–160.

Vellutino, F. R. (1979). *Dyslexia: Theory and research.* Cambridge, MA: MIT Press.

Willows, D. M., & Ryan, E. B. (1986). The development of a grammatical sensitivity and its relation to early reading achievement. *Reading Research Quarterly, 21,* 253–266.

Wong, B. Y. L., Butler, D. L., Ficzere, S. A., Kuperis, S., Corden, M., & Zelmer, J. (1994). Teaching problem learners revision skills and sensitivity to audience through two instructional modes: Student-teacher versus student-student interactive dialogues. *Learning Disabilities Research & Practice, 9*(2), 78–90.

Ysseldyke, J. E., & Algozzine, R. B. (1983). LD or not LD: That's not the question. *Journal of Learning Disabilities, 16,* 29–31.

4

Research on Memory Processes in Children with Learning Disabilities

Introduction

Readers may be amazed or amused to hear me admit that it is a difficult task to summarize or discuss research on memory processes in children with learning disabilities. The reasons are twofold. First, frequently there are considerable difficulties in interpreting the findings. Children's performances in given memory tasks can be much affected by their knowledge base and their repertoires of mnemonic strategies. These factors caution against hasty conclusions of memory deficits in children with learning disabilities when we find them performing poorly in memory tasks. Moreover, an individual's performance on a memory task often involves other, additional cognitive processes over and beyond her or his memory processes (Torgesen, 1988). Second, because of conflicting findings, it is very often impossible to draw unequivocal conclusions or make definitive statements about findings within one particular area of memory research with children with learning disabilities. Despite the difficulty in summarizing and presenting a coherent picture of the research here, I must persevere and press on.

I will introduce certain concepts and theoretical constructs in memory research.

I shall begin with the concepts of encoding, storage, and retrieval, each of which denotes conceptual distinctions in memory processes. Encoding refers to what the individual takes in from sensory (visual or auditory) input, and thus creates a mental representation that can be remembered. In the vast majority of instances, we do not store our sensory experiences for very long in the exact forms in which they originally appear. Rather, we store them in some kind of coded form. Later in this chapter, I will show that when remembering words that are heard or read, we tend to store them in phonological codes (i.e., in terms of their sounds or aspects of their sounds—the phonological features of words). It is important to remember that each person actively constructs his or her own mental representations of stimuli.

Storage in memory refers to "the durability of the memory code, once it has been created" (Torgesen, 1988, p. 350). Retrieval processes refer to the mental operations we mobilize when we try to extract a particular piece of information from memory. Both encoding and retrieval can be automatic or effortful. Torgesen (1988) gave the following as examples for automatic and effortful encoding. Recalling the plot of a television show represents a case of automatic encoding, whereas trying to memorize all the bones in the hand is a case of effortful encoding. An example of automatic retrieval is recalling the names of familiar digits and letters; effortful retrieval is learning new information for a test.

Short-term memory (STM) and long-term memory (LTM) designate another conceptual distinction in memory theories and research. STM refers to brief and limited storage of information that must be rehearsed; otherwise, it is forgotten. Put more technically, the memory trace rapidly decays unless it is kept alive through the individual's active rehearsal of it. In contrast, LTM represents much more stable, and supposedly unlimited capacity for storage of information. Of course, the implicit assumption is that information stored in LTM has been adequately coded in STM, and then rehearsed before being transferred to LTM (i.e., information is thoroughly understood and learning is consolidated).

Working memory (WM) is a more recent theoretical development. The term was coined mainly because theorists and researchers in memory research felt dissatisfied with the construct of STM. They considered it too static, too exclusively focused on the function of storage. They wanted a construct that took on both the storage capacity and active information processing. Consequently, the construct of WM was developed.

With these theoretical constructs, STM, LTM, and WM, cognitive psychologists have theorized about how humans remember things. WM, STM, and LTM are essentially abstract components in theories or models of memory. They can be difficult to understand partly because they seem to take on a life of their own in the context of those theories of memory! But bear in mind that we really do not know if human beings have such memory stores or mechanisms in their heads. Furthermore, these conceptualizations change as newer theoretical models come about, and their arrival changes the direction and focus of memory research. For example, in the 1970s, much research focused on STM. In the mid-1980s, WM emerged as a new theoretical construct, and has eclipsed STM as a research focus. Nevertheless, to gain any insight into how humans remember things, one needs to start with theoretical models that can generate research hypotheses for testing. Because there is no direct way to explore human memory processes, theory-based research appears to be the best solution.

Earlier research on memory processes centered on the storage aspect of memory, in particular, STM (Cohen, 1989). This approach was prevalent even though psychologists have long recognized the conceptual need to consider a memory component that is responsible for both storage and active processing of information. Atkinson and Shiffrin (1971) made the first attempt to develop a theory of memory that incorporated STM. Their model is known as the multistore model and consists of three kinds of memory store: sensory registers, STM, and LTM. Sensory registers are modality-specific stores that receive visual and auditory information respectively and store or hold it in the raw, uninterpreted form for no more than a few (maximum 4) seconds. These sensory registers or stores are constantly bombarded with myriad environmental stimuli. Only a very tiny portion of them is attended to and chosen for further information processing in STM. Processed items are then stored in the LTM. The LTM stores semantic memories and is thought to have unlimited capacity. In contrast, STM is considered to have very limited storage capacity. Unless actively rehearsed, items stored in STM decay rapidly and are forgotten fast (Cohen, 1989).

Cognitive psychologists expended much effort researching these earlier conceptions of human memory. In particular, they focused on designing experimental tasks that test the theorized properties of STM. A typical experimental task is the span test, in which the individual hears a series of digits presented say at the rate of one digit per second, and immediately after presentation, she or he has to repeat verbatim the digits. The order of repetition of digits could be either forward or backwards. This means if I say to you (at the rate of one digit per second) "2913203," and ask you to repeat the digits in a forward order, you would say them back to me as they are. For you to repeat them backwards to me, you would say 3023192. Researchers usually begin with a series of 2 to 3 digits and then increase the number of digits. In this way they scale task difficulty to fit the subjects for their experimental purpose. For example, if the subjects are 6–7-year-olds, you would probably begin with a series of 2 digits. Researchers also begin with digit series or spans, the technical term, involving forward recall. When the subject's performance in recalling digits forward is ascertained (this is indicated when he or she fails both spans at a particular digit length), spans involving backward recall of digits are then given. To give an idea of how researchers can hike the task difficulty in a span test, they can present a series of digits, one per second, then before subjects recall them, subjects do another task first, such as adding a simple sum like 17 + 9. Obviously, this is a distracter task designed to interfere with the retention of the digits.

With the advent of newer models in memory research comes different research foci. Specifically, the old memory models have been criticized in ascribing too many functions to STM. It is believed more appropriate to replace STM, which is a unitary, single memory storage system, with a multicomponent one, the working memory. Moreover, WM has a more dynamic role than STM: it engages in both information processing and storage (Cohen, 1989). Currently, Baddeley's working memory model seems to occupy center stage in research activities and close critical scrutiny by contemporary cognitive psychologists (Gathercole & Baddeley, 1993). Because of its current status and because it is the theoretical framework that guides some of the studies in memory research in learning disabilities, for example, the research of Swanson, I will describe it, explain the functions of its components, and mention some of its shortcomings.

Baddeley's working memory model consists of the all-important central executive and two subsidiary memory systems: the phonological loop and the visuo-sketchpad. The central executive is where most information processing, as well as some brief information storage, occurs. But it also has other functions. These include coordinating activities between and regulating information flow among the two subsidiary memory systems, retrieving information from long-term memory, and providing inputs to the phonological loop and the visuo-sketchpad. The phonological loop handles and stores verbal information. It contains two components: the articulatory control system and the phonological store. The articulatory control system is a verbal rehearsal system, whereas the phonological store is a speech-based storage system. The visuo-sketchpad deals with and stores spatial and nonverbal information. Baddeley currently conceptualizes these two functions of the visuo-sketchpad to be two separate components in it (Cohen, 1989; Gathercole & Baddeley, 1993).

Since the presentation of his model in 1986, Baddeley and associates and some other independent researchers have done much research on the phonological loop. But he has been criticized for lack of research on the most important component of his working memory model, namely, the central executive. Gathercole and Baddeley (1993) admit that the central executive is most difficult to conceptualize and research. Nevertheless, the empirical gap here is most embarrassing for the model developer. It also clearly impedes researchers interested in using his model.

Moreover, critics think that Baddeley ascribes too many functions to the central executive and that this aspect of his theorizing harkens back to the criticisms of the concept of the unitary memory system of STM. They think it is more useful to conceptualize more domain-specific memory processes, and they dismiss the notion of some general executive processor. Although this notion of more domain-specific memory processes has appeal, it lacks unequivocal empirical support. Similarly, the notion of a general executive lacks unequivocal empirical support. In sum, the debate over the role of a general executive in memory processing remains active with no clear winner in sight. But the prediction remains for retaining a general executive in theoretical models of memory, because if human memory systems were all domain-specific, devoid of some central executive (organizer or monitor), there would be chaos in our memory systems (Cohen, 1989). Hence, there seems to be a place for a central executive in human memory systems. How best to conceptualize it, and how to conduct direct empirical assault on it are questions for cognitive psychologists.

In the above, I have briefly described a contemporary theoretical model of memory to provide an example of a model in memory research. Now I shall turn to findings from research on memory processes in children with learning disabilities. To conform to conceptual distinctions typically used in memory research, I shall describe relevant empirical data in encoding, storage, and retrieval processes of memory.

Encoding

Research on encoding processes suggests that compared to normally achieving peers or good readers, children with learning disabilities, or poor readers, have difficulties in phonetic coding. Phonetic coding refers to an individual's transforming words read or heard into speech sounds for purposes of storage in STM. That humans do use phonetic coding has by now been well established by empirical findings of cognitive psychologists.

What does it mean to say that poor readers or children with learning disabilities have difficulties in phonetic coding? It means that they are less sensitive to the sounds of language; and less explicitly aware of the sounds in words (phonological awareness) (Byrne & Shea, 1979; Mann, 1991). These children, as Byrne and Shea (1979) pointed out, know and can distinguish a word from another that differs from it in only one phonetic feature (cat versus hat, for example). Yet they cannot segment the word correctly into its constituent sounds. If you ask these children to say what remains in *mat* if you take away *m,* they would not be able to complete the task successfully.

Numerous studies found that poor readers and children with learning disabilities do not engage phonetic coding efficiently. These studies typically manipulated rhyming and nonrhyming words to highlight differential efficiency in phonetic coding between good and poor readers. The researchers used rhyming words to confuse good readers who use phonetic coding efficiently. Hence, they were predicted to do poorly (more errors/less accuracy) in recalling rhyming words, but to do significantly better in recalling nonrhyming words that do not confuse them. Because poor readers and children with learning disabilities do not use phonetic coding efficiently, their accuracy in recall should not be affected by rhyming words. These predictions have been consistently found in various studies. I shall cite three to illustrate this robust finding.

Byrne and Shea (1979) ran two studies, the first was to research insufficient sensitivity to phonetic (sound) features of words in poor readers; the second explored the possibility that some children could not easily separate form (sounds) of words from meaning of words. Their difficulty here might partially explain their difficulties in phonetic coding.

Thirty second graders, 15 good and 15 poor readers, participated in the first experiment. The materials consisted of 12 clusters, each consisting of five words. Within each cluster, there was one antecedent (A) word, which was paired with a semantically related word, either a synonym or antonym; and a rhyming word. Additionally, each semantic and rhyming word had a control word. For example, an A word would be *home,* the synonym *house,* the rhyming word *comb,* a semantic control word *ship,* and a rhyming control word *glove.* These words were tape-recorded. The 12 clusters of words provided 72 items, which included repetition of each A word. With insertion of filler items that were unrelated to the words in the clusters, there were altogether 121 words presented auditorily to each child. The children's task was to say *new* after any word they had not heard before on the tape, and *old* after any item that they had heard previously.

Byrne and Shea (1979) manipulated the semantic dimension in their study because of this hypothesis: They had found in prior research poor readers were less efficient in using a phonetic code, so they predicted these readers would rely more strongly on using a semantic code. Consequently, they should evidence a high rate of false-positive errors in recognition of semantic items.

The results confirmed their predictions. Poor readers made significantly more recognition errors in semantic items. They made significantly fewer errors involving rhyming words, suggesting that they "did not rely sufficiently upon the phonetic coding for it to cause confusion in recognition" (Byrne & Shea, 1979, p. 334). In contrast, good readers produced more errors involving rhyming than semantic words.

In Experiment II, Byrne and Shea (1979) explored the hypothesis that poor readers might have difficulties separating the forms (sounds) of words from their meanings, and consequently, be slower in developing explicit awareness of phonetic aspects of words or constituent sounds in a word. In turn, such lack of explicit phonetic awareness impedes learning to read, because the latter process involves the child's ability to map speech sounds onto the alphabet and vice versa (Byrne & Shea, 1979; Mann, 1991).

Accordingly, the researchers used nonwords to make the antecedent (A) words their rhyming and rhyming-control words. The procedure was the same as in the first experiment. The results showed indeed poor readers evidenced phonetic confusion on nonwords. However, the extent of their confusion was less than that of good readers. Thus removing semantic aspects of words shows that poor readers can experience phonetic confusion as do good readers. Nevertheless, using nonwords did not remove the performance gap between good and poor readers: Good readers still showed substantially more phonetic confusion than poor readers. Put differently, good readers still demonstrated more efficient use of phonetic coding; otherwise, they would not show such an extent of phonetic confusion.

Using pictures that depicted rhyming and nonrhyming words, Spring and Perry (1983) also demonstrated inefficient phonetic coding in poor readers who were 1.6 years below grade in reading. There were six rhyming and six nonrhyming pictures. Instances of the former included pictures of a cat, hat, bat, can, pan, and fan. Instances of the latter included pictures of a fish, clock, dog, house, bird, and boat.

The task involved the following. Four to six picture cards from the rhyming or nonrhyming set were shown in a random order to the child and placed face down from his or her left to right. Presentation rate of the pictures was 2.5 seconds as the researcher named each. The children had to place each card that was faced down on its matching picture that was attached to a response strip. Altogether there were six response strips, three for rhyming pictures, and three for nonrhyming ones. The researchers controlled for order of the rhyming and nonrhyming pictures, as well as the positioning of the pictures on the response strips.

The results showed clearly that adequate readers had significantly higher memory scores on the nonrhyming pictures than poor readers. But they did not differ on rhyming pictures. Spring and Perry (1983) considered that they had extended prior research findings of inefficient phonetic coding in poor readers to pictures of objects with rhyming and nonrhyming labels.

In three short experiments, Brady, Shankweiler, and Mann (1983) obtained very instructive information on phonetic coding and speech perception in good and poor readers. In the first, they attempted to replicate prior research findings, such as those of Byrne and Shea (1979) and others, that poor readers are less efficient in phonetic coding.

Thirty third graders participated in Brady et al.'s three studies. Of these 15 were poor readers, who were about half a grade below in their reading achievement as measured on the Word Attack and Word Recognition subtests of the Woodcock Reading Mastery Tests. The remaining 15 were good readers, who were reading about two grades above grade.

The stimuli included two sets of rhyming and nonrhyming words, each consisting of 50 words. In the first set, five rhyming words alternated with five nonrhyming words. For example, *chain, train, brain, rain, pain* were followed by *cat, fly, score, meat, scale*. In the second set, the order of rhyming and nonrhyming words was reversed so that the child heard nonrhyming words first. For example, *bell, state, knee, pain, chair*, followed by *fly, pie, tie, eye, sky*. The investigators carefully controlled for word frequency, phonetic structure, and word length in the construction of these stimuli words.

The results indicated that good readers recalled substantially fewer rhyming words than nonrhyming words. In contrast, poor readers showed little difference in their recall between the amount of rhyming and nonrhyming words. Because good readers used phonetic coding more efficiently, they became confused by rhyming words. Consequently, they recalled fewer correct rhyming than nonrhyming words. Poor readers did not suffer from such confusion because they did not have as efficient a phonetic coding as good readers. That poor readers used a phonetic code was seen in transposition errors (i.e., they mixed up letters in the words they recalled). For example, they would recall *trait* and *plane* instead of *train* and *plate*. But the letters they mixed up, *t* in *train* and *n* in *plane* came from other words in the experimental list that they had heard. Hence, like good readers, poor readers did (do) use a phonetic code. The finding of inferior phonetic encoding among poor readers replicated those of prior research.

In Study II, Brady et al. (1983) investigated one possible origin of poor readers' inefficient phonetic encoding, namely, speech perception. They were interested in whether or not poor readers had problems in speech perception that would affect phonetic encoding, resulting in a degraded code being entered into STM, and which in turn led to poor recall.

The same good and poor readers in Study I participated here. The stimuli consisted of 48 high- and low-frequency words that conformed to specific syllabic patterns: consonant-vowel-consonant (CVC); CCVC, CCVCC, and CVCC. There were 12 words per syllabic pattern. Examples of high-frequency words used are *door, team, road, knife, chief, job.* Examples of low-frequency words are *bale, din, lobe, mash, chef, fig.* These words were prerecorded on tape by a male.

A further manipulation was specifically created for the purpose of this study. Brady et al. introduced a masked condition in which the taped words were masked by digitized speech. The control condition was one in which the words were presented as they were taped, devoid of any masking.

The children were told that they would hear a list of words, and to repeat each word immediately after its presentation. In the masked condition, they were simply told that the words had been recorded in some noise. The masked condition always preceded the unmasked one, and the children had practice trials before the experiment proper began.

The results showed that both good and poor readers made many more errors in the masked condition. But poor readers did substantially worse than good readers. In the unmasked condition, both type of readers did well. These findings permit a relatively straightforward interpretation; namely, that poor readers appeared to have less effective speech perception skills than good readers. But their weaknesses here were only observable when they had to respond to degraded stimuli.

Brady et al. (1983) followed up these findings with a very sound question for investigation in Study III. They asked if the poor readers' auditory perception problems were general or specifically confined to linguistic materials. Towards this end, they had the children listen to a tape of environmental sounds, again under two conditions: masked (by white noise) and unmasked.

They used 24 environmental sounds as stimuli, some examples of which are knocking on a door, water running from a faucet, organ playing a wedding march, phone ringing, whistling, airplane engine (noise), door opening and closing, artillery, car starting and driving away, and dialing a phone. Both sets of masked and unmasked noise were presented in one single session; again, the masked condition preceded the unmasked one. Each child was told to identify the source of each sound immediately after its presentation, and to provide as much detail on it as possible. Practice trials involving the unmasked condition were given prior to the experimental proper.

The results clearly showed the poor readers performed similarly to good readers in both masked and unmasked conditions in which they listened to various environmental noises, identified their sources, and elaborated on them. These results are important in that they clearly showed poor readers' auditory perception problems pertained only to linguistic materials. Thus, they have a very specific auditory perception problem, and not a general one. Had it been more general, they would have shown much poorer performance in this study, which involved the use of environmental sounds and not human speech.

To summarize, what are the central themes of Brady et al. (1983)? And why are their findings so significant? The central themes of Brady et al.'s three studies are as follows:

1. Brady et al. wanted to replicate prior research in which the researchers found poor performance on STM tasks in poor readers, and explained their findings in terms of inefficient phonetic encoding in the latter. The STM tasks used permitted phonetic coding. This was the rationale for their first study. Their results confirmed prior research.

2. Brady et al. then investigated one possible origin of poor readers' ineffectual phonetic coding, namely, speech perception (or auditory perception of speech). If poor readers had inferior speech perception, then what got encoded would be degraded auditory input. If that was the case, no wonder that they showed such poor recall (accuracy).

Indeed Brady et al. found that poor readers were very susceptible to deliberate manipulations to degrade (impair the quality of) auditory linguistic input. Compared to good readers, they were markedly inferior in their ability to discern words that were masked by digitized speech. But weaknesses in speech perception were absent in the unmasked condition, in which they performed similarly to as good readers.

3. Brady et al. then asked if poor readers' auditory perception problem was general or specific. To address this question, they used environmental sounds and presented them under masked and unmasked conditions. The results were clear. Poor readers did comparably to good readers under both conditions. Consequently, the investigators were justified in concluding that poor readers' auditory perception problems were of a specific nature, pertaining only to linguistic materials.

The significance of Brady et al. (1983) lies in confirming prior findings of inefficient phonetic coding in poor readers. In turn, they add to the growing body of empirical data on the role of phonological processing problems in reading retardation. More important, Brady et al. highlight the possibility of speech perception problems as one source of inefficient phonetic coding in poor readers. It is insufficient to say that research findings point to inefficient phonetic coding as a valid explanation for poor readers' poor performance on STM tasks. We need to pinpoint mechanisms that in turn explain poor phonetic encoding. The findings in the third experiment of Brady et al. shed some light on this issue of mechanisms of inefficient phonetic encoding in poor readers. Future research addressed to the same issue will surely be enlightening.

Storage

Wong (1978) investigated recall and memory organization in good and poor readers. She was interested in the possibility that poor performance in the latter may on occasion reflect deficient use of task-appropriate strategies, rather than necessarily deficient basic processing. She reasoned that if poor readers were strategically deficient, their recall and organization of memory could be improved with appropriate instruction or cuing. However, if deficient basic processing underlay their poor recall and memory organization, then their poor performances should not be easily modified or improved. Additionally, providing poor readers more time to study items for recall might facilitate them. Experiment I was designed to test the effects of direct cuing and time allotment on recall and memory organization of good and poor readers.

A total of 96 children from grades four and five participated. Of these, half had been formally diagnosed with learning disabilities and were about 1–2 years below grade in reading achievement. The remaining 48 children were normally-achieving, matched in age and sex, randomly drawn from the same classes as the children with learning disabilities. In reading achievement, they were about one grade above grade.

The stimuli consisted of 16 words, with four from each of the following categories: human body parts (arm, head, hand, neck); vehicles (car, plane, meaning airplane, truck, bus); clothing (dress, suit, shirt, pants); and animals (dog, cat, cow, deer). These words were clearly printed in black on white index cards measuring 12.7 cm × 7.6 cm. The category headings were printed on bigger white cards measuring 15.2 cm × 10.1 cm.

Each child was seen individually and given a short practice trial with eight words, different from the experimental ones, to ensure proper understanding of task demands. In the experimental Cued Condition, the experimenter put down all 16 cards before the child. She named each category, for example, "Clothing," and asked the child to point to and name instances that belong to the conceptual category, in this case, that of clothing. Immediately after the child had finished naming all the categorical instances, she instructed her or him to learn conceptually related items together, and to remember them in this way when it was time for recall. Following these instructions, she put down before the child, and on top of the array of stimuli words, the four bigger cards containing the respective conceptual or categorical headings. Thus the child had continuous access to them during the study period before recall.

In the No-Cue Condition, the same procedure applied except that no conceptual or categorical headings were mentioned or provided. In the Timed Condition, children were given 90 seconds to learn the words, whereas in the Not-Timed Condition, they were allowed to self-pace their study, and to inform the experimenter when they were ready for recall.

Two graduate students served as observers to record study behaviors among the children. They targeted three kinds of study behaviors: (a) self-testing, which was operationally defined as looking away from the picture array, and trying to reproduce the items from memory as judged by clearly discernible lip movements; (b) moving pictures, as seen by child's moving them into a conceptual grouping; and (c) verbalizing out loud or whispering with clearly discernible lip movements. Recording occurred for every 15-second interval during the stimuli viewing or studying period.

Wong (1978) found that good readers recalled more words than poor readers, and cuing increased recall. Without cuing, poor readers did very badly, regardless of being timed or not timed in studying. Good readers' recall was affected by the lack of cues only in the Not Timed Condition. In organization of memory as indicated by clustering of words in the children's recall, similar findings were obtained. Again, good readers clustered items in recall substantially more than poor readers. Additional analyses pinpointed two important findings: Good readers clustered more items than poor readers in the Cued Not Timed Condition and in the No-Cued Timed Condition. These findings suggest that in the Cued Not Timed Condition, good readers were more able to capitalize on the cues and additional time in studying to good effect. And in the No-Cued Timed Condition, unlike poor readers, they were likely able to generate mnemonic strategy in aid of learning.

Concerning observations of children's study behaviors, only the category of verbalization significantly differentiated the two groups of readers. Good readers verbalized the names of the stimuli words significantly more often than the poor readers.

The findings of Experiment I suggested strongly that poor readers' poor recall and clustering pointed to a strategy deficit rather than deficit in deep-seated basic processing capacity. In recall, poor readers did worst in the No-Cues Conditions (Timed and Not-timed), worse than poor and good readers in the Cued Conditions. Their performance in clustering also permits a similar analysis, as suggested above. To further explore the feasibility of a strategic deficit view of memory problems in poor readers, Wong (1978) followed up with Experiment II, in which she deliberately chose stimuli words that were harder to learn or cluster because of low interitem associations. In Experiment I, the words had high interitem associations, for example, *dog, cat*. Wong reasoned that if basic processing capacity differences underlie the differences in recall and clustering between good and poor readers, then using words that are more difficult to learn and cluster should widen the performance gap between these two groups of readers. On the other hand, if strategic deficits underlie poor readers' poor performances, then using words that do not lend themselves readily to clustering should reduce the performance gaps between these two groups of readers.

The stimuli words used in Experiment II consisted of 16 words evenly distributed across four categories: food (hot dog, carrots, apples, grapes); clothing (pants, gloves, scarf, dress); animals (cow, rabbit, dog, mouse); furniture (couch, dresser, table, clock). The results substantiated the predictions. Good and poor readers in the Cued Conditions showed comparable performances in recall. Similarly, in organization of memory, good and poor readers in the Cued Conditions (Timed and Not-Timed) did not differ in clustering of items or words in recall. But both groups of good and poor readers in Cued Conditions surpassed good and poor readers in the No-Cued Conditions.

The results of Experiment II clearly showed a narrowing of performance gaps between good and poor readers in recall and organization of memory, when the stimuli were deliberately made more difficult for recall and clustering. Under such conditions, good and poor readers did not differ substantially from one another in performance. The results therefore support the claim that strategic deficiency explains the poor performances in poor readers' recall and clustering in these experiments. Of broader implication and significance from these results is the need to recognize that it is imprudent to attribute unilaterally poor memory performance in poor readers to deficiencies in basic processing capacity. Rather, sometimes, a lack of task-appropriate strategies satisfactorily explains poor readers' dismal performances in certain memory tasks. Consideration of this possibility precludes erroneous conclusions that may precipitate stereotyping of poor readers' memory capacities and functions.

Wong's (1978) finding of less verbalization in poor readers was corroborated in a study by Torgesen and Goldman (1977). They obtained direct indices of insufficient mnemonic activities in poor readers during learning. Consequently their data strengthen the claim that strategic deficiencies partially explain poor recall in poor readers.

Torgesen and Goldman gave good and poor second graders a delayed recall task, which afforded them the opportunity to observe, record, and score the children's use of rehearsal or verbalization as a strategic aid to recall. The children were asked to recall stimuli that consisted of seven achromatic line drawings of the following objects: spoon, baby, apple, bus, ball, flag, cup. All seven objects were presented on each page of a test booklet, each page measuring 8 × 11 in. However, order of the objects as they appeared on each page was randomized.

In the delayed recall task, the researcher held the test booklet before the child and pointed to a specific number of pictures in a prearranged sequence. The presentation rate of pictures was one picture every 2 seconds. After this picture presentation, the child wore a pair of translucent goggles over her or his eyes for 15 seconds, and the researcher turned the page in the test booklet. Subsequent to the delay, the child was asked to raise the goggles and point to the pictures in the order that had been indicated by the researcher.

The 15-second delay period was important because it was here that the children would show spontaneous strategic behaviors to enhance recall of the pictures. Torgesen and Goldman set up a priori three categories of verbalization or lip movement that would indicate the children's active use of mnemonic strategies. These categories included (a) instances where the names of the pictures were actually said or could clearly be lip-read; (b) lip movements that quite definitely represented systematic attempts at rehearsal, but could not be unequivocally identified as corresponding to specific words; and (c) random lip movements or facial expressions. The children were also asked if they did anything special to promote retention of the sequence of the pictures shown. Torgesen and Goldman also used a second recall task, the point and name task. It consisted of each child pointing and naming the pictures during both the presentation and recall stages of the task.

The results of the delayed recall task clearly showed good readers verbalized substantially more than poor readers. They also recalled significantly more items than the latter. These results suggest that poor readers did not spontaneously activate a task-appropriate mnemonic strategy to enhance their recall. Torgesen and Goldman were able to offer some insight into poor readers' strategic passivity. It is recalled that they asked the children if they used any strategy to help them remember the sequence of the pictures. They found a higher number of poor readers had no awareness that any particular strategy would be helpful on the given task. In order for a child to get credit for using a strategy, he or she must describe it clearly. Put differently, the child had to convince the experimenter that he or she did use a strategy. Among the good readers, 15 out of 16 gave clear descriptions of having used verbal rehearsal as a mnemonic strategy, whereas only 9 out of 16 poor readers did the same.

The use of pointing and naming in the second memory task was to increase verbalization in poor readers during the 15-second delay period, which would enhance their recall. The results supported the intended function of pointing and naming for poor readers. They increased markedly both verbalizations and recall, to the extent that their performances here did not differ from those of the good readers. In fact, they improved vastly from the first delayed recall task to the second point-and-name memory task, whereas no such improvement was observed among the good readers.

Torgesen and Goldman's (1977) study provides direct support for the claim that poor readers' dismal performances in recall task is at least in part attributable to their insufficient use of appropriate mnemonic strategies. In turn, their strategic inertia appears to come from a lack of understanding that planful and strategic approaches to learning are very likely to result in successful learning outcomes (Borkowski, Estrada, Milstead, & Hale, 1989). Fortunately, they can be jolted quite easily into using task-appropriate strategies to enhance their learning and recall.

Retrieval

It is difficult to evaluate claims of retrieval problems in children with learning disabilities, because methodologically we cannot separate storage from retrieval processes, however able we are to conceptualize them as separate processes. This methodological problem has been noted by Cooney and Swanson (1987). Thus, if children with learning disabilities cannot recall information as requested at the time of the request, their difficulties may reflect as much poor storage of those items in long-term memory as poor retrieval. And if these children's encoding of to-be-retrieved items had been qualitatively inferior, a finding that has been shown to be possible by Brady et al. (1983), then understandably they would have poorer recall.

However, data from one area in research on retrieval processes involving poor readers and children with learning disabilities is of concern, namely, rapid naming. Researchers using various rapid-naming tasks, for example, naming of letters, digits, and familiar objects, had found poor readers and children with learning disabilities to have a substantially slower naming rate than normally achieving children and good readers (Spring & Perry, 1983; Stanovich, 1986). Spring and Perry (1983) also found digit-naming speed was significantly correlated to memory of pictures of nonrhyming objects (fish, clock, dog, house, bird, and boat), but not to pictures of rhyming objects (cat, hat, bat, can, pan, and fan) in adequate and poor readers. The rhyming objects would induce phonetic confusion and interfere with the subjects' recall. On the basis of the strong correlation, Spring and Perry (1983) hypothesized that high-speed phonetic coding underlies both rapid naming and serial memory tasks, and that phonetic coding speed plays a critical role in reading ability. They concur with Baddeley's (1979) idea that poor readers devote so much cognitive resources to decoding that their ability to maintain the resultant sequence of phonemes in STM becomes severely impaired. Hence, after effortfully sounding out each letter, they might not be able to recall and blend the resulting letter sequence into a word.

Problems in rapid naming among children with learning disabilities apparently persisted into young adulthood. Korhonen (1995) used rapid naming of colors and objects. The subject was asked to name as fast as possible, 50 items shown in five rows. Five colors (red, blue, green, black, and yellow) and five objects (key, comb, scissors, watch, and umbrella) constituted the stimuli. Korhonen (1995) found that at age 18, his subjects still showed slower naming speed and had more errors than the control. But he noted that the between-group differences were not as great as in his initial study when the individuals with learning disabilities were 9 years old.

Summary

Research findings in encoding, storage, and retrieval processes in poor readers and children with learning disabilities indicate that they have encoding problems, more specifically, in encoding phonological aspects of words (sound features of words). Their storage problems appear to reflect strategic deficiencies, or lack of applying task-appropriate strategies. Apparently, children with learning disabilities and poor readers are not aware that they should approach learning in a planful and strategic manner. At other times, their storage problems appear to indicate lack of relevant knowledge base with which to integrate or anchor new learning (Torgesen, 1985). Retrieval problems in these children are confounded by storage problems, or even encoding problems.

Before concluding this chapter on memory processes in children with learning disabilities, I have decided to include a summary of the research of J. K. Torgesen and H. L. Swanson. I am singling them out because of the *sustained* programmatic nature of their research, and the theoretical and empirical importance of their findings. Because of their continual influence in this area of research, and the likelihood that students will repeatedly encounter their names in reports on memory research in various journals of learning disabilities, I judge it important that students learn about their work.

Torgesen and his associates have conducted the most comprehensive and thorough investigations in STM of children with learning disabilities. Although Torgesen has not explicitly linked his memory research to Baddeley's working memory model, his research focus on learning-disabled children's STM would seem to map onto the phonological loop in Baddeley's model. Remember that the phonological loop stores verbal information.

In his research studies on learning-disabled children's STM functions, Torgesen used a well-established experimental task, the span task, in which subjects have to recall verbatim and in the given order, a number of digits. Each presentation of digits is called a span trial, and there are two span trials at each digit length (e.g., two span trials for a three-digit length might be 2-9-4; 8-1-6). Digit lengths are graduated in difficulty and increase systematically by one digit every digit length. In Torgesen's studies involving the span task, digit lengths typically began with two span trials at a three-digit length. The child is presented with two such span trials at each span length until she or he has failed on three consecutively presented spans. Failure on a span trial means either digit(s) omitted or wrong order of digit recall. A complete set of spans given in the aforementioned manner is called a span series.

The subjects in Torgesen's program of STM research were carefully defined and recruited. They conform to what he terms "rationally defined subgroups," which means that the researcher delineates very specific subject selection criteria in forming his or her subject pool in order to conduct focused research on particular subject characteristics. In his case, he was interested in investigating storage problems in children with learning disabilities.

In line with his research focus, Torgesen formed the following two subgroups of children with learning disabilities: those with severe STM problems, (LD-S), those with adequate (normal) STM (LD-N), and a control group of normally achieving peers and on occasion an additional control group of normally achieving first-grade children with similar STM and academic achievement levels as the LD-S children. The LD-S children fit the following a priori criteria: (a) they had measured IQ from 85 upwards on either the Wechsler Intelligence Scale for Children (WISC) or Stanford-Binet; (b) they were between the ages of 9–11 when chosen for participation in the research studies (grades 4 and 5); (c) they were 1.5 years below grade level in either reading or math; and (d) they had no behavioral problems.

The LD-N children were recruited from the same resource rooms as the LD-S children and fulfilled the remaining selection criteria as the LD-S children. Normally achieving children were achieving between 35 and 65% in their academic subjects.

Torgesen's research program focused on investigating the severity, stability, and breadth of LD-S children's memory problems (Torgesen, 1988). Regarding severity of their memory problems, Torgesen and his associates found, on the average, LD-S children recall 4 digits in the correct order. This performance was comparable to normally achieving 5–6-year-olds. In contrast, LD-N and normally achieving peers recalled an average of 5.8 and 5.9 digits in the correct order. This performance was comparable to 9–12-year-olds. Such data attest to the severity of the STM storage problems of LD-S children.

The problem in verbatim recall of briefly stored verbal information in LD-S children was ultimately very stable. It was about 40% less variable than the performance of LD-N and normally achieving children. Torgesen and his associates found little changes in performance of span tasks in the course of a whole year of research in which they saw the LD-S children eight times and gave them many trials of span task. The stability of LD-S children's STM problems was most prominent in the condition in which monetary incentive failed to increase the number of digits recalled (Torgesen & Houck, 1980). Specifically, after they had completed three span series in digit recall, all the children were told that they would be rewarded with money for improved recall in the subsequent second set of three span series. Thus, for each trial that they recalled correctly in the second set of span series that was greater than the number of digits recalled in the first set, they could receive 10 cents.

The children were actually encouraged to compete against their own prior recall performance. The children were shown an actual role of dimes, as well as examples of how much money could be earned by recalling a certain number of span trials correctly. The researcher informed the children of their progress at the end of each of the three span series and exhorted them to continue trying hard at recalling more digits. Although the introduction of money as an incentive slightly increased the number of digits recalled in the correct order in both LD-N and normally achieving children, no such effect was observed among the LD-S children.

Regarding breadth of STM problems in LD-S children, Torgesen, Rashotte, Greenstein, and Portes (1991) found that these children only evidenced storage problems in tasks that required "verbatim retention of verbal items over brief periods of time" (Torgesen, 1988, p. 607). This finding is most instructive because of the range of tasks given the LD-S, LD-N, and normally achieving children. Specifically, Torgesen et al. (1991) gave nine different memory tasks: immediate recall of sequences of abstract visual forms, an incidental memory task entailing recall of meaningfully organized information from long-term memory, two recognition memory tasks, recall of digit series in reversed order, verbatim recall of sentences, recall of digits presented visually, and a typical aurally administered span task. The results clearly indicate that LD-S children were not uniformly deficient in the given memory tasks. Rather, their deficient performances occurred in specific tasks— Picture Sequences, Digit Span Visual, Sentence Recall, and Digit Span Auditory— all of which shared the demand of "immediate verbatim recall of sequences of verbal items" (Torgesen, 1988, p. 607).

How does Torgesen explain STM problems in LD-S children? He thinks their STM problems reflect phonological coding problems. In other words, LD-S children have difficulties storing information through phonological (verbal) codes. The major source of support for Torgesen's view comes from research findings that LD-S children performed comparably as LD-N and normally achieving children when the given information had to be stored visually, but not when it had to be stored phonologically. Specifically, Torgesen et al. (1991) found LD-S children did not differ from the two control groups in the performances in four visual tasks: visual sequential memory, sorting recall, recognition memory, and memory for content. In contrast, they differed from the LD-N and normally achieving children on verbal tasks, such as memory for sequence, numbers visual (digit spans presented visually), sentences, and aurally presented digit spans (for forward recall). In these verbal tasks, LD-S children performed substantially poorer than those in the two control groups. Such findings indicate the specificity in LD-S children's storage problems. They have difficulties storing information in terms of its phonological or verbal attributes (Torgesen, 1988, pp. 607–610).

If LD-S children do not store verbal information efficiently (in more technical terms, they are less efficient in phonological coding or processing), then any task that requires them to hold verbal information briefly and, additionally, to integrate it with subsequent incoming verbal information should be difficult for them. Think of decoding the word *cat*. The LD-S child must recognize the letter *c*, then reach and activate from his long-term memory the sound that corresponds to it. Then he must hold in his mind or more precisely, his STM, the phonological (verbal/sound) information of the letter *c* while he attempts to decode *a*. If he successfully accesses the stored verbal information or sound of *a*, he has to blend (integrate) it with the sound of letter *c*, and so on with letter *t*. Because LD-S children have difficulties storing or remembering verbal information, the simultaneous demands of remembering the sound of *c* and processing (recognizing the letter and retrieving from LTM the sound of) *a* would be very hard for them. Hence, it is not surprising that they would have great difficulty with decoding.

Teachers of LD children would say that it is old news to say they have decoding problems! So what *is* new or instructive about the research findings of Torgesen and his associates? The informative aspect of Torgesen's research on STM problems in LD children concerns the mechanism that underlies those memory problems, and the differentiations in performance between the two groups of LD-S and LD-N children. Specifically, LD-S children have more severe decoding and blending problems than LD-N children. LD-N children did not show decoding difficulties with one-syllable words but showed them with words containing two or more syllables. Moreover, LD-S children had substantial problems in a blending task in which they were presented with sound segments and had to blend them into words (Torgesen, Rashotte, Greenstein, Houck, & Portes, 1987). For example, *mat* is presented in three segments: *m-a-t,* and the child has to say *mat*. In striking contrast, LD-N children did not show blending difficulties. They performed similarly as normally achieving children. On the sound-blending task, the means and standard deviations (*SD*) for LD-S, LD-N, and normally achieving children were, respectively, 8.1 (2.3), 14.7 (2.7), and 13.9 (2.5).

Knowing that severe STM problems impair decoding and blending in LD children, one may wish to ask if these problems also impair their listening comprehension. The answer, surprisingly, is "Apparently not!" Torgesen, Rashotte, and Greenstein (1988) showed the LD-S children's understanding of the gist and their recall of thematically important ideas in expository passages were unaffected by their sever STM problems. But they did have problems remembering specific words and word order in the orally presented expository passages. Moreover, they had difficulty remembering directions sufficiently to enact them. In sum, despite severe STM storage problems, LD-S children showed little impairment in understanding meaningful and well-organized prose. However, their memory problems surfaced whenever they had to remember a series of directions and follow them through. Thus, the adverse impact of severe STM problems appears to be localized in LD-S children's early attempts at learning to read (reading acquisition).

Using Baddeley's model of working memory, Swanson mounted a most systematic research program into memory processes in children with learning disabilities. He painstakingly devised experimental tasks that matched the defining, dynamic aspects of working memory, namely, that it has both information-processing and storage functions (Gathercole & Baddeley, 1993). Moreover, in his experiments, he tried to use a broad range of tasks that provide a balance between those similar to academic tasks and those dissimilar to them. In this way, he enhanced reliability in his measurements.

Swanson (1993a) raised the question of whether or not children with learning disabilities have a generalized or specific working memory deficit. Both verbal and nonverbal tasks were given individually to the child. To illustrate the processing and storage aspects of working memory entailed in each task, I shall cite two examples from his study. In Story Recall, the child heard the experimenter read a paragraph about the celebrated battle of the Spanish Armada in which a tiny fleet of English ships managed to defeat the mighty Spanish fleet. Then she was asked a question (process) such as, "Who won the battle, the large or the small ships?" Subsequently the child was asked to recall the paragraph (storage).

In Picture Sequence, the child was presented with pictures of three shapes: Triangle, circle, and asterisk. Cards containing pictures of these shapes were presented for the child's viewing for 30 seconds. In each picture, the order and location of the shapes varied. After viewing, the cards were collected and removed, and the child was asked a question (process) such as, "Is this card (a distracter card) or this card (card selected from another set) the one I presented?" Subsequently, the child was again presented with the cards and asked to put them in the correct order (order of experimenter presentation). The number of cards in the sets ranged from 3–15.

Altogether six verbal and five nonverbal (visual-spatial) tasks were given to two subgroups of children with learning disabilities, reading disabled and math disabled, a group of children without learning disabilities who matched those with learning disabilities in age (chronological age-matched) and a group of younger children who matched the children with learning disabilities in academic achievement. Swanson found that on his working memory measures, the two subgroups of children with learning disabilities performed similarly. His data therefore suggested a generalized deficit in working memory among children with learning disabilities, regardless of type of learning disability. Such findings differ from those of Siegel and Ryan (1989), which clearly showed specific deficits in working memory as a function of type of learning disabilities. Specifically Siegel and Ryan (1989) showed math-disabled learning-disabled children performed adequately on language-related working memory tasks. The contrasts between the empirical outcomes here can be explained by the nature of the learning-disabled subjects. Swanson's subjects were more severely learning-disabled than those of Siegel and Ryan. Consequently, they were more likely to demonstrate a generalized deficit in working memory.

In two other studies, Swanson (1993b,c) found some indication of deficient executive processes in children with learning disabilities. Specifically, he found that in situations requiring low cognitive effort in remembering, children with and without learning disabilities did not differ in dual-task performance.[1] However, compared to children without learning disabilities, those with learning disabilities showed a clear deterioration in task performance in situations requiring high cognitive effort in remembering. This contrasting performance profile suggests the involvement of central executive processes because monitoring and allocation of cognitive resources are presumed in memory tasks involving high cognitive effort (cf. Gathercole & Baddeley, 1993).

Swanson devised the following task to create low and high cognitive effort involvements. Basically, the task contained sentences that were divided into base and elaborative sentences. In each set, the child was asked to choose by circling one of two nouns to complete the given sentence. See example below (Swanson, 1993b,c):

Base sentences

   Low Effort   Word choice

      The woman wore a pretty _____.   dress   foot

   High Effort

      The _____ went to school.   friends   children

Elaborative sentences

   Low Effort

      The woman wore a pretty _____ at the dance.   dress   foot

   High Effort

      The _____ went to school with their mother.   friends   children

In Swanson's (1993b,c) studies, a low cognitive effort task means decision making was made relatively easy for the child. As you can see in the above sentence: "The woman wore a pretty _____," the child should have no difficulty in deciding on the correct choice of word, *dress*. However, in the high cognitive effort task, the child's decision making becomes harder because either word can fit the sentence nicely. "The _____ went to school": *friends* or *children?*

The child had to decide which would be the correct word for the sentence that he or she had read. Altogether there were 20 sentences: 10 base and 10 elaborative. After the child had circled all the words in the sentences, he or she was given a distracter task for 1 minute, which involved adding one-digit sums. Subsequently, the child was asked to recall all the circled words. One minute later, he or she was asked to recall all the words he or she had not circled. Recall of the circled words constitutes measure of the central task, and that of the noncircled words the secondary task.

---

[1]Dual-task performance is explained at the end of this chapter.

The results indicated that children without learning disabilities recalled much more circled words than those with learning disabilities (i.e., children without learning disabilities were superior in recall of the central task on which they allocated their attention). Regarding the secondary task of recalling words that the children did not circle in the sentences, both children with and without learning disabilities did not differ in the low effort condition, but differences did occur in the high effort conditions in favor of the children without learning disabilities. Taken together, these results, in particular the first result of inferior recall of the central task, suggest deficient central executive processes or function in children with learning disabilities (Swanson, 1993b,c).

Note that the section on Swanson's work is much shorter than the one on Torgesen's. Does it mean that I have less to report on Swanson? It would be very wrong to think that Swanson is less prolific a researcher than Torgesen. Nothing is further from the truth! Swanson is a tremendously active researcher. Like Torgesen, each of his studies contains several experiments! But unlike Torgesen, his research focuses as much on theory testing as on investigating memory processes in children with learning disabilities, for example, the separability of STM from working memory. Hence, in each of his studies, part of the data pertain to theory testing and part to memory processes in children with learning disabilities. What I have summarized from his work are data directly relevant to the topic of research on memory problems in children with learning disabilities, in particular, data that are recent and have been replicated in his own studies. I have therefore deliberately left out data in Swanson's research that contain theory testing because in my view, discussion of them is more appropriate for graduate students in learning disabilities. Consequently, the section on his work is shorter than that on Torgesen's work.

REFLECTIONS

Research in memory processes is very important in learning disabilities because memory problems characterize a vast majority of children with learning disabilities. Thus far, in pinpointing more clearly the loci of memory problems in these children, research findings suggest encoding and rapid naming of letters, digits, and colors. Storage problems appear to reflect more strategic deficiencies.

Although the empirical information is very useful, we need to address the question of how learning-disabled children's problems in encoding and rapid naming contribute to their academic problems in reading (decoding and comprehension) and in arithmetic. Already Swanson is beginning to investigate the role of working memory problems in reading comprehension performance in individuals with learning disabilities. Also, in subtyping research, Siegel has found problems in working memory in arithmetic-disabled children.

Reflecting on the research of Torgesen and Swanson, how does one make sense of their findings? They used vastly different experiment tasks reflecting vastly different research foci, which in turn underscore the differential theoretical aspects of the memory model being researched. The key to understanding the importance and complementary contributions of their research is to ask this question: How do memory problems explain, at least in part, reading problems in children with learning disabilities?

To answer the question, reconsider the definition of reading. What is reading? Reading is meaning construction, right? Yes, but before children can make sense of what they are reading, they must attain a necessary level of decoding proficiency. Otherwise they would be mired in a decoding struggle, and precious little cognitive resources would be left for meaning construction (comprehension)! So, reading really is decoding + meaning construction (comprehension). In light of this more complete definition of reading, I can now explain the importance and complementary contribution of the research findings of Torgesen and Swanson.

Let's recap the research findings. Recall that Torgesen and his associates found clear evidence that LD-S children have severe, stable but specific problems in remembering brief verbal information, and these STM problems may adversely impair their decoding efficiency and, hence, their reading acquisition. On the other hand, Swanson showed that children with learning disabilities have generalized problems in the dynamic processes of working memory: they perform very poorly in tasks that demand simultaneous information processing and storage. Such simultaneous processing is typically involved in reading. Moreover, Swanson showed that children with learning disabilities were deficient in executive processing. Executive processing assumes a cardinal role in reading comprehension. It underlies all the metacognitive coordination and monitoring necessary for effective reading (Brown, 1980).

Together the research findings of Torgesen and Swanson shed important light on how memory problems in children with learning disabilities may explain at least in part, their enormous difficulties in learning to read and in reading comprehension. We may conclude that Torgesen's findings enlighten us on bottom-up processing (decoding) problems, and Swanson's findings on top-down processing (reading comprehension) problems in children with learning disabilities. The significance of their commendable research programs should be clear, as are their complementary contributions to unraveling the causes of reading disability in children with learning disabilities.[2]

[2]*Dual-task technique and the concurrent or interference tasks.*   Concurrent or interference task is designed to induce interference in the subject's performance on the target task. The researcher is not interested in the subject's performance on the interference task, but rather in the extent of deterioration in the latter's performance on the target task, as a result of the interference.

In contrast, in the dual-task technique or design, the research is interested in the subject's performances on both the interference task and the target task. The researcher seeks to determine if a subject's performances on both tasks suffered. If the target and interference tasks differ vastly and yet affect each other, then the researcher can legitimately infer that both tasks involve similar information processes, and that their negative effects or mutual interference signal competition for the same cognitive (attentional) resources of the central executive, which has a limited capacity (Cohen, 1989).

Intervention Research in Memory Processes with Students with Learning Disabilities

As bright, young undergraduates with lots of energy and initiative combing through the journals in the library, or as teachers, high-charged with motivation to learn, you will find various intervention (training) studies designed to increase retention in children and/or adolescents with learning disabilities. With rare exceptions, these are one-shot, episodic research studies. That is, the researchers ran their studies, duly reported the findings, and you never read another intervention study by them on the same topic again! Although I do not discount such findings, nevertheless, I would put much more weight on, or set store by, findings that come from programmatic interventions that are theory-based, and show consistent replications of prior data. Why do I say this? You see, episodic research studies provide piecemeal, fragmentary information. You do not get as full a picture as you do with information gathered from a programmatic research program in which the researcher examines various variables systematically and exhaustively in a series of well-planned and connected studies. As an analogy, think of a jigsaw puzzle. Researchers engaged in programmatic research obtain data that they can piece together and understand, like fitting various pieces of a jigsaw puzzle together to yield the total picture. Integrating research data from their systematic research enables them to provide a comprehensive outlook of a phenomenon under study. Imagine you only had a few pieces of a jigsaw puzzle. Would you be able to make much out of them in figuring out what the jigsaw puzzle is? Of course not. Regardless of the significance of the data, episodic research studies on any topic yield fragmentary or incomplete information. This is why I only present data from memory intervention research in students with learning disabilities that has been obtained through programmatic research.

Margo Mastropieri and Tom Scruggs have produced the most instructive intervention research in enhancing retention of vocabulary, attributes, and content materials in social studies and science in students with learning disabilities and those with mild mental retardation. I shall briefly summarize the history of their intervention research, then highlight the instructional principles across their intervention studies involving different target materials, and conclude with explanations of the significance of their programmatic research.

Mastropieri and Scruggs began their memorial intervention research with vocabulary studies. They taught junior high students with learning disabilities foreign and difficult vocabulary (e.g., Spanish words) through interactive imagery, which is one way of elaborating verbal materials. They obtained very strong and positive results, indicating clear benefits of mnemonic instruction. Parallel studies teaching students with learning disabilities various attributes (characteristics of say, minerals or invertebrate animals) through interactive imagery or elaboration also produced similar positive results of the supremacy of mnemonic instruction.

At this time, Mastropieri and Scruggs began to formulate a model of recon-structive elaborations. Using this model, they extended their intervention research to content learning, specifically social studies and science. Again, the data here repli-cated what they found earlier in the vocabulary and attribute training studies, name-ly, that mnemonic instruction resulted in far better retention of learned materials than traditional instruction.

I will elaborate on the instructional principles in their research. In their mnemonic vocabulary training, Mastropieri and Scruggs utilized the key word method. There are three steps to this method. First, the instructor changes or re-constructs the to-be-learned word, which is typically unfamiliar and meaningless to the students, into a key word that is much more familiar and concrete. Second, they teach students to relate the learned key word to the to-be-learned word through visual imagery. Specifically, the instructor presents students with a picture in which the key word is interacting with the meaning of the to-be-learned vocabulary word. Third, they teach students to use the key word as a retrieval cue for the learned vo-cabulary word. These three instructional principles are Reconstructing, Relating, and Retrieving, the 3 Rs, as Mastropieri and Scruggs (1991) call them.

The following examples of mnemonic vocabulary instruction should clarify what it is about. To teach students the vocabulary word *oxalis* (which is a clover-like plant), students were first taught to use *ox* as the key word because it is familiar and concrete to them and sounds like *oxalis*. Students were next shown a picture of an ox munching clover-like plants. The instructor then taught the students to use the key word *ox* to cue their recall of the meaning of the word *oxalis*. When presented with *oxalis*, they should remember the key word *ox*, use it to recall the interactive imagery in the picture of the ox munching clover-like plants. Then they should be able to recall the meaning of *oxalis* (Mastropieri, Scruggs, & Fulk, 1990). Another application of this key word method can be seen with the word *ranid*, a word found in certain science curricula that refers to typical members of the frog family. Using the key word vocabulary method, students first learn the key word *rain* because it is familiar and concrete to the students and it sounds like *ranid*. Then, they are shown a picture of a frog sitting in the rain. The frog looks rather unhappy as it is being rained on quite heavily (Mastropieri & Scruggs, 1991, p. 11). Finally, students are told that whenever they are asked the meaning of the word *ranid*, they should think of the key word *rain*, and then recall the interactive imagery of the frog sitting in the rain, which would help them to remember what *ranid* means.

Now the actively thinking student may ask: Does this mnemonic vocabulary in-struction work only with concrete words? Does it work with abstract words? Good question! You just don't know how good questions from thoughtful students warm the cockles of our hearts! Why else do professors beam at such students?

Well, the key word mnemonic vocabulary instruction works equally well with abstract words (Mastropieri, et al., 1990). Let me illustrate from the work of Mas-tropieri and Scruggs (1991, pp. 17–21). Suppose students are to learn the definition of the word *buncombe,* which means an empty and insincere speech. The key word is *bun,* and the interactive imagery depicted in a picture shows a speaker being bombarded with buns from the irate audience of three men and a woman. One of the men was shouting, "This speech is empty, insincere, and contrived!"

The key word mnemonic instruction can also be effective in teaching content in history. For example, in the chapter on World War I, students with mild retardation and those with learning disabilities had to learn names of famous individuals with their associated events or functions. One of these individuals was William Jennings Bryan, who was President Woodrow Wilson's Secretary of State. He was known to be a pacifist. Thus, these students had to learn the name, Bryan, and associate it with the two important functions: Secretary of State and pacifist. To make the name Bryan more familiar and meaningful to those two groups of students, Mastropieri and Scruggs modified or reconstructed it to become *lion.* Then to make an interactive imagery between *lion* and the to-be-learned information of Secretary of State and pacifist, a picture was drawn showing the lion atop a secretary's desk pleading for two other animals not to fight. The latter animals were about to begin a fight right in front of the secretary's desk.

Mastropieri and Scruggs (1991) were careful to point out that teachers must ensure that students do not fixate on the key words and forget to relate them to the meanings of the words that have been learned. They found occasionally students would respond with key words when asked for the meanings of the learned vocabulary words. When this occurs, teachers should simply remind students to think back to the interactive images involving the key words and the additional elements (i.e., the vocabulary words). Moreover, teachers should clearly explain to students the functions of each of the three instructional steps in the key word mnemonic approach in vocabulary learning.

Reflections on the Intervention Research of Mastropieri and Scruggs

What is the significance of the intervention research program of Mastropieri and Scruggs that led me to single out their work and focus on teaching it? Let me explain and justify my bias.

The intervention research on memory by Mastropieri and Scruggs is significant for the following reasons: First, they have extensive replications of their findings of superior learning in students resulting from mnemonic instruction. Each replication study added to their prior research because it addressed questions either unresolved in or arising from the previous one. Hence, not only have the researchers shown consistent efficacy of their mnemonic instructional techniques, they have also mapped out various parameters of the reported instructional efficacy, for example, range of students for which the training applies (elementary, middle school, junior high); the range of curricula (foreign vocabulary, attributes, social studies, and science); type of exceptional students (learning disabled, mildly retarded, and be-havior disordered).

Second, Mastropieri and Scruggs's intervention research on memory has eco-logical validity. This means they did not conduct their studies only in experimen-tal labs. They started their vocabulary studies in controlled experimental lab settings. Subsequently, they conducted all their interventions in schools, and involved the special education teachers directly in the teaching. Also, they used school curricu-la. Ecological validity in research is very important, especially for intervention re-search. Without it, we cannot make much use of the findings, even if they support the intervention strategy in the research study. To elaborate, suppose I trained eighth-grade students with learning disabilities through mnemonic instruction (interactive imagery) to remember a list of Chinese letters and found they remembered them better than a control group of eighth-grade students with learning disabilities taught through direct instruction. Is this information very useful or helpful? Not as useful or helpful than if I had taught them to remember names from *Romeo and Juliet* (which is part of their English curricula) through interactive imageries! This is why *ecological* validity is such an important factor in intervention research.

Third, Mastropieri and Scruggs attended to other variables in their intervention research. Specifically, they addressed whether teachers and students were happy with the intervention or training. Did the students with learning disabilities really enjoy learning interactive imageries in the mnemonic instruction condition? Did they re-ally learn more under this instructional condition? Did special education teachers enjoy using such instruction? To all these questions, the answer was *yes!* Both stu-dents and teachers wanted more mnemonic instruction. Their positive response pro-vided *social* validity to the intervention.

Mastropieri and Scruggs also examined whether cumulative strategy instruction might confuse students with learning disabilities (all the imageries presented for learning). The answer was no. They also examined if students with learning dis-abilities could generate imageries for themselves through in-class brainstorming. Al-though they could, it turned out to be very time consuming. Hence, Mastropieri and Scruggs warned that teachers must weigh the cost and benefits of having stu-dents with learning disabilities generate their own interactive imageries. Having them do so would result in less coverage of content because of time lost.

Last, the researchers examined the question of teacher-generated versus exper-imenter-generated materials. They found that the special education teacher who volunteered to make her own instructional materials for interactive imageries found the procedure difficult and very time-consuming. This is understandable because she was tackling a very unusual and unfamiliar task.

In my view, the most important aspects of the programmatic intervention re-search by Mastropieri and Scruggs are (a) the development of the conceptual frame-work that guides their research: the Reconstructive Elaborations Model; and (b) the identification of the underlying mechanisms for the efficacy of their mnemonic instruction of interactive or elaborative imagery. These mechanisms include facilitation of learning through making the materials more concrete, meaningful, and hence more interesting to students with learning disabilities and encoding efficiency (Mastropieri & Fulk, 1990). Why do I consider these aspects of Mastropieri and Scruggs's work so important? Well, a sound theoretical or conceptual framework must guide intervention research. Equally important is the ability to explain the data. It is insufficient to simply say to students or readers that one's intervention has worked, or the training has been effective. That is a functional explanation of the efficiency of the intervention. Students and readers must understand *why* the intervention has been effective. The intervention researcher's task is to clarify and pinpoint for readers the agents or mechanisms that mediated the effective intervention. In short, we must move beyond functional explanations.

References

Atkinson, R. C., & Shiffren, R. M. (1971). The control of short-term memory. *Scientific American, 225,* 82–90.

Baddeley, A. D. (1979). Working memory and reading. In P. Kolers, M. Wrolstad, & H. Bouma (Eds.), Processing of visible language (pp. 355–370). NY: Plenum Press.

Borkowski, J. G., Estrada, M. T., Milstead, M., & Hale, C. A. (1989). General problem-solving skills: Relations between metacognition and strategic processing. *Learning Disability Quarterly, 12*(1), 57–70.

Brady, S., Shankweiler, D., & Mann, V. (1983). Speech perception and memory coding in relation to reading ability. *Journal of Experimental Child Psychology, 35,* 345–367.

Brown, A. L. (1980). Metacognitive development and reading. In R. J. Spiro, B. Bruce & W. F. Brewer (Eds.), *Theoretical issues in reading comprehension* (pp. 453–481). Hillsdale, NJ: Lawrence Erlbaum.

Byrne, B., & Shea, P. (1979). Semantic and phonetic memory codes ion beginning readers. *Memory & Cognition, 7*(5), 333–338.

Cohen, G. (1989). Memory systems: The experimental approach. In G. Cohen, G. Kiss, & M. LeVoi, *Memory: Current issues* (pp. 65–90). Buckingham, PA: Open University Press.

Cooney, J. B., & Swanson, H. L. (1987). Memory and learning disabilities: An overview. In H. Lee Swanson (Ed.), *Memory and learning disabilities: Advances in learning and behavioral disabilities.* Supplement 2 (pp. 1–40). Greenwich, CT: JAI Press, Inc.

Gathercole, S. E., & Baddeley, A. D. (1993). *Working memory and language.* Hove, UK: Erlbaum.

Korhonen, T. T. (1995). The persistence of rapid naming problems in children with reading disabilities: A nine-year follow-up. *Journal of Learning Disabilities, 28*(4), 232–239.

Mann, V. (1991). Language problems: A key to early reading problems. In B. Y. L. Wong (Ed.), *Learning about Learning Disabilities* (pp. 130–162). San Diego: Academic Press.

Mastropieri, M. A., & Fulk, B. J. (1990). Enhancing academic performance with mnemoric instruction. In T. Scruggs & B. Y. L. Wong (Eds.), *Intervention Research in Learning Disabilities* (pp. 102–121). New York: Springer-Verlag.

Mastropieri, M. A., & Scruggs, T. E. (1991). *Teaching students ways to remember.* Cambridge, MA: Brookline Books.

Mastropieri, M. A., Scruggs, T. E., & Fulk, B. J. M. (1990). Teaching abstract vocabulary with the keyword method: Effects on recall and comprehension. *Journal of Learning Disabilities, 23*(2), 92–96, 107.

Siegel, L. S., & Ryan, E. B. (1989). The development of working memory in normally achieving and subtypes of learning disabled children. *Child Development, 60,* 973–980.

Spring, C., & Perry, L. (1983). Naming speed and serial recall in poor and adequate readers. *Contemporary Educational Psychology, 8,* 141–145.

Stanovich, K. E. (1986). Cognitive processes and the reading problems of learning-disabled children: Evaluating the assumption of specificity. In J. K. Torgesen and B. Y. L. Wong (Eds.), *Psychological and educational perspectives on learning disability* (pp. 85–131). New York: Academic Press.

Swanson, H. L. (1993a). Working memory in learning disability subgroups. *Journal of Experimental Child Psychology, 56,* 87–114.

Swanson, H. L. (1993b). Executive processing in learning-disabled readers. *Intelligence, 17,* 117–149.

Swanson, H. L. (1993c). Individual differences in working memory: A model testing and subgroup analysis of learning-disabled and skilled readers. *Intelligence, 17,* 285–332.

Torgesen, J. K. (1985). Memory processes in reading disabled children. *Journal of Learning Disabilities, 18*(6), 350–357.

Torgesen, J. K. (1988). Studies of children with learning disabilities who perform poorly on memory span tasks. *Journal of Learning Disabilities, 21*(10), 605–612.

Torgesen, J. K., & Goldman, T. (1977). Rehearsal and short-term memory in second grade reading disabled children. *Child Development, 48,* 56–61.

Torgesen, J. K., & Houck, D. G. (1980). Processing deficiencies of learning-disabled children who perform poorly on the digit span test. *Journal of Educational Psychology, 72*(2), 141–160.

Torgesen, J. K., Rashotte, C. A., & Greenstein, J. (1988). Language comprehension in learning disabled children who perform poorly on memory span tests. *Journal of Educational Psychology, 80*(4), 480–487.

Torgesen, J. K., Rashotte, C. A., Greenstein, J., Houck, G., & Portes, P. (1987). Academic difficulties of learning disabled children who perform poorly on memory span tasks. In H. L. Swanson (Ed.), *Memory and learning disabilities: Advances in learning and behavioral disabilities* (pp. 305–333). Greenwich, CT: JAI Press.

Torgesen, J. K., Rashotte, C. A., Greenstein, J., & Portes, P. (1991). Further studies of learning disabled children with severe performance problems on the digit span test. *Learning Disabilities Research and Practice, 6*(3), 134–144.

Wong, B. Y. L. (1978). The effects of directive cues on the organization of memory and recall in good and poor readers. *Journal of Educational Research, 72,* 32–38.

5

Social Aspects
of Learning Disabilities

The first researchers in learning disabilities tended to focus more on assessment and remediation issues, but in the 1970s Tanis Bryan pioneered research into social problems of children with learning disabilities. Her research efforts were extremely timely and reflected the growing concerns among professionals who had long observed social relational problems in some children with learning disabilities. These professionals persisted in voicing the need to investigate such nonacademic problems.

The research on social aspects of learning disabilities covers a range of interesting subtopics: (a) the self-system, such as self-concept, self-esteem, self-efficacy, and attributions; (b) social competence (social status); and (c) social cognition, such as role taking (alternatively known as perspective taking), comprehension of nonverbal communication, moral development, social problem solving, and lastly, communicative competence.

Research on Self-Concept, Self-Esteem, and Self-Efficacy

Tanis Bryan (1991) defined these concepts very nicely.

> Self-concept refers to a person's awareness of his or her own characteristics and the ways in which he or she is like and unlike others. Self-esteem refers to the value a per-

son puts on oneself and one's behavior. Perceived self-efficacy refers to a person's judgments of competence to execute courses of action required to deal with prospective situations. Attributions refer to a person's explanations for successful and failure outcomes. (p. 198)

In self-concept research, researchers used certain instruments, for example, the Piers-Harris Self-Concept Scale and the Sears Self-Concept Scale (Piers & Harris, 1969). These scales typically contain statements to which respondents are asked to rate themselves. An example from the Sears Self-Concept Scale is "Being good at sports," where the respondent has to rate himself or herself as excellent, very good, better than most, OK, or not so good.

In general, research findings on self-concept of children and adolescents with learning disabilities indicate that compared to normally achieving children and adolescents, they tend to have lower academic self-concept. This means that they tend to consider themselves to be less able in academic areas than their normally achieving peers. However, they have equally good self-concept in nonacademic areas, for example, in sports, or in looks (Chapman, 1985; Winne, Woodlands, & Wong, 1982).

An important parameter that affects self-concept in students with learning disabilities concerns the social context in which they rate themselves. Apparently, they rated themselves higher in self-concept when they compared themselves with other students with mild handicaps in the resource room. Back in the mainstreamed classroom, they again rated themselves poorer when compared to normally achieving peers (Morrison, Forness, & MacMillan, 1983; Schurr, Towne, & Joiner, 1972). Another important parameter is the classroom climate set by the teacher. If he or she emphasizes evaluative feedback, then the students' self-concept ratings would be adversely affected. On the other hand, if the teacher emphasizes cooperation among the students, individualized instruction, and de-emphasizes evaluativeness, then the students' self-concept ratings would increase. Self-concept ratings in kindergarten children were found to be very susceptible to classroom climate. However, fourth graders were less affected by evaluative classroom climate (Benenson & Dweck, 1986; Stipek & Tannatt, 1984).

Self-esteem scales contain items such as, "I take a positive attitude toward myself"; "At times I think I am no good at all" (see T. Bryan, 1991, p. 202). Respondents are to rate themselves under categories of "Yes" or "No." Thus far, research findings appear to show no differences between children with and without learning disabilities. However, differences were obtained with adolescents and adults, with normally achieving subjects scoring higher in self-esteem self-ratings (Buchanan & Wolf, 1986; Tollefson et al., 1982; White, 1985; Winner, Woodlands, & Wong, 1982).

Having summarized research on how students with learning disabilities perceived themselves let us turn to how significant others, such as teachers, perceive such students. Why are we concerned with how teachers view students with learning disabilities? Because teachers assume a very important place in the eyes of their students within the classrooms, especially in lower grades. Because of his or her authoritative status in the classroom, a teacher's opinion of a student carries much weight. If the teacher holds a student in high regard, for example, thinks that student is very capable, this attitude may well influence how other students perceive that particular student. They too may come to view that student as very capable, because they trust the teacher's opinion. The converse applies equally. In turn, teachers' high or low opinions of a student tend to have direct effects on his or her self-perceptions. This is why we should examine research on teacher perceptions of students with learning disabilities.

Teacher Perceptions of Children with Learning Disabilities

Teachers gave poorer ratings of social competence to children with learning disabilities than their normally achieving peers. They considered children with learning disabilities to be more often off-task, to act out more, and to have disturbed relations with peers (T. Bryan, 1991). Classroom observation studies confirm teachers' ratings of more off-task behaviors and dependency in children with learning disabilities (Feagans & McKinney, 1981; McKinney & Speece, 1983).

However, teachers gave higher ratings of social competence to children with learning disabilities who were receiving remedial help. They considered these children to be more cooperative, more responsible, and more likely to complete assignments and to pay attention (T. Bryan, 1991). Nevertheless, more recent research findings again indicate that teachers rated third- and fourth-grade children with learning disabilities and low achievers to have poorer social competence (e.g., in cooperation with peers in group activities or in controlling temper) (Tur-Kaspa & Bryan, 1944).

Research on Attributions

Attributions, as T. Bryan (1991, p. 198) explained, are the explanations we give for the outcomes of our actions. When we take responsibility for the consequences of our own actions, whether it be rear-ending someone's car or winning an award, we are said to have an internal locus of control. On the other hand, if we habitually shirk the responsibility of our actions, for example, blame the presence of a black cat when we rear-ended someone's car, then we are said to have an external locus of control. Attributions thus are very much tied to whether or not we consider ourselves to be in control of our own fates, or agents of our own actions.

Research on attributions in children with learning disabilities found that they have rather maladaptive attributional patterns. Specifically, they attribute failures to a lack of ability, and successes to luck or teacher favor. In contrast, normally achieving children attribute failures to deficient effort, and success to joint contributions of ability and effort (Pearl, Donahue, & Bryan, 1986).

Students' attributional patterns appear to interact with teacher instructional style with particular effects on learning outcomes. Pascarella and Pflaum (1981) found that children with learning disabilities and poor readers who showed an internal locus of control did well in a less structured reading instructional program. Those with an external locus of control did well in a more structured program. Similar findings had been reported with learning-disabled junior high male students.

If students believe successful learning outcomes are out of their control, for example, a result of luck or teacher favor, they would cease trying and become passive learners. To elicit students' active participation in learning and effort expenditure, it is worthwhile to attempt reattribution training (alternately called attribution retraining) where maladaptive attributions exist. Successful reattribution training has been reported by Borkowski, Weyhing, and Can (1988). In this study, children and adolescents with learning disabilities aged 10–14 were randomly assigned to one of four conditions: (a) treatment condition of reading strategies plus reattribution training; and three control conditions; (b) reading strategies plus attribution (where students were not trained to analyze reasons for task failure, to attribute it to lack of appropriate strategy and insufficient effort in applying strategy, but just trained to summarize and attribute success to strategy-based reading. In short, they did not receive reattribution training); (c) attribution control in which students did not get any attribution retraining, but just received strategy training; and (d) reading strategy control in which students received reattribution training but no strategy training.

The results clearly indicated that only students from the treatment condition of reading strategies plus reattribution training improved substantially. The gains they made surpassed students in the other conditions by a sizable margin. However, improvements in attributions were confined to reading, and did not generalize to mathematics.

A recent study by Tur-Kaspa and Bryan (1993) adds interesting data to prior research on attributions in students with learning disabilities. Specifically, they found these students attributed their successes to *both* external and internal factors! Examples of external and internal factors are others' motives and characteristics of self, such as effort. In attributions for failures, these students with learning disabilities attributed them to personality interactions, then others' moods and motives. In contrast, normally achieving and low-achieving students attributed both successful and unsuccessful outcomes to personality interaction and others' personality. Hence, they did not show the inconsistency in success attributions, whereas students with learning disabilities did.

Tur-Kaspa and Bryan's (1993) data thus indicate a curious inconsistency in the attributions for success in students with learning disabilities. The data suggest that they are capable of taking credit for their success. Nevertheless, such internal attribution (of effort) appears to be offset by an equal emphasis on external factor (of others' motives). The net result appears to be little substantive gains in their self-esteem (Tur-Kaspa & Bryan, 1993).

Consistent with prior research, this new set of data from Tur-Kaspa and Bryan (1993) calls for continual research on the development of attributions in individuals with learning disabilities. Perhaps too, future research studies could include individual interviews with the subjects with learning disabilities so that we have additional verbal data on why they choose certain internal and external attributions for success.

Research on Social Competence (Peer Acceptance and Social Status)

There is sufficient empirical evidence that some children with learning disabilities are very unpopular. They are rejected by their peers. This finding is important because it has been replicated across different samples of children with learning disabilities. The pioneer and leading researcher here is Tanis Bryan (see T. Bryan, 1991).

This empirical finding of remarkable unpopularity among children with learning disabilities, particularly females, sparks the search among researchers for the underlying reasons for it. Thus when examining the data in the areas described below, remember that the research has been driven by the search for answers to the unpopularity of children with learning disabilities (see Figure 2).

Researchers began to ask questions such as, Do peers reject children with learning disabilities because they have deficient social perception or because they are deficient in role-taking skills? Or because they do not comprehend well nonverbal cues in verbal communications (conversations)? Or because they lack comprehension of social mores? Or because they are poor in social problem solving? I examine research findings on each of these questions.

Social Perception

In social perceptions experiments using children with and without learning disabilities, one major criticism has been that attention in the former was not ascertained, thereby confounding data that indicated poorer social perception in them. However, the two studies briefly summarized here do not have that confound.

Pearl and Cosden (1982) presented segments from TV soap operas to children with and without learning disabilities, and assessed their understanding of the social interactions of characters portrayed. They found that children with learning disabilities had much more inaccurate social interpretations. In another study, Weiss (1984) used aggressive and nonaggressive boys who were either diagnosed as learning-dis-

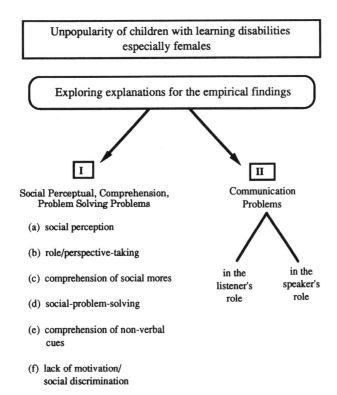

Figure 2 Directions of research in attempts to explain unpopularity (low social status) in children with learning disabilities.

abled or non-learning-disabled. She presented them with four very brief videotapes of 16 seconds each, which contained different social interactions among two or three boys. These social interactions ranged from neutral, friendly, cooperative, teasing, horseplay, fighting, to angry. The task of the subjects was to rate what they had seen in each videotape as very, very friendly to very, very unfriendly. Weiss (1984) found that aggressive boys with and without learning disabilities tended to rate the video scenarios as more unfriendly than the nonaggressive boys with and without learning disabilities. Thus the former appeared to have biased social perceptions.

These early studies on social perception or social information processing shared one shortcoming; they did not measure social perception in a comprehensive manner. They all focused on one specific aspect of social perception. One very recent study attempted to redress this problem. Using Dodge's (1986) model, Tur-Kaspa and Bryan (1994) measured five aspects of social information processing. Additionally, they included a comparison group of low achievers (LA) as well as the usual comparison group of average students. This way, they could examine if low academic achievement per se explains social problems in students with learning disabilities. For example, if LA and learning-disabled students perform similarly in all aspects of social information processing, then low academic achievement may underlie their social problems. On the other hand, if LA students surpass those with learning disabilities in the given social tasks, then low academic achievement and status cannot explain the latter's social problems. They also examined developmental aspects by contrasting two sets of grade levels: grades 3 and 4 versus grades 7 and 8.

In Dodge's model of social information processing, the first step involves the individual's "encoding the social cues in the environment." This basically means reading and remembering the social situation accurately. The next step involves the individual's "mental representation and interpretation process" of the encoded social cues. The third step involves the individual's searching for an appropriate response. In the fourth step, she or he decides on the response to be produced. When a decision is reached, she or he acts it out in the fifth step, "response enactment," which subsumes monitoring and evaluating the effects of the response on the environment (Tur-Kaspa & Bryan, 1994, p. 13). The researchers improved on Dodge's assessment materials by increasing the number of scenarios from two to five to accommodate the age span of their subjects. It is recalled that they used both elementary and middle school students in their study.

What did Tur-Kaspa and Bryan (1994) find? Well, they found that the students with learning disabilities did substantially poorer than both normally achieving and LA students in two specific areas: (a) encoding of social cues, and (b) preference for self-generated solutions. Put more colloquially, students with learning disabilities did not read social situations as accurately as normally achieving and LA students. They also tended to choose less competent solutions from the set of self-generated solutions. Such choice suggests poor evaluation of solutions generated.

The researchers also found developmental changes in that older students in grades 7 and 8 showed improved performance in social encoding (though not among the normally achieving students), in the amount of solutions generated, and in preference for competent self-generated solutions. Last, Tur-Kaspa and Bryan found receptive and expressive language skills to be closely related to social information processing. However, they emphasized that the language tests used by them (The Peabody Picture Vocabulary Test-Revised, and the Expressive One-Word Picture Vocabulary Test) measured semantics and not pragmatics of language. They think that pragmatics may play a more significant role in students' social competence because "pragmatics refers to the rules governing the use of language in context, beyond appropriate vocabulary and syntactic rules" (Tur-Kaspa & Bryan, 1994, p. 21).

This latest finding of social encoding problems in students with learning disabilities corroborates findings from earlier studies in social perception. Similarly, the second finding that students with learning disabilities lack the ability to evaluate the competence of self-generated solutions corroborates the finding from an earlier study with learning-disabled adolescents by Hazel, Schumaker, Sherman, and Sheldon (1982). These findings speak to the need for social interventions for students with learning disabilities.

Role Taking (Perspective Taking)

In this area of research, typically the researchers engineer a study in which children with and without learning disabilities were asked to differentiate between the knowledge or information two characters should have in a story. For example, Wong and Wong (1980) constructed three story sequences: anger, sadness, and fear. Each story was depicted as a cartoon series. Thus, in the one entitled "Anger," a little boy about 7 years old made a sand castle and was seen smiling with pride and joy over what he had built. In the next cartoon, a little girl about the same age came whistling by on a bike and deliberately flattened the boy's sand castle. The third cartoon showed the boy crying bitterly over the destruction of his sand castle. The fourth cartoon depicted him going home, looking very angry, with a black cloud hovering above his head. In the following cartoon, he is shown to be home, being greeted by his little brother who was about 4. The little brother had just made a castle with cards. The sixth cartoon showed the older brother deliberately blowing down the younger brother's castle of cards. The last cartoon showed he marched off, still fuming, while the younger brother looked very confused at the older brother.

Each child was seen individually in Wong and Wong (1980). The child was asked to pretend he was the little boy, and to tell the story from that perspective. Subsequently, the child had to repeat the story from the perspective of the little brother. The idea is that if the child was self-centered and could not switch perspectives from the boy to his younger brother, then he would say that the little brother knew what happened to the older boy, why the latter was in a foul mood, and displaced his anger onto the younger brother. For female subjects, parallel series of cartoons on "Anger," "Sadness," and "Fear" were drawn with female children.

The results indicated that girls with learning disabilities were less able to take a different perspective than non-learning-disabled girls and boys with learning disabilities. Thus, girls with learning disabilities appeared to be more egocentric. Findings from other studies on this topic also indicated that students with learning disabilities did more poorly in role-taking measures than those without learning disabilities (T. Bryan, 1991).

Comprehension of Social Mores

Another hypothesis for learning-disabled children's unpopularity was that they lack knowledge on appropriate social behavior or social mores. To test this hypothesis,

J. Bryan and Sonnefeld (1981) designed the following study. Children with and without learning disabilities were told that they would be getting a visit from a prominent female personality from a TV station. She would interview them individually. If she felt impressed by their conversations, she would give them goodies from the TV station. Hence, the researchers instructed the children to be as nice to this person as possible. In short, they were exhorted to ingratiate themselves with this visitor from the TV station.

The children's individual interviews with the adult supposedly from the TV station took place in a mobile trailer, which was specifically set up to videotape the interview. Of course, the children did not know that they were being videotaped.

The results indicated that children with and without learning disabilities were equally capable of ingratiating themselves with this significant adult. Thus, the hypothesis that learning-disabled children lack social mores was not supported by the data. It seems that when the situation calls for appropriate social behaviors, children with learning disabilities were very able to rise to the occasion and behave appropriately. In this way, they demonstrate clearly that they possess the necessary repertoire of appropriate social behaviors. Thus, insufficient social mores cannot explain the social unpopularity in learning-disabled children. Could it be that they need prompting to behave appropriately?

Social Problem Solving

The research studies in social problem solving tend to involve small-group collaborative discussion, which in turn, involves communications among the group members of children with and without learning disabilities. To understand the outcomes of these studies, we need to consider communication problems in children with learning disabilities. Hence, I shall describe these studies in the section on communication problems.

Comprehension of Nonverbal Cues

Nonverbal cues in social interactions refer to body language such as posture, smiles, and eye contact. Being able to read such nonverbal cues facilitates social interactions. Four research studies examined comprehension of nonverbal cues in children with learning disabilities. They all used a test devised by Rosenthal, Hall, Mateo, Rogers, and Archer (1979) called the Profile of Nonverbal Sensitivity (PONS). It consists of a black-and-white videotape lasting 45 min. This videotape contains 220 2-second shots of a young woman demonstrating various emotional responses. Children with and without learning disabilities were presented with the 200 items under three visual presentations (face, body, figure), and two auditory presentations (scrambled speech and electronically filtered speech). These visual and auditory presentations were presented singly as well as in combination. The children were asked to choose one out of two descriptions of a given scenario as an accurate description of what they had seen. Three studies found less accurate perceptions of nonverbal cues among children with learning disabilities (Axelrod, 1982; T. Bryan, 1977; Jackson et al., 1987), but one found no differences between children with and without learning disabilities (Stone & La Greca, 1984). In their study, Stone and La Greca controlled for attention in children with learning disabilities because they had hypothesized that inattention might have been responsible for the results of previous studies. Their data appear to support their hypothesis.

Clearly, in this area of comprehension of nonverbal cues in children with learning disabilities, data are inconclusive. This means more research is needed before we can make any definitive statements on whether or not children with learning disabilities have serious problems in interpreting nonverbal cues in social interactions. In my view, future research should use other tasks than the PONS test by Rosenthal et al. (1979), because we need convergent data from different kinds of tasks. If when using different experimental tasks, different researchers obtained the same finding, either children with learning disabilities perform same or differently from children without learning disabilities, we would have more confidence in the data because they are not bound to the same task (not task-specific).

Lack of Motivation and Social Discrimination

James Bryan and his associates took a very different route in researching underlying causes of the social unpopularity of children with learning disabilities. They reasoned that the extant studies reporting social rejection of those children, in particular, white female children, involved children and significant others such as teachers who were familiar with those children with learning disabilities. Perhaps the social rejection of those children of their peers stems from the latter's familiarity with them, and the teachers' devaluation of them might in part stem from knowledge of them and their diagnostic labels. Accordingly, Bryan and his associates controlled for such familiarity. They were interested in first impressions of children with learning disabilities in adults who had no knowledge of the latter's diagnostic label, nor had any prior interactions or relationships with them.

In J. Bryan and Perlmutter (1979), 24 female undergraduate students in psychology rated the social desirability of children with and without learning disabilities from grades 3, 4, and 5. The children with learning disabilities had first been taught to play a bowling game. They were than asked to teach a peer of the same age, sex, and race to play the game. Eight videotape recordings involving interactions of children with learning disabilities and eight of those without learning disabilities were used for viewing by the female adults. These videotape recordings lasted on the average 4 minutes and 39 seconds.

The judges saw the 16 videotape recordings in a fixed order. Within each presentation of a tape, student status and sex were balanced such that it contained one male child with learning disabilities, followed by a male child without learning disabilities, one female child with learning disabilities, and one female child without learning disabilities. Moreover, there were three conditions of presentations: (a) Audio-Visual Condition, in which the judges saw and heard the tapes. (b) Audio-Plus-Transcript Condition, in which the judges heard the videotapes (voices of the children), were given the transcripts of the tapes to read or follow along with the tapes, but did not see the tapes. (c) Visual Condition Only in which the judges saw the videotape recordings without the accompanying sounds, as in silent movies of the past.

J. Bryan and Perlmutter (1979) found that judges' impressions or ratings of social desirability in children with and without learning disabilities were based on an interaction between the child's student status (i.e., with or without learning disabilities) and the modality condition (i.e., the Audio-Visual, Audio-Plus-Transcript, or Visual-Only Condition). Specifically, the judges rated the children with learning disabilities to be as socially desirable in the Visual-Only (No-Sound) Condition as they were in the Audio-Visual Condition! The mean ratings in these two conditions were 3.77 and 3.73; whereas the mean rating in the Audio-Plus-Transcript Condition was 3.98. In contrast, the judges rated the children without learning disabilities to be highest in social desirability in the Audio-Plus-Transcript condition (4.22), whereas in the Audio-Visual Condition and the Visual-Only Condition, they gave these (average) ratings: 4.20; 3.98. Additionally, the judges gave the lowest ratings to female children with learning disabilities.

Thus, J. Bryan and Perlmutter (1979) replicated prior research findings of the social devaluation of female children with learning disabilities. Moreover, adult females when observing children with learning disabilities solely on their nonverbal behaviors, as in the Visual-Only Condition, gave them almost the same rating of social desirability as when they viewed these children in the Audio-Visual Condition.

Perlmutter and Bryan (1984) continued to investigate adult ratings of social adaptability of children with learning disabilities based entirely on nonverbal behaviors. The stimuli consisted of 20 videotaped interactions of 20 intermediate children with and without learning disabilities. Half of the children were instructed to ingratiate a female interviewer, and the remaining half to act naturally. The interviewer was to ask each child first the child's favorite TV program, his or her second most favorite TV program, his or her favorite movie, and his or her favorite cartoon. A 10-second videotape was made that focused exclusively on the child's face. A 25-second videotape was made that focused on both the child's face and body. Nowhere on these videotapes was the female interviewer shown. The judges were 21 male and 21 female undergraduate students in psychology. The judges watched the videotapes without the accompanying sounds, as in silent movies.

The results indicated that children with learning disabilities were rated lower on social adaptability than those without. Additionally, children instructed to ingratiate received higher ratings than those not instructed. A significant interaction indicated that children with learning disabilities who were instructed to ingratiate received ratings in social adaptability that were comparable to those received by children without learning disabilities (mean ratings for the former were: 3.65, and for the latter, 3.63). But children with learning disabilities not instructed to ingratiate received the lowest ratings in social adaptability when compared to all the other groups (mean rating of 3.36; that of noninstructed children without learning disabilities, 3.59).

These results suggest that children with learning disabilities who were not explicitly told to ingratiate, but told to act naturally, created very poor first impressions on undergraduate males and females. Interestingly, such unfavorable first impressions were generated entirely on the basis of their nonverbal behaviors! Moreover, these unfavorable impressions were reliably made within an extremely short time (10- and 25-second videotapes), and by strangers! Yet, when explicitly told to ingratiate, children with learning disabilities were equally able to do so as those without learning disabilities! The latter finding clearly suggests that they possessed the ability or knowledge of how to ingratiate. To resolve the discrepant findings in rated social adaptability between children with learning disabilities told to ingratiate and those not thus instructed, Perlmutter and Bryan (1984) suggested motivational factors or lack of social discrimination on when initiating certain actions would render oneself in a favorable light to the observer.

Clearly, it is a most refreshing approach that is taken by James Bryan and his associates in unraveling underlying causes of social devaluation and rejection of children with learning disabilities. They chose to examine the latter's social devaluation and rejection on the part of adults and not their peers, and adults who have no prior knowledge of these children with learning disabilities. The research findings of J. Bryan and Perlmutter (1979) and Perlmutter and Bryan (1984) are important because they showed that social devaluation and rejection of children with learning disabilities occurred on a nonverbal basis. Further research along similar lines as Bryan and associates appears to be very desirable.

Communication Problems

Children with learning disabilities very often have problems in expressing themselves (i.e., problems in expressive language). It is possible that these expressive language problems may result in communication problems that, in turn, adversely affect their social interactions with others.

To investigate whether or not children with learning disabilities have communication problems, Tanis Bryan and her associates conducted the following experiments. In T. Bryan, Donahue, and Pearl (1981), learning-disabled and non-learning-disabled children were asked to rank order individually 15 gifts (e.g., perfume for a teacher, candy, two tickets to a movie, etc.). Then they had to repeat the process of rank ordering in triads; with the composition of triads being one learning-disabled to two non-learning-disabled children or three non-learning-disabled children. The children were videotaped as they discussed their rank ordering of the gifts.

The results showed that learning-disabled children talked as much as the non-learning-disabled children. However, they were less persuasive in getting the non-learning-disabled children to agree with their ranking of the top choices. Their ineffectualness apparently arose from their tendency to agree with the others in the triad, less likelihood to disagree or argue for their own choices. Moreover, they were less likely to monitor the group's progress in discussion and keep it focused. In short, although they talked as much as non-learning-disabled children, the learning-disabled children were not sufficiently assertive in their ranking of the gifts, and ineffectual in persuading others to agree with their top choices of gifts.

Another study had children with and without learning disabilities serve as talk-show hosts. Again, videotapes showed that learning-disabled children talked as much as the non-learning-disabled children. However, they did not ask as many questions of their guests. Nor did they pose open-ended questions to promote conversation and discussion. They tended to ask questions that led to a yes or no answer from their guests. Worse still, their talk-show guests talked more than they did, suggesting that the latter had usurped the learning-disabled children's role as talk-show hosts (Bryan, Donahue, Pearl, & Sturen, 1981).

These two studies suggest that quality and not quantity in communication differentiated importantly between children with and without learning disabilities. The data from both studies converge on the passiveness of children with learning disabilities in their communications. In Bryan, Donahue, and Pearl (1981), they manifested their passivity in not asserting or arguing for their rank ordering of their top choices of the gifts, and in their tendency to agree with the others' top choices. In T. Bryan, Donahue, Pearl, and Sturen (1981), they manifested their passivity in asking fewer questions of their talk-show guests, and in communication problem of asking inferior questions (questions that restrict the talk-show guest to a yes or no answer). Last but not least, they became dominated by their talk-show guests as the latter talked more than they did!

Other studies also demonstrated communication problems in children with learning disabilities. Olsen, Wong, and Marx (1983) found that in teaching younger children to play a board game, children with learning disabilities did not modify their language use. They did not use simpler language nor shorter sentences. In another study, Donahue, Pearl, and Bryan (1980) found that children with learning disabilities did not monitor their understanding of given verbal instructions. The instructor deliberately gave ambiguous or incomplete information in her instructions, with the notion that if children monitored what they heard, they would spontaneously ask for clarification. This was the case with non-learning-disabled children, but not with children with learning disabilities. The latter became aware of incompleteness of the task instructions only when they began to construct the task.

Findings from the above studies clearly showed communication problems in children with learning disabilities. More important, they highlight the nature of their communication problems. In one study, it was lack of adaptivity to the needs of the listener. In the other, it was lack of self-monitoring of what one heard. These communication problems, however, do not seem irreversible. Perhaps suitable interventions can be devised that would increase learning-disabled children's sensitivity to adapting language to a younger audience. As well, cognitive behavior modification (CBM) could be used to increase self-monitoring of their understanding of given verbal instructions. These ideas would profit from empirical tests.

Recent Research on Social Competence (Peer Acceptance and Social Status)

Earlier, I reported that one major finding from Tanis Bryan's research is the low social acceptance or unpopularity of children with learning disabilities. The significance of her original findings is greatly enhanced by replication studies that obtained the same findings.

More recent research into social competence of children with learning disabilities focused on factors that may affect their social competence. A leading research is Sharon Vaughn. Together with her students and research associates, Vaughn embarked on a 5-year longitudinal research project on social competence of children with learning disabilities. They followed the children from kindergarten to grade 5, and investigated the following issues: (a) Do children with learning disabilities show similar or different developmental patterns of social competence as low achievers, average, and high average achievers? (b) To what extent do children with learning disabilities differ from low achieving students, average, and high average students in social competence? The first issue reflects the researchers' use of a developmental framework to examine social competence in children with learning disabilities. The second reflects a more traditional approach in between-group comparisons in social competence. Because of Vaughn and associates' interest in a developmental perspective in researching social competence in children with learning disabilities, they also examined social status in their subjects before and after formal identification of learning disabilities had occurred. Additionally, they also examined the influence of teacher perception of the social competence of these children.

Intraindividual Differences in Social Competence

Vaughn and Hogan (1994) reported longitudinal data on the social competence of 10 children with learning disabilities: 7 males and 3 females, during the period of their attendance in kindergarten to grade 3. They collected data on (a) peer acceptance, (b) reciprocal friendship, (c) self-concept, and (d) social skills. They found that the children's social competence scores fluctuated markedly from year to year as they progressed from kindergarten to grade 3. From their data, they extracted three general patterns of social competence: (a) consistent competence, (b) early problem resolution, and (c) lingering and inconsistent difficulties.

On (a) consistent competence, Vaughn and Hogan (1994) observed four out of 10 children with learning disabilities to show consistently adequate to above-average ratings and reports from peers, teachers, and self in social competence. Except for one female, all of them had at least one reciprocal friendship. (Reciprocal friendship refers to two children naming each other as good or best friends.) On (b) early problem resolution, three children had peer relations problems and low social skills ratings from teachers during parts of the 5 years of the study. But they recovered from such low spells to attain adequate ratings in those areas. All three had reciprocal friendship in second grade. On (c) lingering difficulties, there were three boys with learning disabilities, all of whom show disturbing patterns of declining peer acceptance from beginning of a school year in September to spring of the following year in kindergarten and grades 1 and 2. Their teacher ratings were either low or variable. None reported to have a reciprocal friend in grade 2.

Vaughn and Hogan's (1994) study highlights the relevance of longitudinal research in learning disabilities (Wong, 1994). Devoid of it, we would not have known the instability in the social status of the majority of their subjects. More important, their findings point to the need to search for factors that affect learning-disabled students' social status, self-concept, and social skills in the classroom. Unraveling these factors and determining their relative influence on the various components of social competence (e.g., social status and peer acceptance, absence of maladaptive behavior, social cognition and self-concept, social skills) can guide us toward suitable interventions. For example, what factors affect self-concept in children with learning disabilities? Peer ratings and teacher ratings appear to be the factors involved. But which rating exerts more critical influence on these children depends on the particular child with learning disabilities. For example, in Vaughn and Hogan (1994), of the three males with learning disabilities who showed lingering problems in social competence, Juan was sensitive to teacher ratings. His self-rating scores followed his teacher's ratings of him! If the teacher's ratings of him increased, so would his self-rating scores! In contrast, the remaining two boys' self-ratings were influenced by peer ratings. if these improved, their self-ratings increased and vice versa.

Social Competence of Children with Learning Disabilities before and after Identification

Vaughn and Haager (in press) reported data on children with learning disabilities and other comparison groups from their 5-year longitudinal study in the following areas: peer acceptance, self-concept, behavior problems, and social skills. Regarding peer acceptance (or social status), Vaughn and Haager found that young kindergarten children, prior to being identified as learning disabled, were less popular or accepted by their normally achieving peers in the fall of the school year. By spring, their peer acceptance scores became substantially lower than those of high average children. But their ratings did not differ substantially from those of low achievers nor those of average students. Similarly, from kindergarten to grade 3, children with learning disabilities did not differ from low achievers nor from high average students in peer acceptance. The data therefore suggest that in social status or peer acceptance, children with learning disabilities did not differ much from low achievers. This lack of differences can be masked if researchers lump low achievers, average, and high average children altogether in a comparison group. Put differently, if a comparison group contains low achievers, average, and high average students, then one would likely obtain between-group differences in social status between such a comparison group and a group of children with learning disabilities.

On self-concept measure, Vaughn and Haager did not find any decline in self-concept, including academic self-concept in the children with learning disabilities across the years in their longitudinal study. It was low achievers that showed progressive declined in self-concept. These findings contradict previous findings (see Chapman, 1985). Vaughn and Haager explained their data by suggesting the positive effects of special educational help, or alternatively, lack of realism on the part of the children with learning disabilities in their own self-ratings.

In behavior problems, again Vaughn and Haager found little overall differences between the children with learning disabilities and low achievers. In social skills, again no differences between children with learning disabilities and low achievers were found. However, both groups were rated substantially lower than the average or high average group. In summary, Vaughn and Haager's study found children with learning disabilities cannot be distinguished in measures of social competence from low achievers.

Another study by Vaughn, McIntosh, Schumm, Haager, and Callwood (1993) deserves attention because it contains important methodological improvements and new empirical foci. Specifically, Vaughn et al. controlled for potential teacher bias. Prior research suggested that teacher perceptions of students with learning disabilities tended to be negative, and these negative perceptions could unwittingly get transmitted to the rest of the class. In this way, peers' perceptions of classmates with learning disabilities might become adversely influenced. To control for such potential bias, Vaughn et al. recruited for their study regular classroom teachers who were accepting towards students with learning disabilities. They approached school principals for nominations of such accepting teachers. Subsequently, they asked special education teachers to confirm the principals' nominations. Finally, the researchers interviewed these teachers to ascertain their tolerance as well, the latter rated themselves on acceptance of students with learning disabilities.

The second variable Vaughn et al. (1993) controlled for was academic status. Because low academic status is related to peer acceptance or social status of a student, it is important to control for it. Vaughn et al. achieved this control by forming several comparison groups: low achievers (LA), average students (AA), and high average students (HA). In doing so, they have provided much more careful differentiation of student academic status. Prior research on social competence did not differentiate among student academic status. The typical comparison group was composed of a mixture of LA, AA, and HA students.

Moreover, in their study, Vaughn et al. introduced two new research foci on social competence: (a) the relationship between knowing and liking a person, and (b) reciprocal friendship. On the relationship between knowing and liking a person, Vaughn et al. wondered if unpopularity of students with learning disabilities could in part result from classmates' insufficient acquaintance with them because they are usually pulled out for remedial help several times during the week, ranging from 20 minutes to 1 hour. Pull-out services therefore may have reduced the opportunities for interactions between students with learning disabilities and their classmates. For this reason, Vaughn et al. investigated the relationship between knowing and liking. Reciprocal friendship deserves research because it provides another dimension to social competence among students with learning disabilities.

What did Vaughn et al. (1993) find? Interestingly, they found the students with learning disabilities did not differ from the other groups of LA, AA, and HA students in peer acceptance, peer knowing, and reciprocal friendship. On the relationship between peer knowing and peer liking a person, the obtained correlation was higher for students with learning disabilities than LA students. LA students were found to be the least known and the least liked.

The findings therefore show that when you form more differentiated comparison groups, you find that students with learning disabilities are not necessarily the most unpopular students. Somehow, LA students were far less accepted by their peers than students with learning disabilities in Vaughn et al.'s study. Prior research has consistently found that students with learning disabilities were very unpopular (see summary of prior research by T. Bryan, 1991). How do we resolve the contrasts between the current findings by Vaughn et al. (1993) and prior research?

Vaughn et al. provide some plausible explanations. They suggested that the early studies were pioneer research studies in social competence and could have involved children with more severe learning disabilities and social problems. Also, because in those days, these students were largely not mainstreamed, they would be less known by their peers. Because knowing and liking a person is highly correlated, the lack of familiarity with students with learning disabilities in prior research studies could explain partially the high rejection of them by their peers. Additional explanations involve improved methodology, and the fact that the learning-disabled subpopulation is very heterogeneous, which means some individuals with learning disabilities would show problems in social competence, whereas others would not. Last but not least is the changing research focus from replicating previous findings to one of investigating social functions of students with learning disabilities. In sum, as Vaughn et al. (1993) aptly stated, their findings should be seen as refining our knowledge base in social competence of students with learning disabilities, and not as suggesting that we should dismiss prior research findings.

Research on Social Skills in Adolescents and Adults with Learning Disabilities

Concerning social skills in adolescents with learning disabilities, Deshler, Schumaker, Warner, Alley, and Clark (1980) found little differences between those adolescents and low achieving adolescents. More recent research findings confirmed findings from Deshler et al. (1980). Tur-Kaspa and Bryan (1994) found seventh- and eighth-grade adolescents with learning disabilities did not differ from low-achieving adolescents in the same grades in peer relations, self-control, and empathy. In contrast, replicating results of prior research, they did find children with learning disabilities and low-achieving children in grades 3 and 4 to have problems in these three areas.

Turning to adults with learning disabilities, after reviewing the research literature, Adelman and Vogel (1991) reported social relational problems in those adults. Apparently these adults had difficulties making and keeping friends. Such relational problems resulted in loneliness. Similar findings were found by Barr (1990). Barr also found female adults with learning disabilities had more social relational problems.

Werner (1993), however, reported more positive findings in adults with learning disabilities. In her longitudinal follow-up study of at-risk children who eventually were diagnosed as learning-disabled, Werner (1993) found that as adults in their 30s, they finally have settled down and lead satisfactory lives. They all have jobs, however, these were mainly low-status, semiskilled jobs. They have satisfactory marital relations, and have similar divorce rates as non-learning disabled adults. More important, 71.4% of them reported to have satisfactory relations with friends. The non-learning-disabled adults reported 80% of such satisfactory relations with friends. Clearly, those adults in Werner's (1993) study have indeed triumphed and prevailed over their learning disabilities!

Surely we must all wonder why previous research on adults with learning disabilities had more negative findings than Werner's (1993) more recent study. What is it about her adults with learning disabilities that resulted in these more positive social outcomes? Werner (1993) proffered explanations in what she terms "protective clusters." These have been explicated in the section on adults with learning disabilities on pages 20–21 in Chapter 1.

REFLECTIONS

Now that we have covered details on the research on social aspects of learning disabilities, let us recap consistent empirical patterns and then consider the big picture. In social competence, children with learning disabilities are now found to be similar to low achieving children. These two kinds of students are less competent socially than average and above-average children. To date, research on social cognition appears to yield conflicting data in role taking. But research on social cues perception and interpretations yields more consistent data, indicating that children and adolescents with learning disabilities have poorer (less accurate) social cues perception (Tur-Kaspa & Bryan, 1994). Similarly, research on social problem solving suggests that children and adolescents with learning disabilities are less competent. Although they possessed adequate social problem-solving knowledge, curiously they chose less efficient solutions (J. Bryan and Sonnefeld, 1981; Stone & LaGreca, 1984; Tur-Kaspa & Bryan, 1984). Last, research on self-concept in children and adolescents with learning disabilities consistently showed that they held poorer self-perceptions only in academic domains. Moreover, low academic status does not appear to explain entirely low social acceptance in children with learning disabilities, because low achievers are equally, if not more, rejected than they are! Having recaptured major research themes and findings, let us consider the big picture of research on social aspects of learning disabilities.

So what's the big picture? Well, some children, adolescents, and adults with learning disabilities are found to have diverse problems in the social realm. Because only a portion of them have social problems, this characteristic therefore cannot be considered a primary (causal) defining characteristic. Consequently, it cannot be included in the definition of learning disabilities. To insist on its inclusion amounts to ignoring research findings that strongly and consistently indicate social problems are not ubiquitous among those with learning disabilities. Moreover, such insistence causes confusion. In this regard, I disagree with the Canadian definition of learning disabilities which includes social problems.

Second, children and adolescents with learning disabilities had been found to share the same low social status or acceptance as low-achieving children and adolescents (see research by Deshler et al., 1980; Vaughn et al., 1993; Vaughn & Haager, in press). But it is important to remember that those children and adolescents with learning disabilities in their studies still had (have) social problems. Put differently, just because children and adolescents with learning disabilities do not differ from low achieving children and adolescents in social acceptance, we must not forget that they both have low social status! This important empirical fact leads to two research implications: (a) We have to continue research on causes of their low social status. Moreover, we may profit from asking this question: Are the causes for low social status the same or different for children and adolescents with learning disabilities and low achievers? (b) We must research effective social skills interventions for both children and adolescents with learning disabilities and low achievers to increase their social acceptance.

Third, we still have not been able to explain why some children and adolescents with learning disabilities are (a) poor in social perception, and (b) inept in social problem solving. Hence continual research in search for answers here is very necessary. Finally, because language use (pragmatics of language) plays a vital role in social interactions, we should research how poor language use in children and adolescents with learning disabilities contributes to their problems in social interactions, which in turn may adversely affect their social acceptance. With programmatic longitudinal research, we may answer these questions and others, and eventually, bring satisfactory closure to the diverse causes of social problems in children, adolescents, and adults with learning disabilities.

Social Intervention Research

Underlying Assumption and Theoretical Framework

The assumption underlying social interventions is that learning-disabled children lack social skills, which explains at least partially their social rejection by non-learning-disabled peers. The guiding theoretical framework is the deficits model, which points to the learning-disabled child as the source of the problem and as the focus for intervention.

Intervention Procedures and Outcome Measures

Target learning-disabled children are given social skills training and the effects of training subsequently measured. Vaughn, McIntosh, and Hogan (1990) provided a detailed summary table on the range of training foci and outcome measures. The data on social intervention studies (about 20 of them in 1991) suggest that in general, one can increase social skills in learning-disabled children, but such increase does not necessarily change their social acceptability by non-learning-disabled peers. Apparently negative attitudes among non-learning-disabled peers towards the unpopular learning-disabled children are quite resistant to change.

Critique on Theoretical Framework and Outcome Measures

The deficits model appears to be a poor framework for intervention research because learning-disabled children should not be seen as the sole course of their social problems. These problems arise from their interactions with non-learning-disabled peers and adults within particular contexts. Hence, we need a conceptual framework that encompasses all the players in that context in which the learning-disabled child's social problems are observed. The contextualist model affords such study (Vaughn & La Greca, 1992; Vaughn, 1991).

The contextualist model "assumes that social relationships are a function of interactions between individuals, the social setting, and values. Thus peer acceptance is viewed as a dynamic interactive process in which the child is both influenced by and influences others" (Vaughn & La Greca, 1992, p. 99). Vaughn (1991) illustrated the application of this contextualist model to a case study. A female learning-disabled student was chosen for training in social problem solving. On prior sociometric measures, she was found to be extremely unpopular. None of her non-learning-disabled classmates wanted her as a friend.

Intervention consisted of the following steps. First, the learning-disabled female and another high-status (very popular) non-learning-disabled child were given training in social problem solving involving the FAST strategy (see Table 3). Second, the learning-disabled female and her partner, the high-status non-learning-disabled student, share with the class what they had learned in social problem solving. They were known as "informants," persons who have valuable knowledge or information to share. Third, the learning-disabled female and her partner actively interact with the class to solve social problems that were related anonymously by their classmates. The latter wrote down problems they have at school, home, and with friends and put them in a decorated shoebox located outside the classroom. These problems were used by intervention researchers to train the learning-disabled female and her partner in social problem solving. As well, they were used for class presentations in which the learning-disabled female and her partner taught the class social problem solving. The learning-disabled female in this case study became very popular after training. Table 3 presents the FAST strategy designed by Sharon Vaughn (1991) for training students with learning disabilities who have social skills problems.

In my view, the contextualist model has several merits: (a) to become social skills trainers, both children with and without learning disabilities together learn skills in social problem solving, (b) they learn to generate solutions to social problems presented to them by their classmates. The merits of (a) and (b) lie in the equity between learning-disabled and non-learning-disabled social skills trainers. They begin

Table 3   The FAST Strategy in Social Skills Training[a]

Interpersonal problem solving (FAST)		
F	FREEZE	Don't act too quickly. What is the problem?
A	ALTERNATIVES	What are all my possible solutions?
S	SELECT ONE	What is the best solution in the long run?
T	TRY IT	What do I need to implement the solution? And if it doesn't work, what else can I try?

[a] Reproduced with permission from Sharon Vaughn (1991).

at the same baseline for training in social problem solving. In short, they shared the same status regarding target social skills. Moreover, they have to cooperate with each other in producing solutions to social problems. The whole process of solution-generation has ecological validity because the social problems are real-life problems presented by their classmates. When they succeed in resolving these social problems, they can justifiably feel proud and happy.

Moreover, the learning-disabled student's status of social skills trainer effectively counters her low academic status in class. As she gains credibility in her skills as a social skills trainer and problem solver, she would come to be seen in a new light by her non-learning-disabled peers. This should translate into more positive perception and acceptance.

Additionally, the social problem-solving training occurs in the right context, the classroom! It involves interactions with non-learning-disabled peers. These social interactions with non-learning-disabled peers focus on social problems that are important to learning disabled students. Hence, these interactions may well foster the recognition among the non-learning-disabled peers that the learning-disabled student is quite acceptable after all. In their language, it's a case of "You're OK!"

Vaughn's contextualist model certainly is promising regarding social skills interventions of unpopular learning-disabled students. Obviously it needs extensions to older intermediate and secondary students with learning disabilities. One study that used the contextualist model with 10 learning-disabled boys found partial success. Only five of them showed increased social skills. The remaining five were difficult to train because of additional conduct disorder (Vaughn, 1991). Clearly, for students with learning disabilities whose social problems are compounded with conduct disorder or aggressiveness, alternative or additional training to social skills intervention is necessary. In sum, Vaughn's contextualist model needs both replication and extension.

Turning now to social skills intervention research involving adolescents with learning disabilities, Hazel et al. (1982) did an interesting study. They had three groups of adolescents in their study: those with learning disabilities, a comparison group of adolescents without learning disabilities, and a group of juvenile delinquents. The latter were on probation at the time when Hazel et al. launched their study, and volunteered for the training upon hearing about it.

The presenting social problems of the adolescents with learning disabilities were noncompliance with both parents and teachers and chronic truancy. Age (13–18) and intelligence (IQ from 86–117) ranges of the three groups of adolescents were similar. The areas in which all three groups received training were giving positive feedback, giving negative feedback, accepting negative feedback, resisting peer pressure, negotiation (e.g., negotiating curfew with parent), personal problem solving (e.g., insufficient time to complete an assignment). In all these areas, the adolescents with learning disabilities differed from those without learning disabilities in pretest. They did more poorly.

Pretests, training, and posttests involved role playing particular scenarios. Training consisted of a weekly 2-hour session across 10 weeks. The training procedure consisted of seven steps. Step 1: The trainer introduced, explained, and described the to-be-learned skill. Step 2: The trainer gave the rationale of the to-be-taught social skill and how use of it could profit the trainees' social interactions with others. Step 3: The trainer discussed social situations in which the learned skill can be used. Step 4: Group members were handed a list of components of the to-be-learned social skill. They discussed and came up with the rationale for each skill component. Step 5: The trainer modeled the social skill in a role-playing situation. Step 6: Group members learned the component steps of the social skill. Step 7: In pairs, group members enacted the social skill in role play in a social scenario of their own choice or construction. The following example from Hazel et al. (1982) illustrates the social skill components or steps in resisting peer pressure to shoplift: Face the person, maintain eye contact, have a serious expression, use a concerned voice tone, maintain a straight posture, say something positive to the person, say "No" to the shoplifting suggestion and give a reason, suggest an alternative activity, and leave the situation if necessary.

Hazel et al. (1982) obtained good training results. All three groups gained after training and could generalize to new role-playing situations. More specifically, adolescents with learning disabilities evidenced the same learning rate as the other two groups of non-learning-disabled and juvenile delinquents. They took as many trials as the non-learning-disabled adolescents in learning. However, in social problem-solving skill, they still needed more training because in the posttest, they achieved 50% versus 77% in both non-learning-disabled and juvenile delinquent adolescents. In this area of social problem solving, the adolescent had to generate alternative solutions and evaluate the consequences of them, and choose the best one for implementation.

REFLECTIONS

Social skills intervention research is very difficult to design and conduct. This is because of inherent problems in every stage of such studies: selection of target subjects with learning disabilities, the nature, intensity, and duration of any theory-based intervention (training) program, outcome measures, measuring maintenance and generalizability of training.

Because social skills problems are not ubiquitous among individuals with learning disabilities, it is important that those targeted for social skills interventions indeed lack the very skills contained in the intervention program. Moreover, of those who would benefit from social skills interventions, more individualized programs may be necessary because they are likely to vary in their training needs. For example, some may need training in social perception, some in social problem solving, some may need both kinds of training, and so forth. Obviously this heterogeneous nature of social problems in individuals with learning disabilities also impacts on the intensity and duration of training. Those with more social problems, for example, would need more elaborate and likely longer training.

The issue of generalizability of training is most vexing. As Keogh (1990) astutely pointed out, social skills are very complex skills. Whatever social skill an intervention researcher builds in target children with learning disabilities is at best, a very specific, clearly defined but narrow social skill. It is narrow when we put it in perspective against the entire range of social skills engaged in daily in social interactions. Moreover, social context and time of contact govern our social interactions (Keogh, 1990). Because social cues and elicited responses in such context and time are often unpredictable, it is difficult for intervention researchers to guarantee maintenance and generalization of trained social skills in the target subjects. One needs only to think of the vast differences between home and school where most social skills interventions occur, to have an inkling of the problem of skill maintenance and generalization. There is also, the possibility that trainees' reversion to undesirable social behaviors may come from classmates' reinforcement (Keogh, 1990).

Although the barriers to social skills interventions research are daunting, we must persevere with them. Awareness of these problems and issues should spur us to better designs of social skills interventions. Social skills are indeed complex. And both foreseeable and unforeseeable verbal and nonverbal cues influence social interactions between any two individuals. To the extent that research information enlightens us, we can design training sessions in social skills that particular learning-disabled children and adolescents lack, and painstakingly increase their social skills repertoires in longitudinal research. Through systematic and longitudinal social skills intervention research, we may hope to redress problems that plague some of the children, adolescents, and adults with learning disabilities, and resolve major issues such as maintenance and generalization.

References

Adelman, P. B., & Vogel, S. A. (1991). The learning-disabled adult. In B. Y. L. Wong (Ed.), *Learning about learning disabilities* (pp. 563–594). San Diego: Academic Press.

Axelrod, L. (1982). Social perception in learning disabled adolescents. *Journal of Learning Disabilities, 15,* 610–613.

Barr, P. M. (1990). *The adaptation of adults with learning disabilities in four life domains.* Unpublished doctoral dissertation, University of Calgary, Calgary, Alberta.

Benenson, J., & Dweck, C. (1986). The development of trait explanations and self-evaluations in the academic and social domains. *Child Development, 57,* 1179–1187.

Borkowski, J. G., Weyhing, R. S., & Can, M. (1988). Effects of attributional retraining on strategy-based reading comprehension in learning-disabled students. *Journal of Educational Psychology, 80,* 46–53.

Bryan, J. H., & Perlmutter, B. (1979). Immediate impressions of learning-disabled children by female adults. *Learning Disability Quarterly, 2,* 80–88.

Bryan, J. H., & Sonnefeld, J. (1981). Children's social ratings of ingratiation tactics. *Journal of Learning Disabilities, 5,* 605–609.

Bryan, T. (1977). Children's comprehension of non-verbal communication. *Journal of Learning Disabilities, 10,* 501–506.

Bryan, T. (1991). Social problems and learning disabilities. In B. Y. L. Wong (Ed.), *Learning about learning disabilities* (pp. 195–229). New York: Academic Press.

Bryan, T., Donahue, J. M., & Pearl, R. (1981). Learning disabled children's peer interactions during a small-group problem-solving task. *Learning Disability Quarterly, 4,* 13–22.

Bryan, T., Donahue, M., Pearl, R., & Sturen, C. (1981). learning disabled children's conversational skills: The "TV talk show." *Learning Disability Quarterly, 4,* 250–259.

Buchanan, M., & Wolf, J. S. (1986). A comprehensive study of learning-disabled adults. *Journal of Learning Disabilities, 19,* 34–38.

Chapman, J. W. (1985). *Self-perceptions of ability, learned helplessness and academic achievement expectations of children with learning disabilities.* Unpublished manuscript, Education Department, Massey University, Massey, New Zealand.

Deshler, D. D., Schumaker, J. B., Warner, M. M., Alley, G. R., & Clark, F. L. (1980). *An epidemiological study of learning disabled adolescents in secondary school: Social status, peer relationships, activities in and out of school, and time use* (Research Rep. No. 18). Lawrence, KS: The University of Kansas Institute for Research in Learning Disabilities.

Dodge, K. A. (1986). A social information processing model of social competence in children. In M. Perlmutter (Ed.), *Minnesota Symposium on Child Psychology, 18,* 77–125. Hillsdale, NJ: Erlbaum.

Donahue, M., Pearl, R., & Bryan, T. (1980). Learning disabled children's conversational competence: Responses to inadequate messages. *Applied Psycholinguistics, 1,* 387–403.

Feagans, L., & McKinney, J. D. (1981). Pattern of exceptionality across domains in learning disabled children. *Journal of Applied Developmental Psychology, 1*(4), 313–328.

Hazel, J. S., Schumaker, J. B., Sherman, J. A., & Sheldon, J. (1982). Application of a group training program in social skills and problem solving to learning disabled and non-learning disabled youth. *Learning Disability Quarterly, 5,* 398–408.

Jackson, S. C., Enright, R. D., & Murdock, J. Y. (1987). Social perception problems in learning-disabled youth: Developmental lag versus perceptual deficit. *Journal of Learning Disabilities, 20,* 361–364.

Keogh, B. K. (1990). Commentary: The effectiveness of social and behavioral interventions. In Tom E. Scruggs & B. Y. L. Wong (Eds.), *Intervention research in learning disabilities* (pp. 322–326). New York: Springer Verlag.

McKinney, J. D., & Speece, D. L. (1983). Classroom behavior and academic progress of learning-disabled students. *Journal of Applied Developmental Psychology, 4,* 139–146.

Morrison, G. M., Forness, S. R., & MacMillan, D. L. (1983). Influences on the sociometric ratings of mildly handicapped children: A path analysis. *Journal of Educational Psychology, 75,* 63–74.

Olsen, J., Wong, B. Y. L., & Marx, R. (1983). Linguistic and metacognitive aspects of normally-achieving and learning-disabled children's communication process. *Learning Disability Quarterly, 6,* 289–304.

Pascarella, E. T., & Pflaum, S. W. (1987). The interaction of children's attribution and level of control over error correction in reading instruction. *Journal of Educational Psychology, 73,* 533–540.

Pearl, R., & Cosden, M. (1982). Sizing up a situation: LD children's understanding of social interactions. *Learning Disability Quarterly, 5,* 53–57.

Pearl, R., Donahue, M., & Bryan, T. (1986). Social relationships of learning-disabled children. In J. K. Torgesen & B. Y. L. Wong (Eds.), *Psychological and educational perspectives on learning disabilities* (pp. 194–224). New York: Academic Press.

Perlmutter, B. F., & Bryan, J. H. (1984). First impressions, ingratiation, and the learning-disabled child. *Journal of Learning Disabilities, 17*(3), 157–161.

Piers, E., & Harris, D. (1969). *The Piers-Harris Children's Self-Concept Scale.* Nashville, TN: Counselor Recordings and Tests.

Rosenthal, R., Hall, J. A., Mateo, J. R., Rogers, P. L., & Archer, D. (1979). *Sensitivity to nonverbal commu-nication: The PONS test.* Baltimore, MD: Johns Hopkins University Press.

Schurr, K. T., Towne, R. C., & Joiner, L. M. (1972). Trends in self-concept of ability over 2 years of spe-cial-class placement. *Journal of Special Education, 6,* 161–166.

Stipek, D. J., & Tannatt, L. (1984). Children's judgements of their own and their peers' academic com-petence. *Journal of Educational Psychology, 76,* 75–84.

Stone, W. L., & LaGreca, A. (1984). Comprehension of nonverbal communication: A re-examination of the social competencies of learning-disabled children. *Journal of Abnormal Child Psychology, 12,* 505–518.

Tollefson, H., Tracy, D. B., Johnsen, E. P., Buenning, M., Farmer, A., & Barke, C. R. (1982). Attribution patterns of learning-disabled adolescents. *Learning Disability Quarterly, 5,* 14–20.

Tur-Kaspa, H., & Bryan, T. (1994). Social information-processing skills of students with learning dis-abilities. *Learning Disabilities Research & Practice, 9*(1), 12–23.

Tur-Kaspa, H., & Bryan, T. (1993). Social attributions of students with learning disabilities. *Exceptional-ly, 4*(4), 229–243.

Vaughn, S. (1991). Social skills enhancement in students with learning disabilities. In B. Y. L. Wong (Ed.), *Learning about learning disabilities* (pp. 408–440). San Diego: Academic Press.

Vaughn, S., & Haager, D. (in press). Social competence as a multifaceted construct: How do students with learning disabilities fare? *Learning Disabilities Quarterly.*

Vaughn, S., & Hogan, A. (1994). The social competence of students with learning disabilities over time: A written-individual examination. *Journal of Learning Disabilities, 27*(5), 292–303.

Vaughn, S., & La Greca, A. (1992). Beyond greetings and making friends: Social skills from a broader perspective. In B. Y. L. Wong (Ed.), *Contemporary Intervention Research in Learning Disabilities: An in-ternational perspective* (pp. 96–114). New York: Springer-Verlag.

Vaughn, S., McIntosh, R., & Hogan, A. (1990). Why social skills training doesn't work: An alternative model. In T. Scruggs & B. Y. L. Wong (Eds.), *Intervention research in learning disabilities* (pp. 279–303). New York: Springer-Verlag.

Vaughn, S., McIntosh, R., Schumm, J. S., Haager, D., & Callwood, D. (1993). Social status, peer accep-tance, and reciprocal friendships revisited. *Learning Disabilities Research & Practice, 8*(2), 82–88.

Weiss, E. (1984). Learning disabled children's understanding of social interactions of peers. *Journal of Clin-ical Child Psychology, 13,* 50–55.

Werner, E. E. (1993). Risk and resilience in individuals with learning disabilities: Lessons learned from the Kauai Longitudinal Study. *Learning Disabilities Research & Practice, 8*(1), 28–34.

White, W. J. (1985). Perspectives on the education and training of learning-disabled adults. *Learning Dis-ability Quarterly, 86,* 231–236.

Winne, P. H., Woodlands, M. H., & Wong, B. Y. L. (1982). Comparability of self-concept among learn-ing-disabled, normal and gifted students. *Journal of Learning Disability, 15,* 470–475.

Wong, B. Y. L. (1994). The relevance of longitudinal research to learning disabilities. *Journal of Learning Disabilities, 27*(5), 270–274.

Wong, B. Y. L., & Wong, R. (1980). Role-taking skills in normal achieving and learning-disabled chil-dren. *Learning Disability Quarterly, 3,* 11-18.

6

Metacognition and Learning Disabilities

One current educational goal is to produce and/or promote students to be self-regulated learners. What does it mean for students to be self-regulated learners? It means that they are active, autonomous learners, who initiate, direct, and sustain their cognitions, learning behaviors, and affect towards attaining particular goals that typically involve academic success (Garcia & Pintrich, 1994; Schunk, 1994; Wigfield, 1994). Implicit to self-regulated learners is the motivation to learn, which reflects their valuing learning, and the possession of volition, which is the will to focus on learning or task completion or goal attainment. Such will underlies these learners' deliberate efforts to ward off distractions or negative thoughts that may detract from their academic focus (Corno, 1986; Kuhl, 1987, 1985, 1984). Thus self-regulated learners show initiative and independence in learning. Their motivation to learn is clearly reflected in the commitment of effort in learning. More important, such effort is sustained and unwavering despite possible setbacks and distractions from task completion. Their focus and determination in learning indicate a will to reach academic success.

Upon successful task completion, self-regulated learners give themselves due reinforcement (a pat on the back), and through appropriate attributions of success or academic goal attainment, they increase their own sense of self-efficacy. In turn, this increased self-efficacy fuels planful, strategic learning (Borkowski, Day, Saenz, Diet-

120

meyer, Estrada, & Groteluschen, 1992; Borkowski, Estrada, Milstead, & Hale, 1989; Borkowski & Thorpe, 1994) and predicts future academic success (Schunk, 1994). Thus, the term *self-regulated learners* has a very rich meaning, involving the learners' metacognition, motivation, and volition in active participation in learning (Zimmerman, 1989).

How does metacognition play an important role in defining self-regulated learners? I shall explain this role, and my explanation will introduce the relevance of metacognition to the learning disabilities field.

For learners to be able to select task-appropriate strategies, they must possess an awareness of their own cognitive strengths and weaknesses so as to choose strategies that match their cognitive assets to the task demands. Moreover, in order for them to deploy strategies flexibly, adding or dropping or modifying strategies to suit the tasks at hand, they must continually self-monitor and self-evaluate the effectiveness of the strategies in use. To effect appropriate choice of strategy and subsequent strategy monitoring and evaluation, learners need to have metacognition. This is evident in the definition of metacognition below.

Flavell (1976) originated the theoretical construct of metacognition, which he defined as one's awareness of one's own cognitive processes, one's cognitive strengths and weaknesses, and self-regulation. Basically, he has in mind an individual's turning inwards to reflect on his or her own cognitive processes, cognitive strengths, and weaknesses. Such reflections enable the individual to arrive at certain realizations. For example, that he or she may be relatively more skilled verbally than mechanically; that he or she may be one of the top swimmers in his or her swim club, but only average when compared to the top swimmers from all the swim clubs in the city. And he or she may develop knowledge, such as the concept of swimmer burnout and that someone who learned to swim the front crawl at age 4 is likely to be a far better swimmer than someone learning at age 45.

Flavell's construct of metacognition has a second aspect: self-regulation. How the two aspects of it are connected can best be illustrated in Ann Brown's simple model of learning. Brown shows how an individual's metacognition serves to orchestrate self-knowledge, task demands, and appropriate learning activities to result in his or her successful learning. Ann Brown's model of simple learning contains four factors: characteristics of the learner, nature of the materials to be learned, criterial task, and learning activities.

The *characteristics of the learner* refer to the cognitive and strategic repertoires that the individual brings to the learning situation. Individual differences in knowledge and procedural repertoires affect how the individuals learn (Brown, 1980). For example, students with a psychology background would find it easier to understand the research summaries in this and other chapters of this book than someone without such a background. The *nature of the materials to be learned* refers to the organizational nature of the materials, materials that match the readers' prior knowledge, and so on. The nature of the materials to be learned affects the individual's learning outcome. For example, materials that match the subjects' prior knowledge are more easily understood by subjects (Anderson, 1980; Brown, 1978). Organized lectures facilitate student understanding and note taking. The *criterial task* is the end product in any learning. For example, the criterial task in my course in learning disabilities comprises a midterm and a final examination. The efficient learner is aware of the criterial task, and tailors his or her learning activities accordingly (Baker & Brown, 1984a). For example, knowing that the final examination in a course involves short essay questions would lead a student to rely less on memorization of materials. Instead, she or he would focus on understanding the course material and thinking hard about implications of what is read. Thus, the criterial task sets the learner's purpose in learning, as well as providing him or her with standards for evaluating his or her learning (Anderson, 1980; Brown, 1980). *Learning activities* refer to the activities the student engages in while learning. She or he could spontaneously deploy suitable learning activities or be taught to do so. As children grow older, they gradually learn a repertoire of learning activities. With extensive use, these learning activities and strategies become automatic and their deployment unconscious (Brown & Palincsar, 1982). Engaging in appropriate learning activities greatly influences students' learning outcome. For example, failure to categorize items into discrete categories such as food, clothing, furniture, or vehicles impairs recall in children with learning disabilities. Unobtrusively prompting them to put related items into suitable categories remarkably improved their recall (Wong, 1978).

The literature in cognitive psychology and developmental psychology has shown us clearly how each of the above factors governs the likelihood of a student's successful learning. To demonstrate the point that these four factors and their interactions are important determinants of learning, two illustrative studies are described.

The influence of knowledge of criterial task on students' performances was shown by Wong, Wong, and LeMare (1982). In two experiments involving normally achieving and children with learning disabilities, Wong et al. investigated the hypothesis that poor comprehension and recall in learning-disabled children might stem from vague perception of criterion tasks (task demands), and that provision of clear knowledge of criterion tasks would enhance their performance. This performance enhancement comes about when students focus their study efforts on relevant parts of the exercise, in light of knowledge of criterion task.

In the comprehension task, children given knowledge of criterion task were explicitly told to attend to preparagraph questions in two expository passages, because they modeled test questions the children would receive later. In the recall task, the children in the treatment condition were told to study the two expository passages for subsequent recall.

The results in the comprehension task supported the predictions. Wong et al. (1982) found that both normally achieving and children with learning disabilities given knowledge of criterion task, correctly answered more questions than their respective counterparts in the control condition. However, the results in the recall task did not indicate reliable differences between treatment and control groups. The investigators attributed this outcome to the imprecision in the instructions given to the treatment groups. It is recalled that these children were simply told to expect a recall test. Unlike the comprehension task, they were not guided on which parts of the text to focus on in studying.

In a follow-up experiment, Wong et al. (1982) improved the methodology in the recall task. They instructed the children in the treatment condition to study the passages for subsequent recall, and to attend specifically to certain important parts of the passages in their study. The children in the control condition were simply told to study the passages for subsequent recall. The results clearly indicated that given explicit knowledge of criterion task, both normally achieving and learning-disabled children recalled substantially more of the passages than their respective control groups. In sum, Wong et al. (1982) showed that explicit knowledge of criterion task induced appropriate studying activities in children. The children were able to focus their attention on relevant contents in the passages because of knowledge of criterion task.

Miyake and Norman's (1979) study illustrates the interactive influences between the nature of the to-be-learned materials (in this case, conceptual difficulty) and learning activities employed by students. Miyake and Norman (1979) investigated the effects of prior knowledge on student's questioning behavior. They used two groups of college students. One group knew little about computers and text editors. The other group was given sufficient training in the use of a text editor. The criterion in training was the students' editing one text unaided. Subsequently both groups were instructed to learn to operate a different text editor by following either an easy nontechnical manual or a difficult technical manual. The students were further instructed to verbalize their thoughts and questions as they learned the new text editor. Miyake and Norman (1979) found an interesting interaction in their study: Novice students in computer science asked more questions on the easy manual but very few on the hard manual. The reverse pattern of questioning was obtained for the trained students. Miyake and Norman interpreted the findings to suggest that to ask a question, you have to have an optimal amount of prior knowledge for the particular subject matter at hand. Because educators have long stressed the importance of cultivating questioning behaviors to facilitate learning in students, Miyake and Norman's findings imply that teachers should attend to students' existing prior knowledge as a concomitant condition in teaching students to generate questions. The preceding study of Miyake and Norman (1979) presents a mere glimpse into the web of interactions of various parameters underlying successful learning.

Metacognition and Brown's Model

One impetus responsible for the development of metacognitive theory and research is that an individual's successful learning requires more than background knowledge or learning strategies. Equally, if not more important, the individual must be able to use his background and strategic knowledge effectively during learning (Brown, 1980). If an individual is unaware of his own repertoire of strategies, he or she would be unlikely to deploy suitable strategies flexibly and precisely in tune with task demands. Occasionally, children and adults fail to use appropriate strategies for learning despite having them in their repertoire of strategies (Brown, 1980). Flavell (1976) used the term *production deficiencies* to describe these occasions, whereas Scardamalia and Bereiter (1987) used *inert knowledge*. For the learner to be able to use and control appropriately his background knowledge and knowledge of strategies, he needs to develop metacognitive skills (Baker & Brown, 1984a; Brown, 1980).

It is recalled that metacognition refers to the awareness of knowledge and control and regulation of that knowledge (Baker & Brown, 1984a,b). The distinction between cognition and metacognition is the "distinction between knowledge and the understanding of knowledge in terms of *awareness and appropriate use*" [italics added] (Brown, 1980, p. 453). Metacognitive skills are those that have been attributed to the "executive" in numerous theories of human memory and artificial intelligence. They are the essential characteristics of efficient thinking in a broad range of learning situations, including efficient reading and effective studying (Anderson, 1980; Baker & Brown, 1984a; Brown 1980). The following example gives some flavor of how good students deploy metacognitive strategies in their studying. After being informed that there will be a midterm examination involving short essay answers, the good students begin to plan their study schedule. With 3 weeks left before the midterm, they start reading their lecture notes and corresponding chapters from their textbooks. They underline important parts of these materials, and denote parts that they understand well. In addition, they identify those sections not understood thoroughly. They seek out the teaching assistant and the professor for help with parts of their notes and texts of which they lack thorough understanding. Having received the necessary help or clarification, they concentrate their efforts at studying the important parts of their notes and texts. Remembering that short essay answers rather than multiple-choice questions will be on the midterm, good students spend time thinking about what they are studying, in particular, the implications of what they have studied.

In the above example, good students ascertain what they already know or understand and what they need to clarify in their lecture notes and texts (assessing own knowledge repertoire). Their awareness of the need to get clarification for certain parts of their notes and chapters leads them to seek help from the appropriate sources: the teaching assistant and the professor (awareness leads to proper action). Having clarified their notes and texts, they settle down to diligent studying (self-regulation). However, they are mindful of the criterial task (short essay answers in the midterm), which leads them to engage in appropriate studying behaviors (concentrating on thinking about rather than rote memorization of notes and text). Metacognition enables good students to coordinate their awareness of their state of knowledge with appropriate problem-solving behaviors, and guides them to link up appropriate studying behaviors with the task demands of the midterm. Surely the consequences of such well-coordinated, planful, and intelligent studying behaviors is a first-class performance on the midterm?!

The above description indicates how good students consciously and deliberately coordinate their efforts in studying. The skills they have mobilized in coordinating and regulating their efforts in studying are metacognitive skills. What they have coordinated and regulated are their own knowledge, their notes and texts, their own learning activities, and the criterial task. These are factors depicted in Brown's model. Thus, it can be seen that metacognitive skills are essential in effective coordination of the four factors in that model, and this coordination greatly affects the student's success in learning. Put differently, executive processes are needed to direct, coordinate, and regulate the interactions among those four factors. It is effective coordination or "orchestration" (to borrow the word from Brown, 1980) of these interactions that is responsible for the success of any learning outcome. These executive processes are the individual's metacognitive skills.

In the above section, I have explained the role of metacognition in an individual's successful learning, and in particular, how one's self-awareness yokes up with one's self-regulation to produce successful learning. However, there is a glaring deficiency in Brown's model of simple learning and her exalted role of metacognition in orchestrating the four factors in her model. Specifically, the deficiency concerns the neglect of the essential role of motivation. The individual's motivation comes into play to connect her self-awareness and self-regulation. Without it, for all her self-awareness of her own cognitive processes, assets, and liabilities, she would not pursue the right course of self-regulated action! To illustrate, say on the night the Canucks are playing the New York Rangers, a student knew she should study for the midterm examination the next day. This knowledge represents metacognitive awareness. Moreover, she knew how to study for it, since she had been told it would comprise short essay answers. She planned to think hard about implications of what she had learned in lectures. This planning suggests the student knew the proper course of action to take (self-regulation). However, being weak-kneed and irresolute, she opted for the hockey game rather than studying. She lacked the requisite motivation to link up metacognitive awareness with self-regulation in studying! Various theorists have addressed this problem in their own ways. Specifically, in their metacognitive theory, Borkowski and his colleagues assign an important place to attributions (Borkowski et al., 1992; Borkowski et al., 1989; Borkowski & Thorpe, 1994). Others emphasize self-efficacy (Corno, 1989; Schunk, 1994; Zimmerman, 1989). To illustrate, I shall summarize Borkowski et al.'s (1989) metacognitive model. This model depicts spontaneous and learned development of various cognitive strategies in children as they effectively tackle academic work. Through cumulative development of these cognitive strategies, they develop specific strategy knowledge, which refers to their knowing when, where, and how to use a particular strategy. Thus they have conditional knowledge of strategy use and the range of applicability of each strategy. Moreover, their repertoires of strategies result in the development of relational strategy knowledge with which they compare the usefulness of various strategies and know which are more applicable under specific circumstances.

As children continue to grow, learn, or develop on their own more cognitive and metacognitive strategies to aid learning, they develop a very important piece of knowledge, namely, general strategy knowledge. This knowledge comprises three important aspects: (a) valuing a planful and strategic approach to learning because it increases the likelihood of successful outcomes in learning and performance; (b) realizing that learning involves effort; and (c) most important of all, children come to realize that they are the very agents of their own successful learning as they deploy task-appropriate strategies and effort in learning. Hence, teachers' favor or luck plays no part in their successful learning. In short, they attribute success rightfully to themselves. Such attributions feed their sense of self-efficacy, which is one's objective judgment of one's ability to effectively attain a goal or execute the necessary actions to attain it (Bandura, 1977). Repeated attributions to self as the agent of repeated academic successes naturally increase the child's sense of self-efficacy. Together, appropriate attributions and increased self-efficacy fuel the child's decisions (executive processes) to choose and use strategies in learning and performance (Borkowski et al., 1989). You see then that Borkowski et al. accord important roles to metacognition, attribution, self-efficacy, and executive processes (decision-making processes) in their metacognitive model. Metacognitive knowledge of specific strategies and their use, relational strategy knowledge, and general strategy knowledge guide the child to select and use task-appropriate strategies, and to adopt an intelligent (planful and strategic) approach to learning. Attributions and self-efficacy fill in the gap of motivation in Ann Brown's model of simple learning, which assigns to an individual's metacognition an exclusively central role. And executive processes in Borkowski et al.'s model are energized by attributions and self-efficacy of the child. These executive processes have the important role of directing the child's decision making regarding choice and use of strategies in learning and performance.

How does this discussion of self-regulated learning and metacognition relate to learning disabilities? Can you anticipate what my explanations would be? Try. Take a piece of paper and jot down some ideas. At least two, all right?

Let me begin by pointing out the relevance of what I've covered on self-regulated learners to learning disabilities. Recall the meaning of self-regulated learners. Look back to the beginning of this chapter should you forget. Students with learning disabilities and low achievers lack all those attributes ascribed to self-regulated learners. The former have been called passive learners who do not actively engage in their own learning (Torgesen, 1977). Some of the reasons proffered for their passivity in learning include past histories of failures that erode their motivation to learn and inculcate expectations of failure or low sense of self-efficacy. Another reason appears to be their having been given too much structure in their remediation. A third explanation is their need to learn to value a planful, strategic approach to learning, and that learning requires effort (Borkowski et al., 1989).

In contrast to students with learning disabilities and low achievers, successful students show all the attributes of self-regulated learners (Wigfield, 1994; Zimmerman, 1989). Because teachers want all students, including those with learning disabilities and low achievers to become self-regulated learners, they must attend to and focus on helping them to develop autonomy and self-direction in learning, as well as the attendant motivation to learn and self-efficacy. However, one should remember that students with learning disabilities do possess certain cognitive strategies, but their cognitive strategies tend to be inefficient or faulty. An example of the former is word-by-word reading; an example of the latter is erroneous strategies in arithmetic.

What is the relevance of the construct and research of metacognition to learning disabilities? It lies in demonstrating that students with learning disabilities have less sophisticated metacognition in reading, and very little of it in writing. Consequently, they need instruction in efficient metacognitive strategies in reading and enhanced awareness and understanding of the writing process and the cognitive processes engaged in when composing.

Metacognition and Reading

Before summarizing the research on metacognition and reading, I want to say that although Flavell originated the theoretical construct of metacognition, it is Ann Brown, in her seminal 1980 chapter, who related metacognition to reading. It is important to know this.

Students with learning disabilities behave like younger normally achieving children in their immature understanding of the purpose of reading, and in their repertoires of reading strategies. Metacognitive research in reading can be described according to various topics and the findings summarized accordingly.

Metacognitive Skills and Efficient Reading

Metacognitive skills "involve predicting, checking/self-monitoring, reality-testing, coordination and control of deliberate attempts to solve problems or to study and learn" (Brown, 1980, p. 454). Good readers possess metacognitive skills in reading, are aware of the purpose of reading, and differentiate between task demands in, for example, reading a text for class assignment versus reading a magazine for pleasure. They actively seek to clarify the purposes and task demands through self-questioning prior to reading the given materials (Anderson, 1980). Such awareness leads them to use suitable reading strategies. For example, a good reader varies his reading rate and concentration level as a function of materials being read—text or magazine. It also leads them to monitor their state of reading comprehension. For example, when a good reader encounters a comprehension difficulty, he uses debugging strategies. These problem-solving attempts indicate self-regulation (Anderson, 1980; Brown, 1980). Moreover, good readers evaluate their own comprehension of materials read. Evaluating one's own comprehension of given instructions or of materials read has important consequences (Markman, 1977, 1979). This last reading strategy is a very basic form of self-awareness (Brown, 1980). If a reader does not realize that he or she has not understood a particular part of the given materials, she or he will not employ suitable "debugging devices," such as backtracking, scanning ahead for possible clues to shed light on the part that currently presents difficulties to comprehension (Anderson, 1980; Baker, 1979). In contrast, learning-disabled readers show little indication of such coordination between task demands and suitable reading strategies. They lack the requisite metacognitive skills in reading (Wong, 1985).

Does this not ring a bell? How many times have you found that as you are reading a text for a course (or the chapter on memory processes in this book!), that you find yourself saying out loud, "Wait a minute, what does this mean? What's this sentence saying?" Whenever you experience the aforementioned situation, you are evidencing a comprehension breakdown. For you to utter those sentences suggests that something inside your head has been monitoring how you digest the information you have been reading. You have an internal, unconscious monitor of your reading comprehension. Otherwise, you would read on blithely like students with learning disabilities who habitually do not monitor their reading comprehension! And like them, at the end of the page, you wouldn't have a clue to what you've read! Incidentally, you only mutter things like, "what on earth does this mean?" when you are stymied in reading comprehension. When your comprehension flows smoothly, your internal monitor takes a back seat!

Thus, the fluent or mature reader is rarely conscious of his or her own comprehension monitoring. Only when a comprehension failure arises in reading does the fluent reader realize that comprehension monitoring has occurred (Anderson, 1980). The individual immediately slows down reading and either reviews the difficult section or reads on seeking enlightenment in subsequent text.

It remains to be shown that younger or immature, poor readers, children, and adolescents with learning disabilities have deficient metacognitive skills concerning reading. We shall therefore examine metacognitive research in the following areas: (a) awareness of one's purpose in reading, (b) sensitivity to important parts of text, (c) comprehension monitoring as evidenced in detecting inconsistencies, and (d) deployment of debugging strategies. Because there are two excellent summaries of metacognitive research in reading (Baker & Brown, 1984a,b), the studies described here are only those that have the most relevance to the theme under consideration. Also, because metacognitive research in reading peaked in the 1980s, I choose to cite studies from that decade.

Awareness of the Purpose of Reading

Younger and poorer readers have been found to perceive the purpose of reading to be decoding, rather than reading for meaning (Canney & Winograd, 1979; Garner & Kraus, 1982). Because the instructional focus in reading in the early grades is on learning to read, with much curricular emphasis on decoding and auditory and visual discrimination (Seymour, 1970), the younger readers' perception that the purpose of reading is decoding is legitimate. Because of the nature of the remedial phonics drills that they receive, the perception of poor readers that reading means decoding in the early grades is also legitimate. But for older, poor readers who have learned to decode sufficiently, their perception of reading as decoding reflects deficient awareness of the purpose of reading, that is, a failure to develop the appropriate metacognition about the reading task.

Canney and Winograd's (1979) study illustrates nicely the developmental shift in children's metacognition about the purpose of reading. They interviewed three good and three poor comprehenders from grades 2, 4, 6, and 8 on what they understood reading was about. A particularly good feature of their study was the way they phrased the question on what reading is all about. They asked children in grades 2 and 4, "Suppose you had a friend who had a little brother/sister [same sex as the interviewee] who was going to start school soon. And that little boy/girl said to you, 'My mommy said that when I go to school I will read. [Child's name], what is reading?' What would you tell him/her that reading is?" For children in grades 6 and 8, Canney and Winograd asked, "Many people think that reading is one of the most important things that you do in school. What would you say reading is?"

Canney and Winograd (1979) found that in considering what reading is about, older (grades 6 and 8) good comprehenders referred to comprehension aspects of reading, whereas only two of the three oldest (grade 8) poor comprehenders referred to the comprehension aspects of reading. However, both good and poor comprehenders in grades 2 and 4 focused on the decoding aspects of reading, reflecting the instructional focus of learning to read at school. By sixth grade, good comprehenders showed a shift in their perception of what reading entails. They attended more to the comprehension aspects of reading, whereas the poor comprehenders still appeared to retain a decoding focus in reading. Similar findings had been reported by Garner and Kraus (1982).

Knowledge of Reading and Reading Strategies

Younger and poorer readers were found to lack cognitive and metacognitive skills in reading. Using 144 children from grades 3 and 6, 24 children at three reading levels (good, average, poor) per grade, Forrest and Waller (1980) investigated children's knowledge about decoding, comprehension, and strategies of reading for a purpose (e.g., skimming, studying). In individual interviews, each child was asked 13 standardized questions about the reading skills of decoding, comprehension, and advanced strategies. Examples of the questions on decoding are, "What do you do when you come to a word that you do not know? Is there a difference between what a word 'says' and knowing what a word 'means'?" Examples of questions on reading strategies are "What do you do when you read in preparation for a test?" "Is there anything that you can do to make what you are reading easier to remember?"

Forrest and Waller (1980) found that younger and poorer readers possessed fewer strategies and knew less about decoding, comprehension, and reading proficiency, and that knowledge of these increases with grade and reading proficiency. Also, younger and poorer readers were less sensitive to problems, such as recognition of a comprehension problem, and less able to solve problems, such as a comprehension breakdown. Because older and better readers have more knowledge and strategies in the same areas of reading skills, and use them properly, they have important vantage points in reading.

Sensitivity to Important Parts of Text

Readers' sensitivity to important parts of the text enables their efficient allocation of attention and efforts in focused study of relevant information. There is some research evidence that poor readers lack such sensitivity and awareness.

Winograd (1984) investigated summarization difficulties in eighth graders. He found that good and poor comprehenders held strikingly different notions of important sentences in the given passages. Specifically, poor comprehenders selected as important sentences that contained details, especially details of a highly visual nature. Good comprehenders, in contrast, selected main idea or topic sentences. Moreover, good comprehenders' choice of important sentences paralleled that of adult readers.

Another interesting finding reported by Winograd (1984) was that in the poor comprehenders' summaries of given passage, there was a low correlation between their summary contents and the rated importance of the sentences in the summaries. That is, that which poor comprehenders included in their summaries was less important based on their own judgment or rating. In contrast, good comprehenders were consistent; they included information that they rated as important in their summaries and deleted information that they rated as less important.

Winograd's findings indicated that the eighth-grade poor comprehenders in his study lacked sensitivity to important parts of the text. This deficiency affected adversely the adequacy of their summaries of given passages. An earlier study by Smiley, Oakley, Worthen, Campione, and Brown (1977) found similar deficiencies in Title I children.

Comprehension Monitoring: Detecting Inconsistencies

Many investigators have reported that poor comprehenders and adolescents with learning disabilities do not monitor their reading comprehension (Garner, 1980,

1981; Garner & Kraus, 1982; Garner & Taylor, 1982; Wong & Jones, 1982). The task typically used was the error-detection paradigm in which the experimenter deliberately inserts an intersentential inconsistency or intrasentential inconsistency within the passage(s). The subjects' detection of these inconsistencies is taken to index comprehension monitoring.

Garner and Kraus (1982) investigated seventh-grade good and poor comprehenders' conceptions of reading and their detection of intersentential and intrasentential inconsistencies. We will focus on the second purpose of their study, in which 15 good and 15 poor comprehenders participated. Two narrative passages were first designed—one about a train, the other about a ship's voyage. Each contained five sentences, structured similarly. More important, in each passage, there was conflicting information between the first and last sentences. The inconsistencies involved number changes. In order to contrast intrasentence information inconsistency with intersentence information inconsistency, two additional passages were adapted from the original passages, in which the inconsistent information occurred entirely within the last sentence. Hence a total of four passages was used.

The subjects were seen individually and asked to determine whether any of the passages needed revision by the writer. Garner and Kraus found that of 15 good comprehenders, 4 detected intersentence inconsistency and 12 detected intrasentence inconsistency. None of the 15 poor comprehenders detected either type of information inconsistency. Clearly, poor comprehenders in their study had not engaged in comprehension monitoring.

Debugging Strategies

The term *debugging* was coined by T. Anderson (1980), and it refers to strategies that a person employs to resolve a comprehension difficulty. Although good comprehenders are reported to monitor their listening and reading comprehension (Garner, 1981; Garner & Kraus, 1982; Markman, 1977, 1979), data on whether they also spontaneously employ debugging strategies and on the nature of these strategies were not obtained until Garner and Reis's (1981) study. Nineteen poor comprehenders in grades 4 through 10, with a median of grade 7, and an equal number of good comprehenders participated in the study. For the purposes of their study, Garner and Reis devised a special passage that contained sufficient details for formulating comprehension test questions that would elicit "lookback" behaviors, yet the text did not pose difficulties to the poor comprehenders. Moreover, the passage was broken into three segments, each on a separate sheet to facilitate the experimenter's recording of subjects' lookback behaviors. On each page, the text of the passage appeared on the top half, and the questions appeared on the bottom half of the page. The subjects were seen individually and told to read the first segment silently, and to answer some questions after reading it. When finished reading the first segment and the attached questions, the student was told to continue with the second segment. The page containing the first segment of the passage was left at a 90-degree angle to him or her to facilitate the experimenter's observation and recording of the subject's lookback behaviors. (Some of the questions on the second segment of the passage entailed lookbacks to the first segment for accurate answers.)

Garner and Reis (1981) found that good comprehenders had higher frequency of correct responses in instances of recorded lookback behavior. However, a further examination of the data indicated that there was an unexpected age and experience factor at work among the good comprehenders. The six oldest poor comprehenders showed no differential performance from the group of poor comprehenders in successfully answering questions on which they reviewed (lookback) the text; however, the oldest six good comprehenders were substantially more successful than their entire group. Based on frequency of lookbacks and percentage of accuracy in comprehension test questions, poor comprehenders and younger good comprehenders differed from the six oldest good comprehenders in using lookbacks as a debugging strategy. More important, only these oldest good comprehenders showed spontaneous use of lookback with high frequency.

One important finding from this study was that comprehension monitoring is not necessarily followed by a debugging strategy when a comprehension problem is met. Garner and Reis found that sixth- and seventh-grade good comprehenders did show comprehension monitoring, but such monitoring was not followed by lookbacks. Only the oldest eighth-grade good comprehenders showed *both* comprehension monitoring and spontaneous lookbacks. These findings led the investigators to conclude that in the developmental sequence in the area of detecting and resolving comprehension breakdowns, monitoring precedes deployment of debugging strategies.

Garner and Reis's study is important not only because of their purpose of inquiry and the data obtained, but also because of the use of quantitative *and* qualitative data. They recorded observations of nonverbal and verbal indices of non-comprehension in the subjects (e.g., shrugging shoulders, rolling eyes, shaking head, making faces, saying something such as "That's a hard one; can we skip it?"). Using both quantitative and qualitative information enables a more comprehensive picture of the subjects' cognitive and metacognitive behaviors.

Clearly, findings from metacognitive research in reading paint a picture of students with learning disabilities to be much deficient in metacognition in reading. However, our understanding of their metacognitive deficiencies need to be tempered by the findings of Wong and Wong (1986).

Metacognition in Students with Learning Disabilities

The assumption that students with learning disabilities generally lack metacognitive skills in reading is invalid. Rather, they appear to have *less sophisticated* metacognitive skills than non-learning-disabled peers in reading (Wong & Wong, 1986).

Wong and Wong (1986) investigated how metacognitive knowledge of vocabulary difficulty and passage organization of given passages affected study time of the same passages in above average students, average students, and students with learning disabilities, from grades 5–7. They first interviewed each subject individually on his or her knowledge and awareness of how easy or difficult vocabulary and the organized or disorganized nature of a passage affected the ease of studying a particular passage. Altogether four passages were used. In two of these, level of vocabulary difficulty was manipulated. The "Oyster" passage contained difficult words such as *mollusks, plankton, immediate, environment, unexpectedly, especially,* and *maturity.* In comparison, the "Whooping Crane" passage contained relatively easy words. Passage organization was manipulated through two alternate versions of a passage either about a fox or polar bears. Each passage contained 12 short sentences, which clustered in fours around a specific subtopic about the respective animal: physical features, food, and habitat. One version of the "Fox" and the "Polar Bear" passages was organized so that the four sentences clustering each of the three subtopics were related to the particular subtopic and logically sequenced. In the disorganized version of the passages, thematic cohesion within each cluster of sentences was clearly lacking.

Each child was seen individually and depending on order of passage presentation, was given either the organized or disorganized pair or the pair with hard or easy vocabulary first. With respect to the pair of passages with hard or easy vocabulary, the child was told that two students (A and B) studied the Oyster (hard vocabulary) and Whooping Crane (easy vocabulary) passages. Student A spent 15 minutes studying each passage. Student B spent 30 minutes on the Oyster passage and 15 minutes on the Whooping Crane passage. The child was asked which student would remember more of the passages, especially the Oyster passage, and why. To facilitate the child's responding, a schematic depiction of the hypothetical students' study behaviors and the Oyster and Whooping Crane passages were placed before the child. With respect to the organized and disorganized pair of passages, the child was told that again two students (C and D) studied them. Student C spent 15 minutes on the organized passage, and 30 minutes on the disorganized passage. Student D however, studied them for 15 minutes each. The child again was asked which student would remember more of the passages, especially the disorganized one, and why. Again, to facilitate the child's responding, a schematic depiction of the hypothetical students' study behaviors and the organized and disorganized passages were placed before the child.

About 3 weeks after the interview, the children were again seen individually. Half the children were randomly assigned to receive the passage pair with hard or easy vocabulary first, followed by the organized or disorganized passage pair. The remaining children had the passage pairs in the reverse order. When given the previously seen organized or disorganized passage pair, the child was told to study for subsequent recall of both passages. When given the passage pair with hard or easy vocabulary, the child was told to study for a subsequent reading comprehension test on each passage. Within each pair of passages, the order of passage presentation was randomized. Moreover, there was a 3-minute break between passages within a pair of passages, and a 5-minute break between the two sets of passages. Also, an aide pronounced and carefully explained the meanings of key vocabulary words in the Oyster and Whooping Crane passages. For the benefit of the readers with learning disabilities, words that might pose decoding or vocabulary difficulties were pronounced clearly and explained thoroughly. Additionally, the child was encouraged to seek help with any other decoding or vocabulary difficulties. When ready for the recall or comprehension test, the child signaled to the experimenter. The child was told not to worry about spelling errors in written answers to the short comprehension questions. Study times in minutes and seconds were recorded with a stopwatch. The children's recall was tape-recorded and later transcribed.

Wong and Wong (1986) found a significant interaction between reader and passage. This finding indicated that whereas readers with learning disabilities were most sensitive to level of vocabulary difficulty in a passage, above-average readers were most sensitive to the organization of a passage. Within the pair of passages with easy and difficult vocabulary, only readers with learning disabilities showed reliable differences in study times, studying significantly longer the passage with difficult vocabulary. Within the pair of passages with organized and disorganized sentences, only above-average readers showed reliable differences in study times, studying significantly longer the disorganized passage.

This pattern of differential study times among above-average readers and readers with learning disabilities is important. The data for readers with learning disabilities challenge the ubiquitous assumption of metacognitive deficiency in reading among children with learning disabilities. Readers with learning disabilities apparently do possess metacognitive knowledge about one particular aspect of reading investigated, namely, level of vocabulary difficulty. Moreover, their sensitivity to differential vocabulary difficulty in the two passages led them to deploy suitable reading strategies. They studied much longer the passage with difficult vocabulary. One possible reason for learning-disabled readers' possession of such metacognitive awareness may be due to their decoding problems, from which ensues an acute awareness of vocabulary difficulty in the reading materials, and the development of a strategy to overcome the problems, namely reading slowly and studying such materials longer.

The moral of Wong and Wong's (1986) findings is clear. Students with learning disabilities, through daily struggles with decoding problems, have developed an awareness that when they encounter difficult words in a passage, they must spend more time reading and/or studying it than one with easier words. However, because most of their cognitive resources are consumed (sucked up) in decoding, little are left over for reading comprehension and development of understanding, such as that a disorganized passage is harder to understand, and hence, they should spend more time reading and studying it than an organized passage. Until they master decoding, they will not be in a position to develop higher-order metacognitive skills in reading.

Concerning metacognition in writing, students with learning disabilities have little awareness of (a) text structure (genres); (b) the fact that the writing process involves recursively planning, sentence generation, and revising; (c) their own cognitive processes in writing; and (d) the areas in which they need improvement (Englert, 1992; Graham & Harris, 1993; Graham, Harris, MacArthur, & Schwartz, 1991; Wong, Wong, & Blenkinsop, 1989; Wong, Butler, Ficzere, Kuperis, Corden & Zelmer, 1994; Wong, Butler, Ficzere, & Kuperis, 1996; in press). Moreover, students with learning disabilities tend to equate a good paper with one devoid of spelling errors (Graham et al., 1991; Wong et al., 1996). Last, Wong et al. (1996) found that it took 2–3 years for adolescents with learning disabilities to develop some awareness of their own cognitive processes in writing, and the importance of planning and clarity in writing! In this, Wong et al. vindicated Ann Brown's view that metacognition is slow in development.

Current Status in Metacognitive Research in Learning Disabilities

First, the heydays of metacognitive research in reading appear to be over. This applies to basic research involving both normally achieving students and those with learning disabilities. A major reason may have come from the fruitful realization of the implication from the research findings, namely, that normally achieving students and those with learning disabilities can be taught to good effect various metacognitive strategies in reading. By now, in reading intervention research and practice involving learning-disabled students, metacognitive components have become well ensconced. These metacognitive components typically follow cognitive ones, and involve self-monitoring and/or self-evaluating one's strategy use.

Recently, some researchers have attempted to separate the two aspects of awareness and self-regulation in Flavell's (1976) original definition of metacognition. Specifically, Paris and Winograd (1990) wanted to allocate to the construct of metacognition only the aspects of an individual's knowledge of person, task, and strategy variables, thus leaving out the aspect of self-regulation. Interestingly, they suggested including in those aspects of metacognition the motivational construct of self-efficacy. On the other hand, although they agree with the notion of separating the two aspects of awareness and self-regulation in metacognition, Garcia and Pintrich (1994) do not want to include self-efficacy in it as suggested by Paris and Winograd. It suffices for us to realize that some researchers wish to have clearer, more distinct separation (demarcation) between the awareness and self-regulating aspects of metacognition. Moreover, there are theorists and researchers who focus on and emphasize self-regulation with substantially less emphasis on metacognition (for reference, see Schunk & Zimmerman, 1994).

Second, although metacognitive research in reading appears to have peaked in the 1980s and plateaued since, that in mathematics and writing appears to be gath-

ering increasing interest. Concerning mathematics, Alan Schoenfeld has been doing some very interesting metacognitive research with normally achieving college
students. Marjorie Montague and her associates have been teaching middle school
and high school students with learning disabilities a strategy comprising cognitive
and metacognitive steps in mathematics (see Chapter 8 on arithmetic and mathematics).

Third, in metacognitive research in writing, Graham, Schwartz, and MacArthur's
(1993) findings corroborated those of Wong et al. (1989). All of them found students with learning disabilities to have little awareness of the cognitive processes in
which they engage as writers. For example, they were asked to describe what goes
on in their heads when they write. Typically, students with learning disabilities
would draw a blank and be totally stumped for an answer. Moreover, they lacked
awareness of the audience's need for clarity as the latter read their essays. Wong et
al. (1996) found some nascent awareness of the need to be clear and planful in composing in adolescents with learning disabilities after 2–3 years of writing instruction. These adolescents also showed some awareness of areas that they still need to
improve their writing. Curiously, they were not able to apply their newly developed
insights about their own needs as writers to understand writing problems in other
adolescents. This suggests the nascent (newborn), fragile, and constricted nature of
their metacognitive insights in writing, and points to more research on how to
achieve more broad-based enhancement of metacognition in writing among adolescents with learning disabilities.

In writing intervention research, using self-regulation as an instructional anchor
and goal, Graham and Harris (1994) detailed their success in enhancing writing
in students with learning disabilities. Wong and her associates used writing strategies that contained both cognitive and metacognitive components in teaching
adolescents with learning disabilities and low achievers to plan, write, and revise
three genres: reportive, opinion (persuasive), and compare and contrast essays.
They too were successful in enhancing quality and quantity of writing in those adolescents (Wong et al., 1994; Wong et al., 1996; Wong, Butler, Ficzere & Kuperis,
in press). Self-efficacy in writing was increased in Wong et al. (1994; 1996), but
not in Wong et al.'s last study (in press). Interestingly, an increase in students' metacognition in writing was only evident in the third year of research (Wong et al., in
press).

REFLECTIONS

Why is the theoretical construct of metacognition so important in education?
As supported by Ann Brown's (1980) conceptualization, and by research findings,
its importance resides clearly in the cardinal role it plays in students' effective reading and studying. The role of metacognition retains its importance in the current
zeitgeist of self-regulated learning in cognitive and instructional psychology (But-

ler, 1993, 1995). However, it is complemented with motivational constructs of self-efficacy or attribution.

Let us now narrow the question of the importance of metacognition to the field of learning disabilities. What is its relevance to researchers and practitioners in learning disabilities? It is relevant in the following ways: (a) Metacognitive problems account for some of the performance deficiencies in academic subjects in students with learning disabilities. Hence, we should not unthinkingly or indiscriminately attribute all their academic problems to deep-seated processing problems. (b) Remediation of such students must include inculcation of metacognitive self-awareness and strategies in reading, writing, mathematics, and spelling. In light of the research on metacognition in reading, mathematics, and writing, any exclusive focus on skill building per se is not justified. (c) Simultaneously, in any remedial strategy, teachers must add a self-regulating component. This can come in the form of self-monitoring of accurate strategy use, or self-checking one's own work; for example, students with learning disabilities can check their own arithmetic calculations and answers for errors prior to handing in assignments. Systematic and consistent inclusion of self-regulating components in remedial strategies would make students with learning disabilities into autonomous and self-regulated learners, which is our ultimate instructional goal for these and all students.

References

Anderson, T. H. (1980). Study strategies and adjunct aids. In R. J. Spiro, B. B. Bruce, & W. F. Brewer (Eds.), *Theoretical issues in reading comprehension* (pp. 484–502). Hillsdale, NJ: Lawrence Erlbaum.

Baker, L. (1979, July). *Do I understand or do I not understand: That is the question.* (Reading Education Report No. 10). Center for the Study of Reading, University of Illinois, Urbana.

Baker, L., & Brown, A. L. (1984a). Metacognition skills of reading. In D. P. Pearson (Ed.), *Handbook on research in reading* (pp. 353–394). New York: Longman.

Baker, L., & Brown, A. L. (1984b). Cognitive monitoring in reading. In J. Flood (Ed.), *Understanding reading comprehension* (pp. 21–44). Newark, Delaware: International Reading Association.

Bandura, A. (1977). Self-efficacy: Toward a unifying theory of behavioral change. *Psychological Review, 84*(2), 191–215.

Borkowski, J. G., Day, J. D., Saenz, D., Dietmeyer, D., Estrada, M. T., & Groteluschen, A. (1992). Expanding the boundaries of cognitive interventions. In B. Y. L. Wong (Ed.), *Contemporary intervention research in learning disabilities* (pp. 1–21). New York: Springer-Verlag.

Borkowski, J. G., Estrada, M. T., Milstead, M., & Hale, C. A. (1989). General problem-solving skills: Relations between metacognitive and strategic processing. *Learning Disability Quarterly, 12*(1), 57–70.

Borkowski, J. G., & Thorpe, P. K. (1994). Self-regulation and motivation: A lifespan perspective on underachievement. In D. H. Schunk & B. J. Zimmerman (Eds.), *Self-regulation of learning and performance: Issues and educational applications* (pp. 45–73). Hillsdale, NJ: Lawrence Erlbaum.

Brown, A. (1978). Knowing when, where, and how to remember: A problem of metacognition: In R. Glaser (Ed.), *Advances in instructional psychology* (pp. 77–165). Hillsdale, NJ: Erlbaum.

Brown, A. L. (1980). Metacognitive development and reading. In R. J. Spiro, B. Bruce, & W. F. Brewer (Eds.), *Theoretical issues in reading comprehension* (pp. 453–481). Hillsdale, NJ: Lawrence Erlbaum.

Brown, A. L., & Palincsar, A. S. (1982). Inducing strategic learning from texts by means of informed, self-control training. In B. Y. L. Wong (Ed.), *Metacognition and learning disabilities. Topics in learning & learning disabilities* Vol. 2, pp. 1–17.

Butler, D. L. (1993). *Promoting strategic learning by adults with learning disabilities: An alternative approach.* Unpublished doctoral dissertation, Simon Fraser University, Burnaby, B.C.

Butler, D. L. (1995). Promoting strategic learning by postsecondary students with learning disabilities. *Journal of Learning Disabilities, 28,* 170–190.

Canney, G., & Winograd, P. (1979). *Schemata for reading and reading comprehension performance* (Tech. Rep. No. 120). Center for the Study of Reading, University of Illinois, Urbana.

Corno, L. (1986). The metacognitive control components of self-regulated learning. *Contemporary Educational Psychology, 11,* 333–346.

Englert, C. S. (1992). Writing instruction from a sociocultural perspective: The holistic, dialogic, and social enterprise of writing. *Journal of Learning Disabilities, 25*(3), 153–172.

Flavell, J. H. (1976). Metacognitive aspects of problem solving. In L. B. Resnick (Ed.), *The nature of intelligence* (pp. 231–235). Hillsdale, NJ: Erlbaum.

Forrest, D. L., & Waller, T. G. (1980). *What do children know about their reading and study skills?* Paper presented at the annual meeting of the American Educational Research Association, Boston.

Garcia, T., & Pintrich, P. (1994). Regulating motivation and cognition in the classroom: The role of self-schemas and self-regulatory strategies. In D. H. Schunk & B. J. Zimmerman (Eds.), *Self-regulation of learning and performance: Issues and educational applications* (pp. 127–153). Hillsdale, NJ: Lawrence Erlbaum.

Garner, R. (1980). Monitoring of understanding: An investigation of good and poor readers' awareness of induced miscomprehension of text. *Journal of Reading Behavior, XII,* 55–63.

Garner, R. (1981). Monitoring of passage inconsistency among poor comprehenders: A preliminary test of the "Piecemeal Processing" explanation. *Journal of Educational Research, 74,* 159–162.

Garner, R., & Kraus, C. (1982). Good and poor comprehender differences in knowing and regulating reading behaviors. *Educational Research Quarterly, 6,* 5–12.

Garner, R., & Reis, R. (1981). Monitoring and resolving comprehension obstacles: An investigation of spontaneous text lookbacks among upper-grade good and poor comprehenders. *Reading Research Quarterly, XVI,* 569–582.

Garner, R., & Taylor, N. (1982). Monitoring of understanding: An investigation of attentional assistance needs at different grade and reading proficiency levels. *Reading Psychology, 3,* 1–6.

Graham, S., & Harris, K. (1994). The role and development of self-regulation in the writing process. In D. H. Schunk & B. J. Zimmerman (Eds.), *Self-regulation of learning and performance: Issues and educational applications* (pp. 203–228). Hillsdale, NJ: Lawrence Erlbaum.

Graham, S., & Harris, K. R. (1993). Teaching writing strategies to students with learning disabilities: Issues and recommendations. In Lynn J. Meltzer (Ed.), *Strategy assessment and instruction for students with learning disabilities: From theory to practice* (pp. 271–292). Austin, TX: Pro-Ed.

Graham, S., Harris, K. R., MacArthur, C., & Schwartz, S. (1991). Writing instruction. In B. Y. L. Wong (Ed.), *Learning about learning disabilities* (pp. 310–345). San Diego, CA: Academic Press.

Graham, S., Schwartz, S. S., & MacArthur, C.A. (1993). Knowledge of writing and the composing process, attitude toward writing, and self-efficacy for students with and without learning disabilities. *Journal of Learning Disabilities, 26*(4), 237–249.

Kuhl, J. (1984). Volitional aspects of achievement motivation and learned helplessness: Toward a comprehension theory of action control. In B. A. Maher (Ed.), *Progress in experimental personality research* (pp. 99–171) (Vol. 13). New York: Academic Press.

Kuhl, J. (1985). Volitional mediators of cognition-behavior consistency: Self-regulatory processes and action versus state orientation. In J. Kuhl & J. Beckmann (Eds.), *Action control: From cognition to behavior* (pp. 101–128). Berlin, Heidelberg, New York, Tokyo: Springer.

Kuhl, J. (1987). Feeling versus being helpless: Metacognitive mediation of failure-induced performance deficits. In F. E. Weinert & R. H. Kluwe (Eds.), *Metacognition, motivation and understanding* (pp. 217–235). Hillsdale, NJ: Erlbaum.

Markman, E. M. (1977). Realizing that you don't understand: A preliminary investigation. *Child Development, 43,* 986–992.

Markman, E. M. (1979). Realizing that you don't understand: Elementary school children's awareness of inconsistencies. *Child Development, 50,* 643–655.

Miyake, N., & Norman, D. A. (1978). To ask a question, one must know enough to know what is not known. *Journal of Verbal Learning and Verbal Behavior, 18,* 357–364.

Paris, S. G., & Winograd, P. (1990). How metacognition can promote academic learning and instruction. 1, B. F. Jones & L. Idol (Eds.), *Dimensions of thinking and cognitive instruction* (pp. 15–51). Hillsdale, NJ: Lawrence Erlbaum.

Scardamalia, M., & Bereiter, C. (1987). Knowledge telling and knowledge transforming in written composition. In S. Rosenberg (Ed.), *Advances in applied psycholinguistics: Vol. 2. Reading, writing, and language learning* (pp. 142–175). Cambridge: Cambridge University Press.

Schunk, D. H. (1994). Self-regulation of self-efficacy and attributions in academic settings. In D. H. Schunk & B. J. Zimmerman (Eds.), *Self-regulation of learning and performance: Issues and educational applications* (pp. 75–99). Hillsdale, NJ: Lawrence Erlbaum.

Schunk, D. H., & Zimmerman, B. J. (Eds.). (1994). *Self-regulation of learning and performance: Issues and educational applications.* Hillsdale, NJ: Erlbaum.

Seymour, D. (1970). What do you mean "auditory perception"? *Elementary School Journal, 70,* 175–179.

Smiley, S. S., Oakley, D. D., Worthen, D., Campione, J. C., & Brown, A. L. (1977). Recall of thematically relevant material by adolescent good and poor readers as a function of written versus oral presentation. *Journal of Educational Psychology, 69,* 381–387.

Torgesen, J. K. (1977). The role of nonspecific factors in the task performance of learning-disabled children: A theoretical assessment. *Journal of Learning Disabilities, 10,* 27–34.

Wigfield, A. (1994). The role of children's achievement values in the self-regulation of their learning outcomes. In D. H. Schunk & B. J. Zimmerman (Eds.), *Self-regulation of learning and performance: Issues and educational applications* (pp. 101–124). Hillsdale, NJ: Lawrence Erlbaum.

Winograd, P. (1984). Strategic difficulties in summarizing texts. *Reading Research Quarterly, XIX*(4), 404–425.

Wong, B. Y. L. (1985). Metacognition and learning disabilities. In T. G. Waller, D. Forrest-Pressley, & E. MacKinnon (Eds.), *Metacognition, cognition and human performance* (pp. 137–180). New York: Academic Press.

Wong, B. Y. L., Butler, D. L., Ficzere, S. A., & Kuperis, S. (1996). Teaching adolescents with learning disabilities and low achievers to plan, write, and revise opinion essays. *Journal of Learning Disabilities, 29*(2), 197–212.

Wong, B. Y. L., Butler, D. L., Ficzere, S. A., & Kuperis, S. (in press). Teaching adolescents with learning disabilities and low achievers to plan, write, and revise compare and contrast essays, *Learning Disabilities Research & Practice.*

Wong, B. Y. L., Butler, D. L., Ficzere, S. A., Kuperis, S., Corden, M., & Zelmer, J. (1994). Teaching problem learners revision skills and sensitivity to audience through two instructional modes: Student-teacher versus student-student interactive dialogues. *Learning Disabilities Research & Practice, 9*(2), 78–90.

Wong, B. Y. L., & Jones, W. (1982). Increasing metacomprehension in learning-disabled and normally-achieving students through self-questioning training. *Learning Disability Quarterly, 5,* 228–240.

Wong, B. Y. L., & Wong, R. (1986). Study behavior as a function of metacognitive knowledge about critical task variables: An investigation of above average, average and learning-disabled readers. *Learning Disabilities Research, 1,* 101–111.

Wong, B. Y. L., Wong, R., & Blenkinsop, J. (1989). Cognitive and metacognitive aspects of learning disabled adolescents' composing problems. *Learning Disability Quarterly, 12*(4), 300–322.

Wong, B. Y. L., Wong, R., & LeMare, L. J. (1982). The effects of knowledge of criterion tasks on the comprehension and recall of normally-achieving and learning-disabled children. *Journal of Educational Research, 76,* 119–126.

Zimmerman, B. J. (1989). A social cognitive view of self-regulated academic learning. *Journal of Educational Psychology, 81*(3), 329–339.

7

Informal Assessment
of Reading Problems

In performing any reading assessment, formal or informal, we should first consider the question, "What is reading composed of?" You may wonder why I raise this question, instead of focusing on issues like what do we assess in a reading assessment and how do we go about it? Be patient and hear me out.

You need to know what reading comprises because that knowledge and it alone can guide you to do a thorough reading assessment. Otherwise, you will be robitically performing an assessment without genuinely knowing and understanding the rationales for your actions. I need not elaborate for you the dire consequences of being a robotic technician.

So, what is reading composed of? Please pause and give the answer before reading on. Remember the importance of exercising your brain cells! Yes, reading is composed of decoding and comprehension. Hence, the areas that are covered in a thorough reading assessment reflect component skills underlying decoding and reading comprehension.

Those who embrace and use the whole language approach in teaching reading may be discomforted by the mention of decoding. Don't be. Decoding has a major role to play in a teacher's successful implementation of a whole language approach in language arts in lower and intermediate elementary grades. How so? the skeptic may ask. The answer is this. Children's mastery of decoding skills paves the way for their thorough reading comprehension because with such mastery, they can devote maximum cognitive resources to comprehension. When children lack mastery of decoding (i.e., they cannot produce or say the right sound for the vowel or consonant spontaneously and rapidly), they consequently struggle with associating particular sounds with respective vowels and consonants as they read. In the process of such struggles, their cognitive resources, such as attention, encoding, storage, and retention, are consumed (sucked up) in decoding, leaving very little of them for comprehension. You must remember that human beings have a very limited cognitive processing capacity. We can only devote these valuable cognitive resources to one task at a time. In attending to two task demands simultaneously, we succeed only if we have attained automaticity in one of them. For example, you can talk to your passenger while you are driving in rush-hour traffic because you're now a skilled driver (I hope!). But you wouldn't have done that when you were first learning to drive, especially when you were practicing with the family car!

So, even if you embrace a whole language approach to teaching reading, you cannot brush aside the need to teach decoding skills or their assessment. I shall now differentiate between formal or standardized and informal assessments.

Distinguishing between Formal and Informal Assessments of Reading

Formal and informal tests in reading or mathematics have important differences in (1) their construction, and (2) in the purposes that they serve.

Formal Tests

Formal tests are standardized tests and their construction follows elaborate procedures that are well established in the domain of psychometrics. Specifically, the test developers for a reading achievement test would construct test items that represent components of the theory of reading acquisition to which they subscribe. Then they would pilot the test and revise unsatisfactory test items. The final version of the test would contain items that would discriminate between good, average, and poor performers. This test is then given to a huge sample of subjects (more than 500); for example, the Test of Phonological Awareness (Torgesen & Bryant, 1994) Kindergarten version was normed on 857 children, and the TOPA Grades 1–2 version was normed on 3,654 children, from a representative range of socioeconomic strata (SES). This means the subjects come from working-class, middle-class, and upper-middle-class SES. Such representativeness in SES in the standardization sample is mandatory because the subsequently analyzed data must be applicable to individuals beyond the boundary of a particular SES. The test data are then subjected to sophisticated statistical analyses, which in turn produce tables containing percentiles, grade equivalent scores, standard scores, or even quotients. These tables permit comparison of any individual student's performance against that of the standardization population.

Thus formal or standardized tests provide the data to make a norm-referenced interpretation of any student's test performance. That is, we can compare a student's test score to the known average test score of individuals of his or her age to see how discrepant it is from that average. For example, suppose we have given a standardized reading achievement test to a ninth-grade student with learning disabilities. We then turn to the table of percentiles and grade equivalent scores and find that he is at the 17th percentiles and has a grade equivalent score of 6 in word recognition. The information indicates the severity of his reading disability. Hence, normal or standardized achievement tests provide normative reference to compare testees to individuals from their own age group and comparable SES (Hammill & Bartel, 1995).

Formal achievement tests are important to the learning disabilities field because teachers must ascertain the presence and degree of academic retardation in students who are suspected of having learning disabilities and who await diagnostic assessments. Teachers need to know how the student performs compared to individuals of a similar age, and exactly how far below grade the student is reading. Results from a formal reading test would provide the answers. Some examples of standardized reading tests are the Gates MacGinitie Reading Tests and the Stanford Reading Achievement Test.

Informal Tests

Informal tests are nonstandardized tests that are made by skilled and experienced teachers to answer specific questions. These informal tests in various academic areas pinpoint the student's instructional needs in phonics, reading comprehension, arithmetic, and writing. They also unravel the student's erroneous or faulty strategies. In sum, informal tests provide data for the teacher to set up an individualized educational program (IEP) for the student with learning disabilities.

Why is such information or data not forthcoming in formal achievement tests? Because the items in formal tests sample a broad range of skills, which means they cannot be exhaustive in detailed assessment of a particular skill. For example, in a test passage for oral reading at the seventh-grade level of a formal reading test, the adolescent with learning disabilities cannot decode the word *idol*. He may pronounce the word as *ardol*. He evidences substitution of the long *i* vowel with the r-controlled vowel of *ar*. The next question is whether he makes this substitution consistently, such as when the long *i* vowel sound occurs in the medial and final positions of words. A detailed informal phonics test would be needed to answer the question, for only such tests provide exhaustive comprehensive test items. We need to ascertain consistency in oral reading errors because if a student makes inconsistent errors, it suggests a lack of mastery. If she or he makes consistent errors, it suggests a lack of acquisition of the concept, skill, or procedure. Acquisition and mastery problems involve significantly different remedial goals and emphases, as explained later in this chapter.

Areas of Assessment

A thorough informal reading assessment must cover the following six areas: (a) reading rate, (b) reading accuracy, (c) word recognition, (d) reading comprehension, (e) vocabulary, and (f) spelling. Component skills or processes in these areas relate directly to decoding and reading comprehension.

Assessing Reading Rate

The rationale for assessing a student's reading rate lies in the centrality of automaticity. You should by now be able to explain why a student's excessively slow reading rate impairs his or her reading comprehension. But to drive home the importance of automaticity in decoding for effective reading comprehension, try the following little experiment. When you have your usual hour of relaxation with the newspaper and your cup of tea or coffee, select an item of interest, then read in this particular manner: count at a designated temporal interval between words. If it's a column on equity in employment: You'd read like this: "There (1-2-3-4-5) has (1-2-3-4-5) been (1-2-3-4-5) much (1-2-3-4-5) written (1-2-3-4-5) about (1-2-3-4-5) employment (1-2-3-4-5) equity." Be sure to count at a consistent rate of 1 second per digit. Read the whole news item in that manner. After you have finished reading, try recalling the content of the item, and more importantly, ask yourself the extent of your reading comprehension of it. You should then have a firsthand knowledge of why a slow reading rate hampers reading comprehension, and hence, the realization that you need to test for it in problem learners and remediate it where necessary. If you are puzzled as to why your slow reading rate impeded your comprehension, here's the answer. In reading deliberately slowly, I made you stimulate the decoding of a student with learning disabilities. Remember how decoding problems consumed his or her cognitive resources, leaving little of them for reading comprehension? Clearly, you do not have decoding problems! But by forcing you to read slowly, I overloaded your working memory, thereby impairing your comprehension and retention of what you've read! Sorry to resort to tricks and stratagems, but then it's all for pedagogic reasons!

When you have, with good reasons, singled out a student for an informal reading assessment, you should also select two students who perform consistently in the average range across various subjects in your class for testing. Because they are class-mates of the student suspected to have learning disabilities, they provide you with a valid yardstick against which to measure the extent of academic retardation of the former. If the former's performance turns out *not* to be substantially lower than the two average cohorts, then she or he is unlikely to be a student with learning disabilities. On the other hand, if she or he performs substantially below those two average students, then she or he indeed evidences academic retardation, and the performance levels in reading, math, and so on of those two average peers would provide reasonable remedial yardsticks or goals for the student suspected to have learning disabilities. Clearly, you must always compare your assessment data of students with learning disabilities with those of their average peers.

The reading rate of a student is always expressed in words (read) per minute (wpm). Words (read) per minute could include errors or miscues, or be restricted entirely to words read accurately. It is up to you to decide on the option.

Reading Accuracy

The rationale for assessing a student's reading accuracy lies in the role it plays in reading comprehension. Although certain oral reading errors such as omission of an *s* in plural nouns (e.g., *cats*) may not affect substantially the meaning of the sentence, others do. And certainly, numerous reading errors would erode substance and precision in comprehension. Observe the following sentences:

The turtle was resting ON the floating log in the lake.

The student with learning disabilities reads:

The turtle was resting IN the floating log in the lake.

I focus on oral reading errors in order to analyze the type and degree of such errors. I turn now to the specifics in such analysis. First, you need to have a recording system for student's oral reading errors. Because you need to record his or her oral reading errors in tandem with his or her reading, you have to use a shorthand version of your scoring system. Otherwise, you would not be able to keep pace with the student's reading. There are many ways to create your own shorthand record-keeping system. The important point is to keep a key for the shorthand that you have devised! Failure to do so could be disastrous, for you may not remember whether or not *R* stands for reversal or repetition error! The following represents one way of recording student's reading errors.

Oral reading error	Shorthand
omission	O
insertion	In
repetition	R
reversal	Re
substitution	S/Sub

Always remember that a student's self-correction automatically erases the error count on the corrected word.

Now that your student has finished reading the given passage and you have noted all his or her oral reading errors, you proceed to the next step in reading accuracy assessment. Write down clearly each word that she or he has misread or omitted or substituted on a small index card (measuring 12.6 cm × 7.6 cm). While you are thus engaged, you can send the student off for a drink of water. Then present each of the words successively to the student and ask him or her to recite them. The purpose here is to see if reading the words in isolation would elicit the student's self-correction of the previous errors. If the student can self-correct a previous oral reading error, it suggests that she or he has been inattentive[1] when she or he misread the word. If the error persists, write down the vowels and consonant errors (substitutions) for the purpose of pinpointing areas for remediation.

When you have finished this task of presenting words in isolation (out of context of the passage), examine the student's persistent oral reading errors and answer this question: Can you see any consistent error patterns? For example, does the student consistently err over the short vowel *e* or the more complex vowel patterns *ei/eu/ou/eau?* Look for consistent error patterns because these denote the student's need to learn them, whereas inconsistency denotes a lack of mastery rather than the need for acquisition.

Assessing Word Recognition

The rationale for assessing word recognition is the same as in assessing reading rate and error. The student is given a list of words that should be within his or her sight vocabulary, or knowledge of words commensurate with his or her grade level. She or he is asked to read them aloud. The examiner calculates the percentage of words correctly read or recognized.

In this assessment, you must distinguish between words that the student did not recognize or decode from those that she or he decoded correctly only after much subvocalizing. The student's labored attempts at decoding indicate lack of mastery. However, she or he does have that particular word within his or her knowledge of words. Put differently, the student knows the word, but his or her knowledge is still far from the mastery level, which denotes fast and accurate decoding of the word (automaticity in decoding).

The data from assessments of student's oral reading errors and word recognition necessitate a detailed assessment of his or her knowledge of phonics. Such assessment is necessary because the reading passages and word lists in the word recognition test do not provide an exhaustive test of the student's knowledge and mastery of phonics. The detailed phonics test (Table 4) systematically taps a student's knowl-

---

[1]Stan Auerbach (Delta School District, B.C.) originated this procedure in isolating inattention in oral reading errors.

Table 4   Detailed Phonics Test[a]

Tester's directions

Say: "Here are some groups of letters that are not real words. Some of them sound like real words, though. Say them for me."

Initial consonant sounds

Student's Copy

bem	kis	sem	fet
cil	lum	tud	sap
dor	mub	vip	bis
fum	nad	wos	quan
gid	pid	yeb	gab
hur	quad	zos	jud
om	ron	heb	dod

Initial and final consonant blends

Student's copy

blen	bres	scad	strus	clup	crom
skub	scrat	flis	drud	sprom	glat
frap	smot	twis	pop	gron	sneb
lop	prin	spab	tust	slon	tret
tesk	ston	rasp	swen		

Consonant digraphs[b]

Student's copy

chis	shan	thub	whes	phod	tish
tach	beth	cub	shos	thod	whad
luph	bough	fing	lang	mung	wret
ruck	salk	malf	knup	gnow	knod
palf	malk	leck	wrod	pight	maught

Final consonant sounds—Simple closed syllables
(C—V—C and V—C)[c]

Student's Copy

neb	taj	ip	oz
nic	uk	bor	
ad	el	nos	
sif	rem	hst	
ug	fen	ev	

(continues)

Table 4   *(Continued)*

Controlled vowels

Student's copy

sar	bar	tir	ter	bur
par	ser	nir	bor	sur

Silent *e* principle

Student's copy

nobe	rafe	tife	sobe	lute
poge	nute	bame	kise	dete

Vowel digraphs and dipthongs [d]

fain as in pain or said;	tead as in creed or red;	suif as in suit or build;
sie as in pie;	biem as in beam;	noef as in nose;
meid as in seed;	rue as in true;	feas as in fleas or bread;
moe as in toe;	mead as in need;	tew as in few or sew;
mook as in nook or loop;	saut as in caught;	taw as in saw;
lout as in trout;	noil as in foil;	foy as in boy;
tow as in low or now.		

Student's copy

fain	tead	suif	sie	biem	noef
meid	rue	feas	moe	mead	tew
mook	saut	taw	lout	noil	foy
tow					

Hard and soft *c* and *g* [e]

Student's copy

git	gom	gen	gyp	gup	cof
cil	ces	cam	cos	cyd	cub

[a] Reproduced with permission from R. Parker (1972).

[b] Note: "ough" as in "bought" or "tough".

[c] Note: All vowel sounds should be short except for *o* in *bor*.

[d] Note: The correct vowel sounds are given below in real words.

[e] Note: *c* and *g* are soft only when immediately preceding *i*, *e*, or *y*.

edge and mastery of simple and complex phonic patterns, and highlights areas in need of instruction.

Assessing Reading Comprehension

The rationale for assessing students' reading comprehension is self-explanatory. We need to ascertain that they understand thoroughly what is read and can draw all the expected inferences.

Before assessing any student's reading comprehension, the examiner must ensure that the topics of the test passages are not unduly familiar to the student. This is important because if a student is excessively familiar with the topic of a test passage, then she or he can use prior knowledge instead of textual information to answer the test questions, which means that you have not tested how well she or he understood what was actually read!

Second, analyze the reading comprehension test questions and categorize them according to the kinds of information that the student would need to answer them. There are three kinds of comprehension test questions: text-explicit, text-implicit, and script-implicit (Raphael, 1982). Text-explicit questions ask for factual information in the passage; text-implicit questions ask for text-based inferences; and script-implicit questions ask for information from the student's background knowledge. You must clearly sort the comprehension test questions into their respective categories to analyze the source of a student's comprehension breakdown.

Pinpointing Causes in a Student's Poor Reading Comprehension Test Performance

Decoding Problems as a Cause of Poor Reading Comprehension Performance

If a student has substantial decoding problems (e.g., she read orally at half the rates of two average peers and made two and a half times more errors), it is therefore reasonable to suspect that her poor reading comprehension performance may well reflect decoding problems. To test this hypothesis, repeat the test: read the passage aloud to her while she follows it with her eyes and your finger moves along the lines in the passage. At the end of your reading, repeat the test questions and ascertain if there is any noticeable improvement. If indeed decoding problems were the prime culprit, she should show a vast improvement in her reading comprehension test performance. You can repeat the testing immediately or after a week or two should you be concerned about the student's practice effect or prior exposure to the test passage. I am not very concerned with the possible effect of the student's having seen the test passage once already, because her substantial decoding problems would discount any likelihood of benefits from prior exposure to it!

Vocabulary Problems as a Cause of Poor Reading Comprehension Performance

On occasion, a student's performance on a reading comprehension test hinges on her knowledge of some key vocabulary words. Hence when she does abysmally on the test, we can test the hypothesis that knowledge of those key vocabulary words played a critical role in her test performance. Explain the meanings of the key vocabulary to her and then repeat the test questions that she has just failed, questions that can only be correctly answered if she knew the key vocabulary. Again if our hypothesis or hunch is right, we should see her giving correct answers to those previously failed questions.

Controlling for Retention Problems

Many students with learning disabilities have memory problems. Consequently, they may have difficulty retaining all the information in the test passage well enough to answer the comprehension test questions accurately. To ascertain if indeed retention problems underlie their incorrect answers to factual (text-explicit) test questions, repeat the test question(s), then allow the student with learning disabilities to look back at the test passage and search for the information to answer the question(s).

Controlling for Inferential Problems

Students with learning disabilities often have difficulties with text-based inferential (text-implicit) questions. When they fail to answer correctly this type of question, we need to find out how much scaffolding (support, prompting) they need to draw the correct inference. Use the following procedure. First using a highlighter, box in the paragraphs (often just two) that contain the information from which the student with learning disabilities should draw the inference. Then repeat the test question to her and instruct her to find and integrate the information from the boxed paragraphs and to draw the inference to answer the test question.

If the student fails to extract and integrate the necessary information from the boxed paragraphs for constructing the text-based inference, underline with a highlighter relevant sentences from the two paragraphs that contain the information for student's construction of the text-based inference. Now focus her attention on those underlined sentences and repeat the test question.

Clearly, students with learning disabilities that succeed in drawing text-based inferences from relevant boxed-in paragraphs are easier to remediate than those who require further scaffolding, such as highlighting relevant sentences within the boxed paragraphs.

Ascertaining the Role of Insufficient Prior Knowledge in Poor Reading Comprehension Performance

All reading test designers attempt to control for students' or examinees' prior knowledge regarding the topics of the test passages. Consequently, some of the test passages may be unduly hard. Occasionally, a test passage may prove overly difficult for a particular student because he happens to have extremely little prior knowledge of the topic. If you suspect that is the case, for example, you have an immigrant child from a different culture reading a passage on Halloween, then you may try the following procedure. (I assume the child has learned to read in English.)

After an interval of about a week, take the child aside and teach him about Halloween. Spend about 20 minutes a day on Halloween until he fully understands what it entails. Then retest him on the passage on Halloween. You should find his test performance much improved.

Assessing Vocabulary

The usual way of assessing vocabulary is to ask the individual to explain the meanings of words listed in the vocabulary test. Because individuals with learning disabilities tend to be more inarticulate than those without learning disabilities, they face an undue disadvantage with vocabulary tests. To ascertain their understanding of a particular word despite their inability to define it clearly, *supplement* your testing with this additional procedure. At the end of the vocabulary test administration, return to items that the student with learning disabilities has failed. Ask him or her to make a sentence with the vocabulary word with the constraint that the sentence should explicate the meaning of it, for example, the word *carefully.*

If the student with learning disabilities says, "She walks carefully," you would not give a point. If she or he says, "The old woman walks carefully," you may give him or her half a point. If she or he says, "The old woman walks carefully on the icy road to avoid a fall," you would give him or her a whole point that indicates full understanding of the word *carefully* despite his or her previous failure to articulate its meaning. This additional procedure in vocabulary testing ensures that you accommodate learning-disabled individuals' inability to express themselves, thereby avoiding a floor effect in your test data. A *floor effect* refers to a student's bottoming out in testing, giving data that indicate excessively poor performance. When that happens, all you can deduce from the test data is that the subtests in the test, or the items in a subtest, are too hard for the student, which is not very informative. Data must indicate differential performance linked with differential test conditions, so that you can map out the examinee's areas of cognitive strength and weaknesses, and provide instructional attention to his or her needs accordingly.

Assessing Spelling

In assessing spelling in individuals with learning disabilities, note that those with additional language problems would produce more bizarre spelling errors than those without. You should expect a student with learning disabilities to show parallel patterns of data in his or her errors from three assessment sources: word recognition (sight vocabulary), oral reading accuracy, and spelling. The reason is straightforward: If a student does not know how to decode a word (in Word Recognition), it means she or he has not learned or mastered the vowel(s) and consonant combinations in that word (i.e., the phonics). Hence, when she or he encounters the same vowel(s) and consonants in oral reading, she or he would make decoding errors. Likewise, if she or he does not know those vowel(s) and consonants, how would she or he spell them accurately?

There are various standardized spelling tests for use, for example, in the spelling subtest of the Wide Range Achievement Test (WRAT), the Edmonton Spelling Ability Test.

Conditions for Students' Optimal Performance in Our Assessment

In assessing students' reading and mathematical performances, we must create an environment that would elicit optimal performance. Failure to do so would be most irresponsible on our part and unfair to them. Here are five pointers for creating such an assessment environment.

Establish Rapport Prior to Testing

It is important to spend time establishing rapport with the student before testing. Preferably, you should have observed the student sufficiently prior to testing.

Why is good rapport important? Because it reduces test anxiety in the student. All students tend to feel anxious in any test situation. This test anxiety impairs their performance because it distracts them. Impaired performance attributable to student test anxiety can be most clearly seen in timed test items or those requiring speed. Hence, prior to testing, you must ensure that the student feels genuinely comfortable with you as the examiner.

Discover Student's Optimal Time for Cognitive Functions

Each person has a different body rhythm regarding his or her optimal time for intellectual work. Some of us work best in the morning, some at night. Thus early-birds peak around 7 A.M. or earlier, whereas nighthawks peak at 10 P.M. or later.

If we want to elicit optimal test performance from the student, we should find out when she or he functions best at school. Is the student most attentive and productive academically in the morning? After recess and a good snack? Or in the afternoon from 1 to 2 P.M.? If you can match test time to the period when she or he is observed to peak in cognitive work, then you would surely get optimal test performances.

Inform the Student of the Test's Purpose Beforehand

Yes, I am asking you to lay the cards on the table! Any student realizes that something is afoot when she or he is taken out of class or asked to go with the teacher to a more quiet corner in the classroom. They have an unmistakable hunch why they are going with you. The purposes range from being a guinea pig in an experiment to testing. Hence, it would be to your detriment to play footsy with the student! Besides, you should remember that many students with learning disabilities have been much tested. They are test-wise! So, level with them!

A Good Examiner Never Rushes to Complete All the Testing

Rather, she or he spaces them out so that the student does not get fatigued. The younger the student, the more you should attend to when she or he is getting tired from testing. The first sign of test fatigue should indicate to you to stop testing and continue on a subsequent test session. If you ignore student's fatigue and persist in continuing testing, you will obtain useless test data because they are invalid, confounded by the student's test fatigue. Oral reading errors may increase due to inattention caused by fatigue. Inaccuracies in his or her answers to your reading comprehension questions could well have resulted from his or her inability to focus attention on relevant information from the test passage. So the dictum is clear: You must pace testing according to how much your student can process before she or he gets tired.

Tester or Examiner's Competency

When you give a reading or mathematics assessment, your competency as a tester is assumed.

1. This means that you are well versed in administering the test (i.e., that you have learned and practiced sufficiently the test procedures, and understand how to interpret your test data). Imagine the impact on the child or adolescent when an examiner says: "Wait a minute" in the middle of testing, and then frantically hunts for the page that contains parts of test instructions that the examiner has forgotten! He forgot because he had not exerted himself to learn them well. Similarly, consider the examiner who is too lazy to rehearse test administrations prior to testing a child with learning disabilities. One former student in our practicum gave an entire reading comprehension test as an oral reading test precisely for this reason! Alas, guilt and shame cannot atone for her laziness! She obtained useless data!

2. You must be thoroughly prepared for the testing. The test form(s), materials, and supplementary instruments are well organized, impressively laid out, and ready for use. There is no loose page flying around or a last-minute dash for a sharper pencil for data recording or for the student's use.

Why is such preparation important? The reason is to ensure that you do not lose credibility with the student. Any student can see when a tester is ill prepared. Although younger students may not sneer, older students may be less restrained to let known their feelings and disrespect! They will demonstrate it through half-hearted cooperation in testing. That is what ill-prepared examiners deserve. They lose credibility with the student immediately. Unfortunately, they don't get a second chance!

3. Discreet recording of test data. In recording data, you must remember not to distract the student. After all, you must always keep in clear view your goal of obtaining optimal test performance from the student! And any noisy recording of test data makes him or her anxious, such as using a loud clicking stopwatch!

Interpreting Test Data

What is a useful way of interpreting test data gathered from a student with learning disabilities? One way is to view data in terms of its being either a problem of acquisition or one of mastery.[2]

Acquisition Problems

An acquisition problem indicates the student with learning disabilities has not learned the concept, skill, or procedures, and must be taught them. What signals acquisition problems? Acquisition problems are indicated in the following: (a) nonreaders, (b) insufficient knowledge of prereading skills, (c) poor knowledge of phonics, and/or complex phonics patterns, or (d) process problems that impede acquisition of certain prereading skills.

1. Nonreaders. These are children, adolescents, or adults who have not learned to read. You may encounter them in grades 2 or 3, or in high school, or in adulthood.

2. Insufficient knowledge of prereading skills. Prereading skills refer to the ability to recognize rhyming, to segment words into their constituent sounds (segmentation skills), to blend separate sounds into a word.

3. Poor knowledge of phonics or complex patterns of phonics. Individuals with learning disabilities tend to show poor knowledge of phonics, such as the vowels of *a, e, i, o,* and *u;* double vowels, such as *ea, ai, eu, ou,* etc., and complex vowel combinations, such as *eau,* and vowel and consonant combinations, such as *eigh, tion,* (sc) (t)*ious, augh,* and so on.

4. Process problems in children with learning disabilities can impede their ability to blend. For example, children with blending problems can say the individual

---

[2]The credit of differentiating acquisition and mastery problems goes to Stan Auerbach (Delta School District, B.C.)

sounds in *mat* but when asked to blend the three separate sounds into the word *mat,* would persist in saying the respective sounds of *m-a-t* and not be able to produce the word *mat* from blending them.

Mastery Problems

These problems indicate that the student has learned the concept, skill, or procedure; however, learning has not been consolidated. It has not reached the point of automaticity, where the student's performance is not only accurate, but also fast and smooth without hesitancy. How does a student indicate a lack of mastery applying a concept, skill, or procedure?

Lack of mastery is evidenced in the following examples. In reading, the student takes a long time to say a word and manages to do so only after much subvocalizing, and occasionally repetition of parts of the word can occur. This example suggests that the child does know the specific letter–sound associations in the word. However, he has not learned those associations well, hence the hesitation and need for subvocalizing. He is unsure of the letter–sound associations contained in the word. If he has mastered those letter–sound associations, he would have promptly without hesitation, automatically decoded the word accurately and fast. Let us turn to an example in arithmetic. We see the child falters with the multiplication tables, half guessing or repeating himself thus: "5 × 7 is, 5 × 7 is, er 32 . . . no, 40, . . . no, 35, yes, 35." This example suggests that the child has learned the 5 times table, but his learning is still far from mastery. He will demonstrate mastery of the 5 times tables when he can say the content of the entire table fast, without hesitation, and accurately!

Clearly, mastery of a concept, skill, or procedure means the individual's application of it is automaticized, fast as well as accurate. Mastery in performance is always measured or expressed in speed of errorless performance.

With students with learning disabilities, one should expect that in certain areas they evidence acquisition problems and in others, mastery problems. Identifying the nature of their problems in this way enables us to apply appropriate remedial focus. Specifically, with acquisition problems in students with learning disabilities, we focus on teaching them what they have not learned. Once we insure that they have learned the needed concept or procedure, we help consolidate their learning through practice so that they master what they've learned. With mastery problems, we begin with reviewing what they have already learned, and then, using motivating drills, provide them with needed practice of the conceptual application, skill, or procedure till mastery is clearly and firmly reached. You can see that acquisition problems require much more instruction from the teacher of students with learning disabilities whereas mastery problems require ingenuity in designing motivating games for drill practice.

I end this chapter with some suggested remedial strategies that I designed and have found to be effective with students with learning disabilities.

Remedial Strategy to Improve Reading Rate or Fluency

Method

1. Preview about four pages in the book selected for reading before your instructional session, noting words which you anticipate your tutee will have decoding or vocabulary difficulties.
2. Write down each of the words you think your tutee does not know how to pronounce on small index cards or small pieces of paper.
3. Write down the same words in (2) in the tutee's vocabulary book.
4. During your instructional session, first teach your tutee how to decode and pronounce all the words on the small index cards (or pieces of paper). Explain clearly the meanings for him or her if your tutee is in grades 1 and 2, and record them in the tutee's vocabulary booklet. Older tutees should write down the meanings themselves in their vocabulary booklet.
5. Preview these with your tutee till he or she can say all of them twice in a row without error. When this criterion is reached, begin reading.
6. Have the tutee listen to you read the whole page at a natural pace and pitch. Where necessary, follow your reading with your finger or a pencil or pen to help indicate to your tutee where you are located in the row of words.
7. a. Have the tutee shadow you as you read the page again.
   b. Repeat shadow-reading with tutee on the same page *if* tutee is a nonreader or reads at less than half the reading rate of average peers at baseline testing before proceeding to step 8.
8. Subsequently, the tutee reads the page aloud to you.
9. She or he shadows you in reading the same page a second time.
10. The tutee reads on his or her own again.

Steps 7–10 are repeated until tutee reaches the criterion of not more than the permitted amount of errors per page. Upon reaching that criterion, you turn to a new page and repeat the whole procedure.

You should spend about 20 to 30 minutes for the entire activity of repeated reading, starting with vocabulary preview.

Permitted Number of Oral Reading Errors
To Be Met by Students with Learning Disabilities
before Proceeding to a New Page

Examine the amount of reading errors made by the student at baseline testing. If the child with learning disabilities made more than 10 oral reading errors at baseline testing, set the permitted number of oral reading errors in repeated reading at eight per page for the first week in remediation. For the second week, set it at five per page, and for the third, three, and so on. The student must meet the designated criterion before he or she can proceed to a new page in repeated reading. However, remember that two errors per page is an ideal that needs to be gradually approximated in some students with learning disabilities.

Additional Instructional Activities in Repeated Reading

After the day's session in repeated reading give the student with learning disabilities homework in the following three areas:

Vocabulary Learning

Instruct the student with learning disabilities to learn some of the vocabulary arising from the day's repeated reading. In assigning the amount of vocabulary words to be learned, the teacher should take into consideration the age of the student. Children in grades 1 and 2 should take home four or five words. Those in grades 3, five or six, and so on. It is recalled that each vocabulary word has been written by the teacher on small index cards for initial drills before repeated reading begins. She now gives them to the student with learning disabilities to take home for study.

The student will learn those words for testing the next day, before the repeated reading procedure begins. Any word not learned will get piggybacked to the next batch of vocabulary words for homework. Words learned are immediately pinned up on a corkboard facing the student as the teacher praises him or her for having worked hard. This constant visual reminder of work well done motivates him or her to continue to expend effort at learning new vocabulary because all students with learning disabilities enjoy seeing their corkboard mushroom with pin-ups of vocabulary words. Various imaginative ways of visual presentation of student's vocabulary growth can be attempted. For example, with young children, the teacher can have an apple tree, and each new word learned is written on individual cutouts of apples and pinned on the paper tree. Thus the children with learning disabilities can see how well their apple trees are growing. For boys in intermediate grades, the teacher could make a train engine and a caboose, with the cars being the parts that bear the vocabulary words. Thus, these intermediate students with learning disabilities can see their train getting longer as they accumulate new vocabulary words.

Vocabulary Books

In the vocabulary book kept by each student with learning disabilities, the teacher ensures that after each vocabulary word and its meaning have been written down, she and the student locate a sentence on the page from the book read that contains the word. She copies the sentence down for the primary child. Older students with learning disabilities can copy it down themselves.

The teacher instructs students to study these sentences as they are learning the vocabulary words. The purpose is to increase their repertoires of model sentences, as well as making them attend to the proper contexts of usage of those vocabulary words.

Sentence Generation

When students have learned more than 20 words, the teacher can ask them to write sentences with those newly learned words.

Learning to Spell Vocabulary Words

At the end of the first week of repeated reading, each student with learning disabilities would have learned quite a number of new vocabulary words. It is now time to introduce spelling as additional homework. From the vocabulary words the student has already mastered, the teacher asks the student to choose a set of words to take home to learn to spell. Again, he or she shows consideration to the child's age and concurrent load of homework in vocabulary. Hence, for children in grades 1 and 2, she assigns only three words (this is because they have to continue to take home four or five new vocabulary words to learn the same night). For children in grades 3 and 4, she assigns four words, and so on. The teacher simply retrieves pinned-up words from corkboard and gives them to the student to take home to learn to spell. Any word that a student failed to spell correctly in the spelling test the next day gets piggybacked to the batch of spelling words for the following day. Words that the student with learning disabilities can *both* explain the meanings of, and spell correctly, are prominently and separately displayed from those that he or she has merely mastered the meanings. Students with learning disabilities derive a lot of pride and joy from such separate displays of words because such displays speak to their effort and achievement. Moreover, teachers and parents readily understand those visual displays and smile on them approvingly. What more effective builder of self-esteem can we get than these displays?

A Strategy for Teaching the Short Vowels

Instructional Steps

1. Teach this pair of short vowels first:

Rationale: To provide maximal facilitation for the learning disabled (LD) child in his or her learning of the five short vowels, you need to begin with a pair that is *most* distinct in *both* sound and mouth (lip) movements. The short *a* sound differs sharply and clearly from the short *i* sound. In addition, to make the short *a* sound, you have to open your mouth quite widely in the vertical direction. To make the short *i* sound, you produce it from your throat. You should be able to feel its production if you place two fingers on your throat. Your mouth opens slightly in making the short *i* sound.

Now you may argue that the short *o* and short *e* sounds match the same criteria regarding sound production and mouth movements. But start with the short *a* and short *i* first because quite a number of children find the short *e* sound hard to learn (remember). In teaching an LD child a pair of short vowels that are easier to learn and master, you make *success* readily accessible. With mastery of short *a* and short *i*, you will make him or her happy and confident and ready to take on a harder short vowel! Remember for an LD child who is struggling with decoding, access to success in learning assumes tremendous importance vis-à-vis motivation to learn and self-concept.

2. Make prompts for short *a* and short *i*. Involve the LD child in making your teaching prompts. (Example: before making a prompt of an apple, does the child you are teaching like apples?)

The prompts should be sufficiently large, preferably 8 × 11 (in.), with the picture cue on top, and the letter *a* on the second half of the sheet of paper. Laminate it to increase durability in use. Make another prompt for short vowel *i*. (Example: *igloo*).

3. Make CVC words with *a* and *i*, using consonants that are within the LD child's repertoire. However, if the LD child has a very restricted range of known consonants, then use these to begin with in constructing CVC words. After a week or so, expand to consonants that you want to teach him or her. Do not introduce more than three new consonants at a time; otherwise you are overloading him or her cognitively. (He or she has to learn to discriminate between *a* and *i* to mastery, that is your primary instructional goal. If you make the LD child learn simultaneously more than three new consonants, then you are taxing his or her cognitive resources! Remember what I said about human information processing being very limited?)

If the LD child has a reversal problem with *b* and *d*, or even *p*, avoid using these consonants unless you are also working on eliminating his or her *b–d* reversal problem. In which case, you can use *b*-words. (When *b* is mastered, then *d* words, but not *b* and *d* CVC words in the same lesson, for example: bad).

4. Teaching:

a. Direct explanation

Explain clearly to the LD child what sound the short *a* makes. Point to your mouth movement. Ensure the child attends to the sound you are making. Then point to the prompt to help the LD child associate it with the short a sound.

GOVERNORS STATE UNIVERSITY
UNIVERSITY PARK
IL 60466

Using a mirror, look into it, produce the short *a* sound, make exaggerated mouth movements and loud short *a* sound.

Looking into the mirror to watch his or her mouth movements, the LD child then produces the short *a* sound.

You provide praise or corrective feedback.

Repeat procedure once more.

Then turn to the short *i*.

The procedure with the short *i* sound follows a similar format. Make the short *i* sound. Then put the LD child's hand or two fingers on your throat so he or she can feel the *i* sound generating from there. Keeping his or her fingers on your throat, make the short *i* sound again. Point out how narrow your mouth is, compared to how your mouth looks in making the short *a* sound. Have the LD child look at the prompt so he or she can associate it with the short *i* sound.

Looking into the mirror, you and the LD child both make the short *i* sound. Make sure the LD child puts his or her hand on his or her throat while making the short *i* sound.

5. Drill Work

   a. Display prominently in front of and at the LD child's eye level, the two prompts for *a* and *i*.

   b. Inform LD child you are going to teach him to read pairs of words containing the short *a* and short *i* sounds. You will show him or her one word at a time, you will say it for him or her. He or she will repeat the word back to you.

   c. You will use five pairs of CVC words containing short *a* and short *i*. For example:

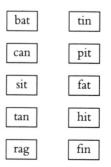

bat	tin
can	pit
sit	fat
tan	hit
rag	fin

Present each CVC word clearly printed on a small index card. Say the word, repeat the short *a* sound, pointing to the prompt, saying, *a* as in apple (or whatever prompt you and the child together have generated). Repeat with the CVC word containing the short *i* sound.

After you have gone through the five pairs of CVC words once, shuffle the pile of CVC words containing short *a* and short *i*. Then pick up the first CVC word from the pile, ask the LD child to say it, prompting him or her to look at the prompt. (You see why the prompts have to be in front of the LD child and at his or her eye level? Not placed at his or her side!) If the LD child hesitates, help him or her. Say the CVC word, repeat the short vowel sound, connect it with the prompt. Have the LD child say that CVC word twice, the word over which he or she hesitated. Remind child to use the prompt to help him or her recall the appropriate short vowel sound.

Repeat the drill until the LD child can say all the CVC words without error twice consecutively. Make sure that with each new drill, you shuffle the index cards containing the CVC words. Make sure that you do *not* always present the first CVC word containing the same short vowel sound. You must always randomize the presentation order of these CVC words containing the short *a* and short *i*. If you always present the LD child with CVC words containing the short *a* sound first, followed by those containing the short *i* sound or vowel, he or she will very soon stop paying attention to the vowels because he or she has learned to rote memorize your presentation order! Hence the LD child will not have really mastered the discrimination between short *a* and and short *i*!

Then give additional practice with these CVC words in the context of phonic games.

6. Testing

After the LD child has reached two consecutive errorless performances in your drill work, give him or her one more practice, then test him or her. In testing, you simply reshuffle the CVC words, then have child pronounce each of them as you present them one at a time to him or her. Record the results. If the child without hesitation, correctly says four of the short *a* CVC words, you will record for that day, 80% accuracy in acquisition of short *a*. If he or she without hesitation, correctly says three of the short *i* CVC words, then you will record 60% accuracy in acquisition of short *i*.

These results will then go onto the graph for that day's instructional session.

You wrap up this session with a 10–15-mins repeated reading with the child, using a passage that contains short *a* and short *i* words. The idea here is to reinforce the LD child's acquisition of short vowel sounds by getting him or her to learn to apply his or her new phonics skills in a sentential context.

For next day's instruction, you will substitute new CVC *a* and *i* words for the ones that the LD child has learned the day before.

For example, new items could be as follows:

man	dim
fan	hit
rib	cat
pin	Jan
lap	fib

7. Review

You teach in the above-described manner daily or at least three times a week. Before the end of the week, have an additional session with the LD child in which you concentrate on giving him or her a good review. You go through all the CVC words he or she has learned with you in past sessions. You remind the child to use his or her prompts.

You present the CVC words to the child, paying close attention to randomization in presentation of them. Drill till the LD child can say every word without hesitation correctly twice consecutively. Then test by choosing randomly five CVC words containing short *a,* and five short *i*. Record results on graph.

8. Repeat this teaching procedure until the LD child has mastered short *a* and short *i* vowel sounds. Mastery is defined as 100% accuracy across 2 consecutive days or instructional sessions. Then carry on teaching for one more week to enable him or her *overlearn* the discrimination. Overlearning promotes maintenance of his or her learned skills.

Please remember the importance of graphing your daily teaching (i.e., the LD child's accuracy scores in acquisition in every instructional session).

9. When step (8) is clearly attained, go to

Use the same teaching and testing procedures.

10. When step (9) is achieved, teach short *u* on its own.

11. When you are teaching short *o* and short *e*, review with the LD child the short *a* and short *i* sounds twice a week in the first week of acquisition of the new vowel pair. After that, review once a week.

When you are teaching the LD child the short *u* sound, review the short *o* and *e* with him/her twice a week in the first week of his/her learning the short *u* sound. Thereafter, once a week review with him/her the short *o* and short *e* sounds. During acquisition of short *u*, review with him/her short *a* and short *i* sounds once every two weeks.

Reminder: You can apply the same instructional principles and method to double vowels (e.g., *ai, ea, ou*, etc.).

A Strategy for Teaching the Concept of Main Idea Sentence

The Importance of Teaching the Main Idea Concept

Students must learn the concept of a main idea within a paragraph and to locate the sentence that contains it within the paragraph. The reason is twofold: First, the main idea sentence informs the student the general nature of the content of the paragraph. Second, if a student does not know the concept of a main idea, she or he can in no way allocate attention to important textual parts, and can ill self-monitor her or his reading comprehension. Thus, teachers who assiduously exhort their students to monitor their own state of reading comprehension without ensuring that the latter have mastered the main idea concept are putting the cart before the horse! Little wonder that they get frustrated with the lack of comprehension monitoring among their students!

How do we proceed to teach the main idea concept? Mark Aulls (1978) had devised a three-step verbal rule approach in teaching it. These three rules are listed in the following prompt card (see prompt card). In my teaching of students with learning disabilities across 18 years (you see how ancient I am!), I found these three verbal rules insufficient. I added a fourth rule, and in conjunction with the use of a diagram, managed to teach the main idea concept effectively with students with learning disabilities and low achievers.

To facilitate student learning, these four rules are typed on a prompt card measuring 8 × 5 in. (the largest index card you can purchase at any stationery store). Explanation on the teaching strategy follows.

Prompt Card

Finding the Main Idea Sentence in a Paragraph

1. The main idea sentence is the most important sentence in the paragraph.
It tells you clearly about the topic in the paragraph.
2. All the other sentences in the paragraph talk about it (refer to it).
3. All the other sentences in the paragraph give you more details about it.
4. Take away the main idea sentence in the paragraph, that paragraph
won't make sense.

Try it. Use this step to check if you have picked out the correct sentence as the main idea sentence.

Our instructional experience indicates that the most efficacious way of teaching
a main idea concept is to use self-made simple single paragraphs during initial conceptual acquisition to demonstrate the rules in locating the sentence containing the
main idea. To illustrate:

Ten-year-old Mark was feeling really scared. His face was turning white. His body
felt chilled. His legs were beginning to feel rubbery. He seemed to have lost his voice
suddenly.

The teacher uses an 8 × 11-in. piece of paper and writes out the first sentence in
the middle of it and boxes it in. He or she then writes down the remaining sentences one at a time, each sentence sufficiently distanced but circling the first one.

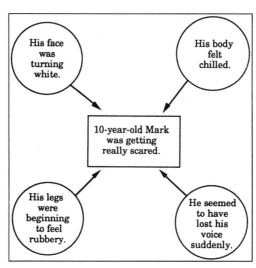

The teacher then explains to the student the first three rules used by Aulls (1978) to teach the main idea concept. As I explained earlier, in my teaching experience with learning-disabled students and low achievers, I have found it necessary to add one final rule. Covering the main idea sentence, which is clearly boxed in and in the middle of the page, ask the student to read the remaining sentences, and then ask, "Do those sentences make sense now that I've covered up the main idea sentence? Whom are they referring to? Whose legs were beginning to feel rubbery? If I came into the room and said all those sentences, would I have made sense?" The use of this extra rule greatly helps students grasp the fact that when you remove the main idea sentence, the semantic integrity of the paragraph collapses. The student is also taught to use this additional rule to self-check and self-test, whether or not he or she indeed identified the correct sentences as the main idea sentences in paragraphs of a given exercise.

Simple single paragraphs are used first, with attention paid to rotating the position of the main idea sentence so that it does not occur invariably in the first sentence. Initially, the instructional sessions should start with the teacher using direct instruction on one simple paragraph; then both teacher and student work on a second paragraph together. The student then is watched closely while working on one new paragraph independently, with the aid of a prompt on which the four rules are typed out clearly. The prompt is a laminated index card measuring 5 × 8 in. Subsequent to satisfactory performance, the student gets five new single simple paragraphs to work on independently. *The teacher watches to be sure the student uses the prompt.*

This instructional procedure is followed until the student demonstrates mastery in identifying the main idea sentence in simple single paragraphs. Mastery is defined as 100% accuracy across 3 successive days or instructional sessions, where the student works independently on five paragraphs per day. Thereafter, the student proceeds to work with single complex paragraphs containing two main ideas. When mastery is reached here (90% accuracy across three successive days or instructional sessions), the student is given more complex paragraphs, each containing two main ideas. The paragraphs in main–idea identification were teacher-made as well as from the Boning Specific Skills series and Barnell Loft series.

If the student uses the prompt card as directed, in particular, step no. 4, then she or he would be able to identify correctly respective main idea sentences in the five given paragraphs. Teacher help or feedback comes in when student is stymied and cannot identify the main idea sentence.

Reminders for teaching the concept of a main idea sentence.

1. Step 4 is of cardinal importance both for teaching and the making of a self-regulated, independent student out of your LD student.

Be sure to teach the LD student to use this step both for his or her own learning and for self-monitoring.

2. Initially, you may have to devise simple paragraphs to facilitate the LD student's learning. One way of doing this is to get together with several other student teachers or practicing regular classroom and/or specialist teachers, each of you make one paragraph of about five sentences. It saves labor and promotes cooperative learning and teaching.

Take care to make some paragraphs in which the main idea does not occur in the first sentence. (Vary the position of the main idea sentence. Otherwise the LD student would just unthinkingly select the first sentence all the time as the main idea sentence.)

3. Then proceed with paragraphs from specific skills series like the BONING (Teaching Main Ideas). Be careful to check each paragraph before you use it. Sometimes, the paragraph really contains an inference rather than a main idea.

4. Use very stringent mastery criterion in this acquisition phase of the skill: 100% accuracy across 3 consecutive days or instructional sessions, on independent work on about 5 paragraphs. When the LD student achieves this, continue next week to ask for 100% accuracy for 2 consecutive days or instructional sessions to achieve overlearning.

Thereafter, proceed to use longer and more complex paragraphs, containing two main idea sentences.

Remember how to teach this concept? Check your notes. If need be, check with me. Call or e-mail me if you wish. I am always happy to dialogue with interested professionals.

Strategies for Inclusive Settings

The preceding strategies to increase rate and phonics proficiency are obviously more appropriate for use with young children with learning disabilities on a one-on-one basis in the resource room (United States) or learning assistance center (B.C., Canada). The strategy for teaching a main idea can readily be used in a moderately inclusive classroom, one in which only high-incidence special needs students, such as those with learning disabilities, are included. One way of implementing this strategy in such a classroom is to have the special needs teacher teach the entire class the main idea sentence concept, and then give additional instructional attention to those integrated special needs students. The teacher can write the strategy steps on the blackboard and have each student construct his or her own prompt card by copying them onto an index card. A teacher or peer can help the students with learning disabilities construct theirs.

Other comprehension strategies that can be effectively used in inclusive classrooms include Palincsar and Brown's (1984) reciprocal teaching strategies in summarizing, question generating, clarifying, and predicting. Scott Paris' (1987) "Reading and Thinking Strategies" are very applicable in teaching reading comprehension in both inclusive and one-on-one instructional settings in the resource room or learning assistance center.

Currently, researchers are attempting to investigate and identify effective teaching strategies for use in inclusive settings (see special issue in the *Journal of Special Education*, 1995, Vol. 29, No. 2, in particular the article by Scruggs and Mastropieri). We should expect to read about them in the next few years. I am, therefore, confident that when I revise this book in due time, I will have much to write about on the topic of effective instructional strategies for inclusive classrooms.

REFLECTIONS

The purpose of assessing a reading problem in any student is to pinpoint the severity and loci of it, with the goal of setting up an appropriate educational program for him or her. The key to a successful assessment that pinpoints a student's relative strengths and weaknesses in reading is thoroughness on the part of the tester. This thoroughness simply reflects thoughtfulness on his or her part. She or he thinks clearly and carefully about the kinds of information she or he seeks regarding the student's reading. This thinking guides her or his testing.

Thoughtful testers never routinize their informal testing. On the contrary, they are ever vigilant about being flexible and adaptive in such testing. Thus, if an adolescent cannot define the meaning of a given word, the thoughtful tester asks for a sentence that clarifies for her or him the adolescent's understanding of it. If a child evidences an inferential problem in reading comprehension, she or he attempts various forms of scaffolding to help resolve it. Using quick and good thinking, she or he engages in dynamic assessment that feeds into remediation.

To become skilled informal testers involves your willingness to expend sufficient effort and time in learning to master informal test procedures, and in understanding proper ways of interpreting test data. Additionally, and more importantly, it involves constant use of thinking on your part as you engage in actual informal reading assessment.

References

Aulls, M. W. (1978). *Developmental and remedial reading in the middle grades*. Boston: Allyn and Bacon Inc.

Hammill, D. D., & Bartel, N. R. (1995). *Teaching students with learning and behaviour problems* (6th ed.). Austin, TX: Pro-Ed.

Palincsar, A. S., & Brown, A. L. (1984). Reciprocal teaching of comprehension-fostering and comprehension-monitoring activities. *Cognition and Instruction, 1*(2) 117–175.

Paris, S. G. (1987). *Reading and thinking strategies.* Lexington, MA: Collamore Educational Publishing, D.C. Heath.

Parker, R., (1972). *Informal test of phonics.* Texas A & M University, College Station, TX. Unpublished.

Raphael, T. E. (1982). Teaching children question-answering strategies. *The Reading Teacher, 36,* 186–191.

Scruggs, T. E., & Mastropieri, M. A. (1995). What makes special education special? Evaluating inclusion programs and the PASS variables. *Journal of Special Education, 29*(2), 224–233.

Torgesen, J. K., & Bryant, B. R. (1994). *Test of phonological awareness* (TOPA). Austin, Texas: Pro-Ed.

8

Arithmetic and Mathematics and Students with Learning Disabilities

On the topic of arithmetic computation problems in students with learning disabilities, two points come to the fore: (a) There hasn't been much research done on arithmetic problems of students with learning disabilities. (b) What we do know about these problems comes from research information and astute observations gathered from normally achieving students by researchers and teachers in mathematics education. In particular, the latter researchers had been able to identify systematic arithmetic error patterns and to categorize them (e.g., Ashlock, 1976). Moreover, they have mapped out the most common error patterns in addition, subtraction, multiplication, and division. All this information serves a most useful function because it provides a benchmark or reference frame for diagnosing various systematic arithmetic error patterns in students. Armed with the diagnostic information, the teacher can embark on a proper course of remediation with the student.

Arithmetic error patterns denote a student's use of erroneous strategies in computation. Curiously, as the following examples in Table 5 illustrate, despite using an erroneous strategy in arithmetic computation, a student can still achieve 50% accuracy in performance. These examples clearly show that a student's use of an erroneous arithmetic strategy does not necessarily lead to a failed assignment! She or he can still salvage a respectable 50% of it! What is likely to cross the teacher's mind

Table 5   Illustration of Erroneous Strategies in Arithmetic Computation

Student[a]				
Alex	287	142	363	425
	−152	−69	−51	−76
	135	127	312	451
Scott	214	$\overset{1}{91}$	524	$\overset{6}{476}$
	+674	+23	+174	+292
	888	15	698	6114
Teresa	320	$\overset{1}{241}$	$\overset{15}{437}$	$\overset{11}{623}$
	× 12	× 4	× 28	× 5
	320	964	916	3115

[a] Fictitious names

when he or she marks an assignment of a student who consistently gets 50% on given assignments? Would the teacher think the student has not grasped the concept or computational procedure? She would if the student consistently fails or gets less than 50%! But the student hasn't failed! He or she always manages to squeak through with a bare pass of 50%! Very likely, the teacher would just shake her head and think the student needs to be much more careful and attentive in completing the given assignments. In this way, the student's erroneous arithmetic strategy escapes detection.

The examples in Table 5 also explain why arithmetic computation problems are less frequently detected or harder to detect than reading problems. Children's reading problems are more readily detectable because as they engage in oral reading, teachers witness directly their struggles in decoding and their slow reading rates.

How do we identify students' erroneous patterns in arithmetic computations and through them pinpoint the underlying erroneous strategies used by students? First, we need a system that enables us to separate students' careless errors from those that signal a problem. Linda Cox (1975) provided a very useful means of doing so. She suggested a set of five problems to identify student errors. If a student makes three or more errors out of five given problems, and if these errors show a clear and consistent pattern, then the student has a problem that needs redress. More diagnostic attention follows for his or her consistent errors.

Remember, you devote additional time and design set or sets of five problems for informal assessment of the student *only* if he or she has made three or more errors out of five problems, and *if* these errors contain a consistent pattern. Should the student make one or two errors that contain no consistent pattern, then it is likely that he or she has been careless. In such cases, there is no need for further diagnostic attention (Cox, 1975).

Should a student make three or more errors out of five problems, but these errors do not contain a consistent pattern, then they are termed *random errors* (Cox, 1975). Again, no further diagnostic attention is given to random errors because it is impossible to analyze underlying causes of or how to remediate errors that spring up in a random fashion.

Before proceeding to the type of consistent error patterns in students' arithmetic computations, I'd like to draw your attention to one important point: When you encounter a consistent error pattern in a student's arithmetic assignment, that student has already been using the erroneous strategy for a long time. For him or her to demonstrate it in the form of a consistent error pattern means the use of that erroneous strategy has become a habit. What implication does this have for you as his or her teacher? Please try to think of an answer before reading on.

The implication is that not only do you have to reteach the correct computational procedure to the student, but you need also to provide ample practice to ensure overlearning. Only thus can you break his or her habit of using an erroneous strategy. Merely teaching him or her the correct way to compute does not eliminate the possibility of a spontaneous return of his or her use of it, no matter how inadvertent its use may be!

Error Patterns in Arithmetic Computations

For a detailed examination of various idiosyncratic error patterns found in normally achieving children's arithmetic computations, I strongly recommend Robert Ashlock's (1976) excellent paperback. He has assiduously compiled a singularly interesting and immensely useful documentation of children's erroneous patterns in arithmetic computations, a guide to careful diagnosis and analysis of them, and suggestions for remediation. Here, to facilitate your learning, I simply summarize into broad but major categories the types of arithmetic computation error patterns that Ashlock had so astutely observed. In my summary I shall give illustrative examples of students' arithmetic computation error patterns, which are modeled on those collected, identified, and compiled by Ashlock (1976). However, I have omitted examples involving fractions because in Canada, we are supposedly focusing on using and teaching the metric system. As you study them, ask yourselves two questions: (a) *How did this student come to develop such an error pattern in arithmetic computation?* (b) *If I were his or her teacher, what would I have done in my teaching to have prevented his or her developing such an error pattern?* I want you to keep in mind these two questions as you pore through the illustrative examples of student computation error patterns below. You would learn best if you make the effort of jotting down your answers on a scratch pad as you read on. Otherwise, your brain cells won't get the necessary exercise, and you'd have stunted development in thinking skills!

Errors Due to Partial Completion of the Given Problem

In this type of error, the student just completes half the problem, leaving the rest untouched. See the following examples:

$$
\begin{array}{r}
45 \\
-\ 2 \\
\hline
3
\end{array}
\qquad
\begin{array}{r}
66 \\
-\ 4 \\
\hline
2
\end{array}
$$

$$
\begin{array}{r}
51 \\
\times\ 6 \\
\hline
56
\end{array}
\qquad
\begin{array}{r}
271 \\
\times\ 8 \\
\hline
278
\end{array}
$$

$$
\begin{array}{r}
39 \\
+\ 5 \\
\hline
34
\end{array}
\qquad
\begin{array}{r}
86 \\
+\ 8 \\
\hline
84
\end{array}
$$

Errors Due to Incorrect Placement and Regrouping

This type of error denotes faulty procedural applications of placement and regrouping. The student has not learned to discriminate when regrouping should occur, or he or she discerns properly the conditions for regrouping but fails in correct placement. See the following examples:

$$
\begin{array}{r}
59 \\
+\ 6 \\
\hline
515
\end{array}
\qquad
\begin{array}{r}
74 \\
+\ 8 \\
\hline
712
\end{array}
$$

$$
\begin{array}{r}
63 \\
-\ 7 \\
\hline
64
\end{array}
\qquad
\begin{array}{r}
42 \\
-\ 9 \\
\hline
47
\end{array}
$$

$$
\begin{array}{r}
{}^{5\ 18}\,68 \\
-21 \\
\hline
317
\end{array}
\qquad
\begin{array}{r}
{}^{3\ 17}\,47 \\
-25 \\
\hline
112
\end{array}
$$

$$
\begin{array}{r}
17 \\
7\,\overline{)749}
\end{array}
\qquad
\begin{array}{r}
28 \\
3\,\overline{)624}
\end{array}
$$

Errors Due to Incorrect Procedures in Computation

In these errors, students clearly have not learned the correct procedures in arithmetic computation. For example, in the first illustration, instead of completing the addition in the ones column, and then continuing to the tens column, the student does this: 2 + 1 + 3 = 6. As you peruse each example, decipher how the student computes the problem to produce his or her answer. The erroneous strategies in their arithmetic computations are not difficult to discover.

$$
\begin{array}{r} 21 \\ +\ 3 \\ \hline 6 \end{array}
\qquad
\begin{array}{r} 17 \\ +\ 4 \\ \hline 12 \end{array}
$$

$$
\begin{array}{r} 16 \\ +\ 2 \\ \hline 38 \end{array}
\qquad
\begin{array}{r} 42 \\ +\ 7 \\ \hline 119 \end{array}
$$

$$
\begin{array}{r} 35 \\ +\ 3 \\ \hline 32 \end{array}
\qquad
\begin{array}{r} 44 \\ +\ 8 \\ \hline 36 \end{array}
$$

$$
\begin{array}{r} 56 \\ -\ 7 \\ \hline 63 \end{array}
\qquad
\begin{array}{r} 34 \\ -\ 3 \\ \hline 37 \end{array}
$$

$$
\begin{array}{r} 65 \\ -\ 2 \\ \hline 43 \end{array}
\qquad
\begin{array}{r} 73 \\ -\ 2 \\ \hline 51 \end{array}
$$

$$
\begin{array}{r} {}^{1}38 \\ \times\ 2 \\ \hline 36 \end{array}
\qquad
\begin{array}{r} {}^{1}45 \\ \times\ 3 \\ \hline 45 \end{array}
$$

$$
\begin{array}{r} {}^{2}26 \\ \times\ 4 \\ \hline 164 \end{array}
\qquad
\begin{array}{r} {}^{2}35 \\ \times\ 5 \\ \hline 255 \end{array}
$$

$$
\begin{array}{r} 11 \\ 7\overline{)98} \end{array}
\qquad
\begin{array}{r} 21 \\ 4\overline{)96} \end{array}
$$

$$
\begin{array}{r} 16 \\ 6\overline{)636} \end{array}
\qquad
\begin{array}{r} 18 \\ 5\overline{)540} \end{array}
$$

Errors Due to Failure in Mastering the Concept of Zero

This type of error is self-evident in the following examples.

$$
\begin{array}{r} 20 \\ \times\ 4 \\ \hline 84 \end{array}
\qquad
\begin{array}{r} 400 \\ \times\ 7 \\ \hline 2877 \end{array}
$$

$$
\begin{array}{r}
\overset{2}{5}07 \\
\times\ 4 \\
\hline
2068
\end{array}
$$

$$
\begin{array}{r}
\overset{2}{5}07 \\
\times\ 4 \\
\hline
2088
\end{array}
$$

Now that we have covered students' error patterns in arithmetic computation and seen how those patterns reflect erroneous strategies, and you've also tried to think about how you might have taught to avoid such error patterns developing, it is time to give you an ominous bit of information. Unless students' erroneous strategies are corrected through suitable remediation, their problems in arithmetic computation will persist. Hence, if you are a teacher and you encounter a student who *consistently* obtains about 50% accuracy in his or her arithmetic assignments, that red light bulb in your head should be flashing! *Arithmetic computation problem alert!* You may have a student with a potential problem here! Scrutinize his or her assignments in search of clear and consistent error patterns. If found, conduct an informal assessment to pinpoint his or her erroneous strategy in arithmetic computation, and follow up with appropriate remediation till overlearning is reached. Remember why you need to devote time to ensure overlearning in this student? If you forget, return to the previous section of this chapter. (Don't worry, no penalty for forgetting. Just make sure you learn the information after you have located it.)

Informal Assessment of Arithmetic Computation Problems

When we need more in-depth and specific information on a student's arithmetic computation problem, we typically resort to informal assessments. This is because formal or standardized assessments, such as the Peabody Individual Achievement Test (PIAT), while providing breadth in sampling various kinds of arithmetic computations, may only contain one item in the area (or of the type) where our student is failing. Thus, to map out more comprehensively the nature of the student's failed item, we need to generate many more items or problems like the one that he or she has failed in the formal or standardized test. This is where informal assessment comes into play.

Let's assume that you have a student who consistently attains between 40–50% in arithmetic performance in subtractions of two-digit problems involving regrouping. Upon diligently examining his homework assignments, you observe a consistent and distinct error pattern in which he never regroups when necessary, rather he simply subtracts from the larger digit, for example:

$$\begin{array}{r} 32 \\ -19 \\ \hline 27 \end{array}$$

To proceed to an informal assessment of this student's computation problem, construct two sets of five problems involving subtractions of two-digit sums that necessitate regrouping (borrowing). Each set of five problems should be neatly presented on an 8 × 11 in. piece of blank paper. Pay attention to the spacing of them. They should be evenly spaced, not bunched together on the upper half of the piece of paper, for example.

Provide a quiet corner for the student's informal assessment. Say to him or her that you'd like him or her to do the five problems for you. Watch his or her performance closely but quietly. After he or she has completed two problems, stop the student. Say to him or her: "Now I'd like you to say out loud what you are thinking as you continue to do problems 3, 4, and 5." Listen carefully to the student's thinking aloud. You want to see if his or her thought processes confirm your hunch on his or her erroneous strategy in the computation procedure.

If you are satisfied with the results of the first set of five problems in your informal assessment (i.e., you have gathered sufficient information on the student's erroneous strategy—you understand how he or she got the wrong answers), and have confirmed your hunch about it, you can stop and not use the second set of five problems. However, if you are in doubt regarding the nature of the student's erroneous strategy, or your hunch about it, then use the second set of problems. But be sure to give the student at least a 5-minute break in between the two sets of five problems in your informal assessment!

Informal Assessment of Arithmetic Computation Problems in Students with Learning Disabilities

At the start of this chapter, I pointed out that not very much research has been done on arithmetic or mathematics problems in students with learning disabilities, but that sufficient information exists regarding error patterns in normally achieving children (Ashlock, 1976). Extant research literature comparing students with learning disabilities and normally achieving students indicate quantitative rather than qualitative differences between their task performances (i.e., they simply make *more* errors of the same types than normally achieving children). Hence, we can legitimately use the information on error patterns in arithmetic computation found in normally achieving children to identify and diagnose computation problems in children with learning disabilities. However, we must add to the informal assessment procedure described above the following questions:

1. Does the student with learning disabilities have conceptual or computational problems or both?
2. How do processing problems figure in this student's arithmetic problem? (Processing problems in understanding the problem, interpreting the problem, memory problems that impede computations involving timetables, etc.)

These additional questions remind you to consider the role played by the characteristics of students with learning disabilities in their arithmetic computation problems, and make good our adaptation of an informal assessment procedure originally used with normally achieving students. To elaborate, we can promote comprehension of a given story problem by asking the student with learning disabilities to first explain it to us. Then where he or she hesitates or informs us of incomprehension, we can provide the needed help. Another way is to ask him or her to draw what he or she has understood from the given story problem or word problem.

Remediation of Arithmetic Problems

Similarly in remediation of arithmetic computation problems in students with learning disabilities, we adapt effective instructional and/or remedial methods with normally achieving students. In our adaptation, we focus on designing effective prompts to ease memory load in students with learning disabilities. For example, for a student with learning disabilities who has just been taught the computational procedure of long division, we may use a large index card measuring 8 by 5 in., on which a display of the computational procedure is shown step-by-step in one column, and a display of verbal statements corresponding to each computational step is shown in an adjacent column. The computational steps shown should come from the same demonstration example used in the teacher's instruction. Thus, on the *same* side of this large index card, the student with learning disabilities sees the long-division problem that the teacher has just explained and taught him or her, each computational step is laid out clearly before him or her, with the accompanying verbal statements typed right next to it in the adjacent column. The student can refer to this prompt card whenever she or he needs to, as she or he tackles long division problems in the assignment during remediation. Laminating the prompt card increases its durability. Permitting the student to put his or her name to it, and keep it is his or her folder gives the student ownership and responsibility of its safe-keeping.

For detailed information on remediation of students' arithmetic computation problems, see Ashlock (1976); for remediation of similar problems in arithmetic and mathematics in students with learning disabilities, see Mastropieri and Scruggs (1987, pp. 205–258); Bos and Vaughn (1988, pp. 221–253); and Fair (1988, pp. 340–377 and 379–415). In the event that you are unclear about the distinction between two commonly used terms, arithmetic and mathematics, here is a clarifying explanation. Arithmetic is generally understood to refer to skills in computation in addition, subtraction, multiplication, and division. Mathematics on the other hand, "is broader in definition, including arithmetic as well as numeration, number systems, fractions, decimals, problem solving, geometry, measurement, time, money, algebra, calculus, and interpretation of charts, tables, and graphs" (Mastropieri & Scruggs, 1987, p. 205).

Empirical Approaches to Mathematics Instruction with Adolescents with Learning Disabilities

Although one can find research studies in mathematics instruction involving adolescents with learning disabilities in *The Journal of Learning Disabilities, Learning Disabilities Research & Practice,* and *Learning Disability Quarterly,* I'd like to describe two empirically substantiated instructional approaches because of their uniqueness. They are Nancy Hutchinson's (1986) doctoral study on teaching adolescents with learning disabilities algebraic word problems, and Marjorie Montague's research. Although Hutchinson published her study in 1993 in *Learning Disabilities Quarterly,* I have her permission to reproduce materials here that greatly facilitate teacher use and empirical replications of her teaching strategy. Hutchinson's research was unique in that she put to test a very sound instructional approach advanced by Mayer (1985) in teaching mathematics problem solving. Mayer (1985) proposed a two-step approach that involves first teaching problem representation, and then problem solution. It basically corresponds to teaching declarative knowledge followed by procedural knowledge. Hutchinson (1986) validated this two-step approach in teaching algebraic word problems to adolescents with learning disabilities.

In her intervention procedures, Hutchinson (1986) first performed a cognitive task analysis on the type of problem to be taught. Such task analyses enabled her to map out (as much as possible) the cognitive processes to be activated that would result in students learning the three algebraic problem types targeted for instruction. These cognitive task analyses served as broad blueprints in her instruction. Tables 6, 7, and 8 contain Hutchinson's cognitive task analyses of relational and proportional problems, and two-variables two-equations problems. They are reproduced here with her generous cooperation.

Hutchinson (1988) also designed several scripts; one for orienting students to the task, another general script for helping students to learn general knowledge and vocabulary about word problems and to relate them to extant knowledge. More specific scripts focused on teaching students construction of problem representation and, subsequently, solution of the problem pertaining to the type of word problem being taught. There was also an instructional script to acquaint students with the structured worksheet both she and they would be using.

The Orientation Script was used on the first day of instruction with the adoles-

Table 6 Task Analysis and Problem Solution of Relational Problems[a,b]

Problem representation	Problem solution
1. Read problem aloud.	8. Check to be certain that an equation has been written.
2. Evoke schema (kind of problem identified by relational statement).	9. Simplify equation by doing work to remove brackets.
3. Draw and label diagram showing implicit relationships (sum or difference of two unknown but related quantities represented concretely).	10. Combine like terms (combine unknowns).
4. Write goal.	11. By applying inverse operation to both sides of equation, remove term added to or subtracted from unknown.
5. Write unknown (let X = simplest unknown; elaboration of X = related but more complex unknown).	12. By applying inverse operation to both sides of equation, remove term that multiplies or divides the unknown.
6. Write knowns (sum or difference, and relational statement).	13. State equation in terms of $X =$ __
7. Represent problem in equation (abstract unknowns inserted into equation whose form is isomorphic to diagram).	14. Refer to goal for meaningfulness.
	15. Write statement(s) meeting goal(s).
	16. Check accuracy of answer(s) by checking consistency with knowns and substituting into equation.

[a] The novice may write the goal, unknowns, and knowns prior to evoking schema and making diagram. The novice will reread the problem frequently, whereas the more experienced solver will carry out quick lookbacks.
[b] Reproduced with permission from N. Hutchinson (1986).

Table 7 Task Analysis and Problem Solution of Proportion Problems[a,b]

Problem representation	Problem solution
1. Read problem aloud.	8. Check to be certain that an equation has been written.
2. Evoke schema (kind of problem identified by complete and incomplete ratios comparing two factors).	9. Simplify equation by doing work to remove brackets.
3. Draw and label diagram showing implicit relationships (given ratio set equal to ratio for new case with labels for all terms, and concrete representation).	10. Cross-multiply, or apply inverse operation to both sides of equation to reduce one side to 1.
4. Write goal.	11. By applying inverse operation to both sides of equation, remove term that multiplies or divides the unknown.
5. Write unknown (let X = unknown term in incomplete ratio).	12. State equation in terms of $X =$ __
6. Write knowns (given ratio, and one term of new case).	13. Refer to goal for meaningfulness.
7. Represent problem in equation (abstract unknown inserted into equation whose form is isomorphic to diagram).	14. Write statement(s) meeting goal(s).
	15. Check accuracy of answer(s) by checking consistency with knowns and substituting into equation.

[a] The novice may write the goal, unknowns, and knowns prior to evoking schema and making diagram. The novice will reread the problem frequently, whereas the more experienced solver will carry out quick lookbacks.
[b] Reproduced with permission from N. Hutchinson (1986).

Table 8   Task Analysis and Problem Solution of Two-Variable Two-Equation Problems[a,b]

Problem representation	Problem solution
1. Read problem aloud. 2. Evoke schema (kind of problem identified by need for two variables and need for two equations). 3. Draw chart showing implicit relationships (sum of two simple unknowns equal to total of simplest factor; sum of two quantities dependent on simple unknowns equal to total of complex factor, with labels for terms). 4. Write goal. 5. Write unknown. Let $X =$ one unknown, $Y =$ other unknown. 6. Write knowns (the two sums). 7. Represent problem in two equations. First is a statement involving simple unknowns. Second is derived from first equation combined with prior knowledge.	8. Check to be certain two equations have been written. 9. Set up table with two simple unknowns, their total, two complex terms involving unknowns, and their total across the top, with labels on each line. 10. Fill in the table with terms that sum to the simple total. Complete the table. Check outcome for complex total against that listed at top of column. Describe outcome as low or high or correct. 11. Select new values for unknowns based on whether result was too low or too high. Complete the table and check outcome against that listed at top of column. Describe outcome as low, high, or correct. 12. Repeat step 11 until outcome is correct. 13. Refer to goal for meaningfulness. 14. Write statements meeting goals. 15. Check accuracy of answer(s) by checking consistency with knowns and substituting into equation.

[a] The novice may write the goal, unknowns, and knowns prior to evoking schema and making diagram. The novice will reread the problem frequently, whereas the more experienced solver will carry out quick lookbacks.
[b] Reproduced with permission from N. Hutchinson (1986).

cent with learning disabilities. In it, Hutchinson focused on explaining to the student various possible reasons for the difficulties with word problems. These range from insufficient care in reading the information contained in the given word problem to inadequate understanding (incomplete representation) of it, failure to break it down into manageable steps, such as representation and solution, to solving the equation. Hutchinson took pains to explain to the adolescents with learning disabilities the relationships between each of these difficulties. For example, careless reading of a word problem impedes their understanding of it. Incomplete understanding in turn would adversely affect their ability to produce the proper equation for the word problem. She concluded the orientation by informing the students that they would learn a self-questioning strategy that comprised a list of questions to guide them in constructing proper understanding (representation) and solving the word problems.

The function of the general script about word problems was to focus students on important pieces of information, and to avoid being distracted by nonessential information in a word problem. For example, Hutchinson pointed out that each problem type has its own specific form, which has its own predictable characteristics. On the other hand, all of them have or can involve nonspecific characteristics such as money, age, distance, and so on. Using this general script, she taught students to understand the need to hone in on important information in the word problem, and to decide what type of word problem with which they were presented.

Subsequently, using specific instructional scripts for each problem type, Hutchinson taught the adolescents with learning disabilities first to construct appropriate problem representation (i.e., their complete and proper understanding of the problem). She encouraged them to demonstrate their understanding verbally or through drawing of a picture. Only when they had attained criterion here would she continue to the next phase of instructing them on solving the problem (solving the equation that they had constructed as a result of their complete understanding of the problem, i.e., derived from problem representation).

Tables 9, 10, and 11 contain Hutchinson's (1986) instructional scripts for three types of word problems taught: Relational, proportional, two-variables two-equations.

With each problem type, Hutchinson began her instruction by modeling for the student with learning disabilities how she would approach the given problem. She used thinking aloud to share with the student her thoughts, to show what statements in the problem to focus on in constructing a proper problem representation, and how self-questioning played a vital role in guiding her construction (complete understanding of the problem). She would think aloud for two problems, then watched the student do the third, prompting and guiding student and ensuring the student used think-alouds. For the fourth and fifth problems, the student did them alone. She or he would think aloud as she or he proceeded. But as training progressed, students did their work silently. The same instructional procedure applied in Hutchinson's instruction of problem solution. Student learning was greatly facilitated by the use of structured worksheets. Tables 12 and 13 present the Self-Questioning Strategy and examples of structured worksheets for the three problem types.

Hutchinson was very successful in teaching adolescents with learning disabilities those three types of algebraic word problems. In her 1986 dissertation study, she taught 12 such adolescents from grades 8, 9, and 10. There were seven females and five males. All were taught individually. Hutchinson has since replicated her study in the classroom and on a much larger scale. I have singled out her thesis study because the instructional approach she used demonstrated effective applications of the tenets of instructional psychology.

I turn now to describe another recent instructional approach in mathematics with middle school and junior high students with learning disabilities: the work of Marjorie Montague. Why her instructional approach is unique lies in several aspects: (a) Montague uses a very comprehensive instructional approach, which comprises

Table 9   Task Analyses of Relational Problem Types in Algebraic Word Problems[a]

Teaching representation for relational problems	Teaching solution for relational problems

The first type of problem we are going to study I have called RELATIONAL. In each of these problems you will find a relational statement. Finding a relational statement will help you to identify a problem as a relational problem. A relational statement is a sentence that tells you about one thing you don't know (or one unknown quantity) in terms of its relationship to something else that you don't know (another unknown quantity). For example, a problem may say that I am twice as old as you. Does this problem say how old you are? (Student is expected to say no.) Does it say how old I am? (Student is expected to say no.) But it does tell us that one thing we don't know is twice as much as something we don't know. This is what I mean when I say that one unknown (my age) is expressed in terms of its relationship to another unknown (your age, which has not been given either).

Let's consider another example. A relational problem contains the statement that Jane has $4 more than Mary. Do we know how much money Jane has? Do we know how much money Mary has? What do we know? That's right, we know that Jane has $4 more. What do we call this kind of statement? What do we call this kind of problem?

In relational problems we are given some additional information about the quantities. For example, we may be told that the sum of our ages is 45. That means that when we add the two unknown ages together we will get 45. This information will help us to write an equation or a true mathematical sentence about the quantities in the problem. Or we may be told that the difference between two unknowns is 20. In this case we would know that if we write down the larger quantity minus the smaller quantity equals 20, we will get a true mathematical sentence or equation.

You have written an equation. You will be working to find the values of the unknowns or letters in this equation. That is your subgoal. Your real goal is to answer the question that you wrote down beside GOAL on the worksheet. You want to find the goal. And write a sentence that answers that question.

The equation that you wrote helps you to do that. But an equation is a special sentence. It says that the left side is equal to the right side. This is like a delicately balanced scale. Think about the balances that you have used in science: (hold out hands to show an equal-arm balance). If you place more weight on one side of a scale, then what must you do to make both sides equal again? Right, add the same amount to the other side.

Equations are like this, too. Whatever you do to one side you must do to the other side. Because the two sides are equal. If you add anything to the equation from outside, take anything away, or multiply or divide one side of the equation by a number that you introduce, then you must be certain to do the same thing to both sides of the equation. Remember that the equation is like the equal arm balance.

When you are adding terms that are already in an equation, there are a couple of things you must remember. You can only add terms that are like each other. You have heard the expression that you can't add apples and oranges. Well you can't add $X + 2$ and get 3. $1X + 2X = 3X$ and $1 + 2 = 3$, but $X + 2$ is $X + 2$. That is why we will be trying to isolate the unknowns, that is get all the X's together on one side of the equation. Then we can say $3X = 30$, or something like that. After that it is easy to find the value of $1X$. Usually we add and subtract before we multiply and divide in solving these equations. You could see in what I was showing you that we need to collect all the X's together in order to find the value of each one.

(continues)

Table 9   *(Continued)*

Teaching representation for relational problems	Teaching solution for relational problems
How can we figure out what two things are that we don't know, if we have the relational statement and the total? Remember I told you about using a letter to take the place of something you don't know. In relational problems we usually let the simplest unknown equal X or Y or any other letter you like. Let's say that X stands for your age which we don't know. If I am twice as old, I must be 2 times X years old. That is because twice means 2 times and 2 times X is $2X$. In relational problems we let the letter stand for the simplest unknown. Then we state the second unknown in terms of its relationshiip (relational statement) to the first unknown.	I want to remind you about operations that are the opposite or obverse of each other. If you add 3 to your money, how can you get back to what you had to start with? Right, you subtract 3. If you multiply what you have by 5 and then want to undo that operation, what must you do? Right, divide by 5. In solving our equations we will frequently be using the opposite operation after we have collected (added, subtracted) like terms.
Suppose the simplest unknown was X and the other was 30 more. What is 30 more than X? $X + 30$ is 30 more than X. If a man is 7 years younger than X how old is he? $X - 7$.	It will be necessary to check your answer with the goal you stated in the representation when you have finished. Make a sentence to satisfy that goal. Some people highlight their answer by circling or underlining.
The relational statement in a relational problem tells you the relationship between two variables. Sometimes this is a complicated sentence. Try to find the simplest variable and set it equal to X. Then figure out the value of the other variable in relation to X.	Then you must check your answer against what you wrote down that you knew in the representation. Your answer must be consistent with these findings. Is the relational statement still true when you substitute these values into it? If so you are finished, if not check your solution, if problem not found, check your representation, if problem is still not found, ask for assistance.
Now I will show you how to use the self-questions to represent relational problems on the worksheet.	Now I will show you how to use the self-questions to find the solution to relational problems on the worksheet.

[a] Reproduced with permission from N. Hutchinson (1986).

both cognitive and metacognitive strategies. These strategies in turn, embody cognitive and metacognitive processes. (b) Her instructional approach befits the present zeitgeist in mathematical instruction, namely, the emphasis on constructivism and on problem solving. (c) It befits the general zeitgeist in process-based instruction in reading and writing (Wong, 1992).

Do I hear someone wondering aloud what constructivism in mathematics education is all about? Well, constructivism refers to the conceptual view that students actively derive meaning from what they hear, read, and learn. They are not passive recipients of information. They do not passively soak up information doled out by the teachers. Using their prior knowledge, which may sometimes contain miscon-

Table 10   Task Analyses of Proportion Problem Types in Algebraic Word Problems[a]

Teaching representation for proportion problems	Teaching solution for proportion problems
The next type of problems we will work on are proportion problems. They have ratios in them: You often need to compare one quantity with another. You get 9 questions correct on a recent test. There was 10 questions in all on the test. You compare the number correct to the number of questions: 9/10 or 9:10. Both are read as "9 compared to 10" or, for short "9 to 10." 9 and 10 are called the "terms" of the ratio. Sometimes in a problem we have two equivalent ratios. That means that they are equal to each other. Equivalent ratios make up a proportion. For example: $$\frac{9}{10} = \frac{18}{20} = \frac{27}{30}$$ To obtain 18/20 from 9/10, you multiply both the numerator (top) and the denominator (bottom) by 2. How do you obtain 27/30 from 9/10? In proportion problems, you will find one complete ratio such as 4/5, which we will call the given ratio or the ratio. You will also find one incomplete ratio such as something you don't know compared to 25. This will be the new case. Let X take the place of the something you don't know. For example, you have obtained 4/5 problems correct. If there had been 25 problems, and you were just as successful, how many problems would you have had correct? 4/5 is equal to X/25. When you have a complete ratio and an incomplete ratio, then you know that it is a proportion problem. 5 is equal to X compared to 25. Now I will show you how to use the self-questions to represent proportion problems on the worksheets.	A proportion is a mathematical sentence that states that two ratios are equivalent. Using the equivalent ratios $$\frac{2}{5} \text{ and } \frac{6}{15},$$ we may write the proportion 2/5 = 6/15. This proportion may also be expressed as 2:5 = 6:15. The proportion in both forms is read "2 is to 5 as 6 is to 15". There are four terms in a proportion as shown: first → 2 = 6 ← third second → 5 = 15 ← fourth The first term (2) and the fourth term (15) are called the <u>extremes</u>. The second term (5) and the third term (6) are called the <u>means</u>. Observe that the product of the extremes (2 × 15) is equal to the product of the means (5 × 6). In the form $\dfrac{2}{5} = \dfrac{6}{15}$ observe that the cross products are equal. 2 ⤬ 6 5 15 2 × 15 = 5 × 6 If any three of the four terms of the proportion are known quantities, the fourth may be determined. Multiply the numerator of the first fraction by the denominator of the second fraction. Multiply the denominator of the first fraction by the numerator of the second fraction. This is called cross-multiplying. Write one product equal to the other. Then solve the resulting equation. You may use another procedure instead of cross-multiplying.

(continues)

Table 10   *(Continued)*

Teaching representation for proportion problems	Teaching solution for proportion problems
	If $\dfrac{4}{5} = \dfrac{X}{25}$, you may multiply both sides of the equation by the inverse of the complete ratio.
	In this case, multiply $\dfrac{4}{5}$ and $\dfrac{X}{25}$ each by $\dfrac{5}{4}$.
	This will give you $1 = \dfrac{5X}{100}$.
	This means $5X = 100$
	Now you can solve this equation to find the value of X.
	Now I will show you how to use the self-questions to find the solution to proportion problems.

[a] Reproduced with permission from N. Hutchinson (1986).

ceptions, they construct meaning from their learning across the curriculum. Constructivism as a conceptual view has dominated education since the 1970s. It has vast implications for those of you who are teachers or student teachers. How should you teach so that you capitalize on students' propensity for constructing their own meanings while learning? How do you eradicate misconceptions from their prior knowledge?

For those of you puzzling over the term *process-based instruction,* read Wong (1992). It is a very short article. You can read it over coffee and a big piece of cake or pie! Briefly, it refers to teaching the cognitive and metacognitive processes that underlie a particular concept or skill. For students to learn a concept or skill, they need you, the teachers, to inform them of these processes and to demonstrate through modeling their activation.

Moreover, like Hutchinson (1986, 1993), Montague's instructional approach has been empirically validated, both involving individualized and small group instruction of adolescents with learning disabilities. It reflects 10 years of research.

To summarize, Montague's instructional approach in mathematics instruction with adolescents with learning disabilities involves teaching those adolescents various cognitive and metacognitive strategies. Specifically, she targets for instruction the following cognitive strategies: READ (by this she means student's reading comprehension of the given math problem); PARAPHRASE (student translates for his

Table 11   Task Analyses of Two-Variable Two-Education Problem-Types in Algebraic Word Problems[a]

Teaching representation of two-variable two-equation problems	Teaching solution for two variable two-equation problems
These new problems, our third type, are called two-variable, two-equation problems. That is because in order to represent and solve them you will need to use two variables or two unknowns. Let one of the things that you don't know equal X. Let the other equal Y. You will read over the problem and find that there are two relatively simple unknowns, such as the number of dimes and the number of quarters. And you will also find that you know the total of these two unknowns, such as 15 coins in all. That means $X + Y = 15$. However, there will be more information given in the problem. This additional information will enable you to write a second equation. The unknown quantities in this second equation will be more complex. For example, instead of just having numbers of coins, you may find that you have the total value of the coins. In order to write an equation it will be necessary to use the information given in the problem and information that you already have in your head. You know there are X dimes. How much is each dime worth? Right—10 cents. How can you find the value of X dimes? Right—multiply X by 10 cents. You will get $10X$ cents. Now how many quarters did we say we had? And how much is each quarter worth? How much are Y quarters worth? You can see that $10X + 25Y$ cents will equal the total amount of money given in the problem. That will be your second equation.	Now, we have two equations, each containing the same unknowns, say X and Y. These are much more complex problems than we have solved before. To do the solution for our first two kinds of problems (relational and proportion) we learned an algorithm that worked for each kind of problem. Sometimes you will come across a complicated problem or a new kind of problem. In these cases you may not know an algorithm or a set of steps for solving the equation. We are going to learn a new procedure that you can always try once you have written the equation(s). This is especially helpful for unfamiliar problems. This procedure is called systematic trial-and-error. You try numbers—not just any numbers. You choose them for a reason. And you keep a record of the numbers you try, the results you obtain, and the outcome. Did the numbers satisfy the two equations? Was the result too large, or too small? In order to keep the record it will be necessary to draw a chart. The chart will have headings for X, Y, and the values in the second equation, along with totals. We will try this procedure in a two-variable two-equation problem, so you can see how it works.

(continues)

or her own understanding the verbal information in the math problem by stating the problem in his or her words); VISUALIZE (student forms a mental picture of his or her understanding of the math problem); HYPOTHESIZE (student develops a plan to solve the given problem); ESTIMATE (student predicts the answer); COMPUTE (student proceeds to solve the problem); and CHECK (student self-

Table 11   *(Continued)*

Teaching representation of two-variable two-equation problems	Teaching solution for two variable two-equation problems
These new problems will require two variables (*X* and *Y*) and two equations—the simplest equation will involve *X* and *Y*. The more complex equation will involve derived values that include *X* in one case and *Y* in the other case. There will be two totals given in these problems. And you will have to use two unknowns. These problems may be about age, work, distance, and numbers, as well as money. Suppose you got one book each year and your friend got two books each year. We know the total number of books the two of you have and the total of your ages. Then we could use two variables. We could write two equations—one telling a true sentence about the total number of years. The other telling a true sentence about the total number of books. That would be a two-variable two-equation problem. Let's try some now. Remember to watch for two quantities that will have to be represented by unknowns. Remember to watch for two totals that you can use to write equations.	

[a] Reproduced with permission from N. Hutchinson (1986).

Table 12   Self-Questioning Strategy in Guiding Students' Problem Representation and Solution[a]

Self-questions for problem representation
1. Have I read and understood each sentence? Are there any words whose meaning I have to ask?
2. Have I got the whole picture, a representation for this problem?
3. Have I written down my representation on the worksheet? (goal; unknown(s); known(s); type of problem; equation)
4. What problem features should I focus on in a new problem so I can know whether I can use the representation I have been taught?

Self-questions for problem solution
1. Have I written an equation?
2. Have I expanded the terms?
3. Have I written out the steps of my solution on the worksheet? (collected like terms; isolated unknown(s); solved for unknown(s); checked my answer with the goal; highlighted my answer)?
4. What problem features should I focus on in a new problem so I can know whether I can use the solution I have been taught?

[a] Reproduced with permission from N. Hutchinson (1986).

Table 13   Examples of Exercises in Three types of Algebraic Word Problems[a]

Relation problem exercises
1. Mike has cycled 13 more km than Sam. Together they have cycled 121 km. Find the number of km Mike has cycled.
2. The sum of two numbers is eight, and one of them is two greater than the other. Find the numbers.
3. Jean gave twice as much money to the Red Cross as Ann did. If the sum of their gifts was $2.13, how much did each give?
4. Ellen is 7 years older than her sister, and the sum of their ages is 21 years. How old is Ellen's sister?
5. A grocer packs 70 kg of cookies. There are 28 more kg of chocolate cookies than peanut butter cookies. Find the number of kg of chocolate cookies he packed.

Proportion problem exercises
1. The ratio of the age of a boy to a girl was 7:6. If the age of the girl was 126 months, find the age of the boy.
2. A machine produces 9 items in 5 hours. How many items will it produce in 20 hours?
3. Of every 15 km I run, I wear weights for 11 km. If I run 330 km, how many km will I run wearing weights?
4. Find the regular price of a suit that sold for $41.25 at a 25% reduction.
5. Last baseball season the number of times John went up to bat was 30. In those 30 times at bat, John got 18 hits. What percent of John's times at bat resulted in hits?

Two-variable two-equation problem exercises
1. I drove my bike and walked for a total of 3 hours. I went at a rate of 30 km/hr on my bike and 5 km/hr walking. The total distance was 65 km. Find how far I walked.
2. John packed 10 crates in all. Each big crate costs $1,000. Each small crate costs $600. The total value of the crates he packed was $4,200. How many crates of each size did he pack?
3. The sum of a woman's age and her daughter's age is 35. If the woman has made three friends every year and her daughter has made two friends every year, find the number of friends the woman has made. In all, the two of them have made 99 friends.
4. A number of cars took the 24 passengers to the picnic. There were some cars that held 6 people and some that held 2 people. If there were 8 cars, how many of them held 6 people? (all the cars were full.)
5. Ann has $75 in $5 bills and $10 bills. She has 12 bills in all. How many $10 bills does she have?

---

[a] Reproduced with permission from N. Hutchinson (1986).

checks what has been done to ensure that proper computations have been performed).

The metacognitive strategies that are targeted for instruction include SELF-QUESTION (strategy knowledge and use); SELF-INSTRUCT (strategy knowledge and use); and SELF-MONITOR (strategy control) (Montague, in press). These two sets of strategies are designed to help adolescents with learning disabilities to solve one-, two-, and three-step mathematical word problems. Table 14 presents the cognitive–metacognitive strategy designed by Montague to facilitate students' mathematical problem solving.

Montague's instructional program contains three components: (a) assessment, (b)

Examples of Structured Worksheets (Relation Problem)[a]

Problem _____   Date _____   Name _____

Exercise   *Relat.*_____   Exp. Phase _____   Session _____   Ob. _____

Goal: *To find how far the child drove.*_____

What I don't know: *Let distance child drove = X km*_____
                        Distance Dad drove = X + 320 km

What I know: *Dad drove 320 km farther than son*
                Total distance driven = 1546

I can write/say this problem in my own words or draw a picture.

Kind of problem: *Relational*_____

Equation:

$$X + X + 320 + 1546$$

Solving the equation:

$$X + X + 320 = 1546$$
$$2X + 320 = 1546$$
$$2X + 320 - 320 = 1546 - 320$$
$$\frac{2X}{2} = \frac{1226}{2} \quad X = 613$$

Dad and I drove to Calgary. It is 1546 km. He drove 320 km farther than I did. How far did I drive?

Solution:
   Child drove 613 km
[compare to goal]

Check: *613*   *933*
            + 320   *+ 613*
             933 (Dad)   *1546*

---

[a]Reproduced with permission from Hutchinson (1986).

Examples of Structured Worksheets (Proportion Problem)[a]

Problem _____   Date _____   Name _____

Exercise   _Prop._____   Exp. Phase _____   Session _____   Ob. _____

Goal: _To find Mrs. Jones's age_____

What I don't know: _Let Mrs. Jones's age = X_____

What I know: Ratio of Mr. Jones's to Mrs. Jones's age is 8:7.
                  Mr. Jones is 96 years old.

I can write/say this problem in my own words or draw a picture.

	Ratio	New Case
Mr. Jones	$\vdash\!\!\frac{8}{}\!\!\dashv$	$\vdash\!\!\frac{96}{}\!\!\dashv$
Mrs. Jones	$\vdash\!\!\frac{7}{}\!\!\dashv$	$\vdash\!\!\frac{X}{}\!\!\dashv$

Kind of problem: _Proportional_____

Equation:

$$\frac{8}{7} = \frac{96}{X}$$

Solving the equation:

$$\frac{8}{7} = \frac{96}{X}$$

$$\frac{\not{8}X}{\not{8}} = \frac{\overset{12}{\not{9}6.7}}{\underset{1}{\not{8}}} \qquad X = 84$$

> The ratio of Mr. Jones's age to Mrs. Jones's age is 8:7. Mr. Jones is 96 years old. Find Mrs. Jones' age.

Solution:
   Mrs. Jones is 84 years old.
[compare to goal]

Check: $\frac{8}{7} = \frac{96}{84}$ $8 \times 12 = 96$

$7 \times 12 = 84$

---

[a]Reproduced with permission from Hutchinson (1986).

Examples of Structured Worksheets (Two-Variable Two-Equation Problem)[a]

Problem _____   Date _____   Name _____

Exercise ___*2-v. 2-e.*___   Exp. Phase _____   Session _____   Ob. _____

Goal: ____*To find the number of goats.*_____

What I don't know: ___*Let X = number of goats*_____

_____ *Let Y = number of ducks*

What I know: *Total number of animals = 15*
                 Total number of feet = 44
                 Goats have 4 feet.
                 Ducks have 2 feet.

I can write/say this problem in my own words or draw a picture.

	goats		ducks		
animals	X	+	Y	=	15
feet	4X	+	2Y	=	44

Kind of problem: ____*2-variable 2-equation*_____

Equation:

$$X + Y = 15$$
$$4X + 2Y = 44$$

Solving the equation:

X	Y	15	4X	2Y	44	outcome
8	7	15	32	14	46	too large
7	8	15	28	16	44	√

Solution:
  There were 7 goats
  and 8 ducks

[compare to goal]

> *There were a number of goats and ducks in one pen, 15 in all. There were 44 feet in the pen. How many goats were there?*

Check:	7	7	8	28	
	+ 8	× 4	× 2	+16	
	15	28	16	44	√

[a]Reproduced with permission from Hutchinson (1986).

Table 14   A Cognitive–Metacognitive Strategy for Mathematical Problem Solving[a]

Read (for understanding)
SAY:	Read the problem. If I don't understand, read it again.
ASK:	Have I read and understood the problem?
CHECK:	For understanding as I solve the problem.

Paraphrase (your own words)
SAY:	Underline the important information.
	Put the problem in my own words.
ASK:	Have I underlined the important information?
	What is the question? What am I looking for?
CHECK:	That the information goes with the question.

Visualize (a picture or a diagram)
SAY:	Make a drawing or a diagram.
ASK:	Does the picture fit the problem?
CHECK:	The picture against the problem information.

Hypothesize (a plan to solve the problem)
SAY:	Decide how many steps and operations are needed.
	Write the operation symbols $(+, -, \times, -)$.
ASK:	If I do . . . , what will I get?
	If I do . . . , then what do I need to do next?
	How many steps are needed?
CHECK:	That the plan makes sense.

Estimate (predict the answer)
SAY:	Round the numbers, do the problem in my head, and write the estimate.
ASK:	Did I round up and down?
	Did I write the estimate?
CHECK:	That I used the important information.

Compute (do the arithmetic)
SAY:	Do the operations in the right order.
ASK:	How does my answer compare with my estmate?
	Does my answer make sense?
	Are the decimals or money signs in the right places?
CHECK:	That all the operations were done in the right order.

Check (make sure everything is right)
SAY:	Check the computation
ASK:	Have I checked every step?
	Have I checked the computation?
	Is my answer right?
CHECK:	That everything is right. If not, go back.
	Then ask for help if I need it.

---

[a] Reproduced from M. Montague (in press). Copyright © PRO-ED, Inc. Reprinted by permission.

explicit instruction, and (c) evaluation. The first component is self-explanatory. Without it, a teacher cannot begin instruction! You tell me why. If you forget the rationale of assessment, review the section on Informal Assessment in Reading. Montague has quite an elaborate assessment procedure that results in a detailed profile of the strengths and weaknesses of the student assessed. Readers interested in her assessment procedures should read the original studies (Montague & Applegate, 1993; Montague, Applegate, & Marquard, 1993).

The second component of instruction included direct instruction: cognitive–behavioral procedures that included modeling, rehearsal, feedback, and mastery tests. These instructional elements reflect the diverse theoretical and empirical influences on Montague. Such influences are widely observed in the work of numerous intervention researchers in learning disabilities.

In the third component of evaluation, Montague directs attention to specific questions on student acquisition, application, maintenance, and generalization of her combined cognitive and metacognitive strategies package. She has been moderately successful in obtaining generalization in her trained adolescents with learning disabilities. She cautions that effective use of her instructional program appears to be constrained by cognitive maturity in the trainees. Apparently, sixth graders with learning disabilities did not profit from it, whereas middle school and junior high students with learning disabilities did.

REFLECTIONS

Readers, do you not find children's error patterns in arithmetic computation fascinating? Do you not wonder how they develop such error patterns? Perhaps some of you are muttering under your breath that their error patterns come about because of teacher disability?

Indeed, to some extent, teachers must accept the responsibility in children's development of erroneous strategies in arithmetic computations. Nevertheless, we must refrain from being too harsh or judgmental towards teachers because if we accept the tenets and importance of constructivism in mathematics learning, then learners too, must share the responsibility in their own development of erroneous strategies in arithmetic computation. For in their own active learning, they might have misconstrued teachers' words and instructions. Moreover, they might have brought misconceptions from their prior knowledge to bear on the teachers' lessons in arithmetic or mathematics.

In my view, it is unprofitable to assign blame to children's development of erroneous strategies in arithmetic computations. Rather, from extant computation error patterns compiled by mathematics researchers such as Ashlock (1976), we should learn where children's arithmetic learning appears to be most vulnerable to misunderstanding, and susceptible to developing errors in computational procedures. For example, a scrutiny of error patterns involving misapplications of regrouping suggests the need to emphasize in the lesson on regrouping *when* it should occur. This way children would learn to discriminate among the conditions in which they should regroup in addition and subtraction, as well as execute correctly the computational procedure in regrouping.

Moving to mathematics learning in students in upper elementary grades or middle school and in high school, there appears to be an increasing preference in using a process-based instructional approach that attends to both cognitive and metacognitive processes. Mathematics learning for these students, especially those in high school, frequently demands problem solving in the form of word problems in many areas (e.g., algebra, geometry). The more explicit teachers inform and model for students the cognitive processes that underlie successful problem solutions in given algebraic or other mathematics problems, the more they facilitate student learning. To the extent possible, teachers should think aloud their thought processes as they solve word problems. In thinking aloud, they model explicitly the kinds of cognitive processes that students should activate in their own heads. Additional metacognitive components of self-checking, self-monitoring, and self-evaluating help make students with and without learning disabilities into autonomous, self-regulated learners.

Finally, we need to continue our research in effective instructional strategies to teach arithmetic (e.g., computations; multiplication tables; addition and subtraction facts, etc.) and mathematics (e.g., algebra, geometry, etc.) to students with learning disabilities. To be effective, these strategies must accommodate their processing problems (i.e., match their characteristics).

References

Ashlock, R. B. (1976). *Error patterns in computation: A semi-programmed approach* (2nd ed.). Columbus, OH: Charles E. Merrill.

Bos, C. S., & Vaughn, S. (1988). *Strategies for teaching students with learning and behavior problems.* Boston, MA: Allyn & Bacon.

Cox, L. S. (1975). Diagnosing and remediating systematic errors in addition and subtraction computations. *The Arithmetic Teacher, 22*(2), 151–157.

Fair, G. W. (1988). Mathematics instruction in junior and senior high school. In D. Kim Reid (Ed.), *Teaching the learning disabled: A cognitive developmental approach* (pp. 378–415). Boston, MA: Allyn & Bacon.

Hutchinson, N. L. (1986). *Instruction of representation and solution in algebraic problem solving with learning disabled adolescents.* Unpublished doctoral thesis, Simon Fraser University, Burnaby, B.C.

Hutchinson, N. L. (1993). Effects of cognitive strategy instruction on algebra problem solving of adolescents with learning disabilities. *Learning Disability Quarterly, 16*(1), 34–63.

Mastropieri, M. A., & Scruggs, T. E. (1987). *Effective instruction for special education.* Boston, MA: Little, Brown and Company, Inc.

Mayer, R. E. (1985). Mathematical ability. In R. J. Sternberg (Ed.), *Human abilities: An information-processing approach* (pp. 127–150). New York: Freeman.

Montague, M. (in press). Cognitive strategy instruction in mathematics for students with learning disabilities. *Journal of Learning Disabilities.*

Montague, M., & Applegate, B. (1993). Mathematical problem-solving characteristics of middle school students with learning disabilities. *The Journal of Special Education, 27,* 175–201.

Montague, M., Applegate, B., & Marquard, K. (1993). Cognitive strategy instruction and mathematical problem-solving performance of students with learning disabilities. *Learning Disabilities Research & Practice, 8,* 223–232.

Wong, B. Y. L. (1992). On cognitive process-based instruction: An introduction. *Journal of Learning Disabilities, 25,* 150–152.

9

Assessment and Instruction of Writing Skills

Developing writing skills in students has always been a major interest and concern among teachers and educational researchers. Although there has been research in students' writing or composing skills in the past, more focused research appeared in the 1970s. Parallel interests in the writing skills in students with learning disabilities appeared sporadically in the 1970s, while more programmatic research began to appear in the 1980s. Thus far, research informs us that the composing problems of students with learning disabilities go beyond mechanical ones such as spelling, punctuation, and grammar (Poteet, 1978; Houck & Billingsley, 1989) to include higher-order cognitive and metacognitive problems (Newcomer & Barenbaum, 1991). Specifically, they lack knowledge of the writing process and metacognition about writing, such as what writing is about, its purpose, and what constitutes a good writer (Englert & Thomas, 1987; Graham, Schwartz, & MacArthur, 1993; Wong, Wong, & Blenkinsop, 1989).

The research information on the nature of composing problems in students with learning disabilities led to various attempts at designing assessment tools and interventions. I shall first focus on assessment tools, and then on writing strategies that have been empirically validated.

Formal Assessments of Writing or Composing Skills

Pro-Ed have published two very good standardized writing assessment tests: The Test of Written Language (TOWL) and the Test of Adolescent Language (TOAL). The TOWL is designed for assessing writing skills in elementary school students, and the TOAL in high school students. Moreover, the TOAL is very discriminating in that results from its subtests can reliably separate normally achieving adolescents from those with learning disabilities. The two subtests of Writing Vocabulary and Writing Grammar are routinely used by intervention researchers for obtaining screening (pretraining) measures in their students with learning disabilities, in order to show that these students perform poorly therein, and hence would profit from writing strategy instruction.

The strength of TOWL-2 as an assessment tool for writing in elementary students resides in its comprehensiveness: It covers both aspects of contrived and spontaneous writing in students. In contrived writing, specific component skills are assessed in isolation and general quality of student writing is ignored. Moreover, students are assigned a more passive role. In contrast, spontaneous writing assesses students' abilities to communicate meaningfully. Students assume a more active role in generating writing, spelling, and use of punctuation. Readers will readily understand the difference between these two kinds of writing, contrived versus spontaneous, as you read the following paragraph. The main point to grasp now is that testers obtain more limited information on a student's writing skills from (sub)tests in contrived writing. They need complementary information from students' functional performance in spontaneous writing to form a more comprehensive and precise idea of their writing skills.

The TOWL-2 contains 10 subtests: 5 assess Contrived Writing, and 5 address Spontaneous Writing. Contrived Writing consists of Vocabulary, Spelling, Style, Logical Sentences, and Sentence Combination. Spontaneous Writing consists of Thematic Maturity, Contextual Vocabulary, Syntactic Maturity, Contextual Spelling, and Contextual Style. A few examples between subtests in Contrived Writing and Spontaneous Writing would suffice to illustrate and explain the differential task demands on students. On Vocabulary, in Contrived Testing, a student is given a stimulus word that he or she must use in a sentence. There are 30 words in this vocabulary subtest, some examples of which include might, pastel, dazzle, heathen, jocular, obdurate. In Spontaneous Writing, a student's score in the subtest Contextualized Vocabulary is derived from the number of different words used in his or her written story that contains seven or more letters. The test developers provide ample guidelines on how to locate such vocabulary in the student's story, as well as what to include and exclude as seven-letter words (see Hammill & Larsen, 1988, p. 35). The story from which the tester obtains the Contextualized Vocabulary score is one that the student has written in response to one of two given pictures that depict either a prehistoric or a futuristic scene.

In the subtests on Spelling and Style in Contrived Writing, the tester dictates sentences to students. Subsequently, the tester scores student accuracy in spelling and punctuation. Two separate scores result from the scoring: one for Spelling, the other for Style. There are 25 items to this subtest on spelling. In the corresponding subtests in Spontaneous Writing, a student's raw score for Contextual Spelling is the number of words correctly spelled in his or her written story. This number in turn comes from subtracting the number of words misspelled from the total number of words in his or her story. The student is scored in Contextual Style on a three-point scale. For any punctuation or capitalization rule found in his or her written story, he or she can get either 1, 2, or 3 points. Specifically, using a period at the end of a sentence earns the student 1 point, whereas using a colon correctly before a series earns him or her 3 points. Again, the test developers have provided ample guidelines and help in scoring here (see Hammill & Larsen, 1988, p. 37).

I shall describe briefly the remaining subtests in TOWL-2. In the subtest Logical Sentences in Contrived Writing, students are simply asked to rewrite stimulus sentences that contain deliberately planted nonsensical words. Students are asked to remove the nonsensical words and reconstruct the sentence into a sensible one. To help readers obtain a substantial grasp of this subtest, I mention three examples:

(1) John blinked his nose. Student rewrites sentence to make it sensible.
(15) The student is bored is why he dropped out.
(25) Bill likes candy better than Nancy.

In Sentence Combining, students are presented with short stimulus sentences, and instructed to make them into one sentence. In this as well as the Logical Sentences subtest, there are 25 items. Scoring guidelines are provided on pages 22 and 28 of the TOWL-2 manual.

The remaining subtests come under Spontaneous Writing: Thematic and Syntactic Maturity. Thematic Maturity assesses students' ability to write in a logical and orderly manner; their capacity to develop a focused theme, to describe the characters in their stories, and other writing skills such as use of humor and dialogue. Students are given a choice of two pictures about which to write a story: One that presents a prehistoric scene of hunters and prehistoric elephants, the other a futuristic scene of aliens on a planet. Again, the manual provides detailed guidelines on scoring (see pp. 31–36 of TOWL-2).

Syntactic Maturity assesses students' ability to use complex sentences that contain clauses and adjectival or adverbial phrases. Testers peruse the students' written stories to denote grammatical errors. Careful attendance and adherence to scoring guidelines are necessary to produce raw scores of student performance. Fortunately, the test developers have attended to the needs of testers (see p. 36 of TOWL-2 manual).

Clearly, the TOWL-2 provides a very thorough assessment of elementary students' writing skills. For those interested in using parts of it for research purposes (for example, in doing master's or Ph.D. research on writing with students with learning disabilities and control comparison students without learning disabilities in grades 2–7), you can use Thematic Maturity and Syntactic Maturity subtests (see Thomas, 1993).

The Writing Vocabulary (WV) subtest in TOAL-2 assesses students' usage rather than their ability to define words. The test developers, Hammill, Brown, Larsen, and Wiederholt (1980) provide the following rationale in assessment. They had used in test development, three forms of vocabulary assessment: (a) definition of words, (b) using a word in a sentence, and (c) both. They found that the second assessment procedure yielded the highest test reliability. This is the major reason for their choice of word usage in assessing vocabulary in students. Other reasons included ease of administration, and their opinion that a student's word usage rather than its definition provides a more realistic gauge of his or her functional understanding of the word. This subtest contains 30 items, and a dichotomous scoring system, (i.e., items are scored as 0 [incorrect] or 1 point [correct]). The following are sample items of this subtest: brilliant, clay, captivity, solitary, improvised, gaunt.

The Writing Grammar (WG) subtest assesses students' usage of syntax in writing. In designing it, the test developers chose a sentence combination technique, which they think is a favorite instructional activity. Students are given several short sentences and told to make one sentence out of them while incorporating all the important information in the stimulus sentences. This activity requires from students adequate knowledge of syntax ranging from changing tenses, transforming sentences into phrases, to using possessives. This subtest also contains 30 items and is scored on a dichotomous system. Sample items follow.

Item (3) in WG presents three short sentences that students must combine and make into one:

We ran in the race.
It rained.
It was Thursday.

Item (14)

The girls loaded the gear into the car.
They were going on a trip.
It was a fishing trip.

Item (28)

The artist is drawing.
He is skilled.
He is sitting under a tree.

He is watching.
He is watching the players.

Informal Assessment of Writing

Informally, teachers can assess writing skills in a student with learning disabilities by the following procedure. First spend time getting well acquainted with the student, and discover his or her hobbies. Then settle on time, date, and place of testing. Present the student with 5–8 pictures of his hobby. For example, the teacher discovers the ninth-grade male adolescent with learning disabilities loves cars. She would then present him with eight pictures of brand new models of cars that would appeal to him, such as the Acura, Mazda sports cars, the CRX, and so on. She would ask him to choose one of the pictures about which he is to write a paragraph of eight sentences. Similarly, for an eighth-grade female adolescent with learning disabilities who loves fashion, the teacher would present eight pictures of beautiful models modeling the latest teen fashion for the impending season. This adolescent's task would parallel that of the ninth-grade male.

In analyzing writings of the students with learning disabilities, one should note the disproportionate amount of time taken to produce the desired amount of writing; the monotonous and unvarying format of the sentences (usually of this form: subject–predicate); the paucity of vocabulary; poor spelling; occasional grammatical and punctuation errors. Additionally, one should note sentences or parts of sentences that are ambiguous.

Writing Strategies

There are numerous books on teaching writing to elementary school children and high school adolescents. I shall therefore not regurgitate their contents. Rather, I shall venture a new route and concentrate on informing you, my readers, on selected writing strategies that have been validated in intervention research. Notice, I state "selected writing strategies." There are many interventions on writing involving students with learning disabilities. I will describe a few and add three that my research associates and I have recently validated. The intervention strategies that I shall present are chosen on these grounds: (a) They have been designed by recognized, programmatic intervention researchers in writing within the field of learning disabilities. (b) With the exception of the Early Literacy Program, an integrated reading and writing program for grades 1–3, all the writing intervention strategies that I shall describe were in widespread use after the researchers had validated them. The Early Literacy Program (ELP) has just been reported in 1994, and appears to be very promising concerning its use in integrated reading and writing instruction in primary grades.

Early Literacy Program

I begin with an ELP by Carol-Sue Englert and her associates. I choose it for the following reasons: (a) It has a sound conceptual base; (b) it integrates reading and writing; (c) it contains curricular activities that have either conceptual or empirical justification; (d) it has been shown to have positive literacy effects on participants; and last but not least, (e) it is produced by instructional researchers who have a fine reputation for their programmatic research in reading comprehension (Taffy Raphael) and writing (Carol-Sue Englert).

S. E. Englert, Raphael, and Mariage (1994) have developed a program that fosters reading and writing in grades 1–3: the ELP. They used Vygotsky's theoretical perspective in conceptualizing their program. Vygotsky postulated that children's cognitive development occurs in a sociolinguistic environment in which interactive dialogues with adult caregivers play a pivotal role. Adults shape and scaffold children's cognitive development. As children internalize strategies in cognitive domains and self-regulation, adults fade out of their directive roles. You will see Vygotsky's conceptual influence on the ELP as I describe principles underlying ELP.

The four principles of the ELP concern how teachers enable children's cognitive development.

1. Instruction is embedded in "meaningful, purposive, and contextualized activities."

2. Strategies are taught to make children into self-regulated learners.

3. Children must be involved in "social and dialogic interactions with others, and responsively supporting and scaffolding their learning in their zones of proximal development."

4. "build literate communities where literacy is shared among all members" (Englert et al., 1994, p. 3).

Instructional activities were chosen that involved oral and written literacy. Examples of oral literacy include storytelling, children dictating stories to teacher, and listening to stories read aloud. Examples of written literacy include reading and writing stories. Combined oral and written literacy instructional modes include silent reading, partner reading and partner writing, sharing chair (in which children share stories, with the help of a peer to overcome decoding difficulties), morning news, and authors' center (using strategies previously modeled by teacher, children write their papers on topics they know much about) (C.-S. Englert et al., 1994). These activities were interrelated and contextualized in thematic units that highlighted different expository topics, such as "Turtles," "Circus," "All About Animals." For full details on curriculum activities that reflect faithfully the four principles underlying the ELP, and how they are knitted together across the principles, please read C.-S. Englert et al. (1994). Preliminary data from an evaluation study of the ELP suggest that it benefited the participants.

Writing Strategies for Intermediate Grades

Karen Harris and Steve Graham are justly viewed as pioneers in programmatic research on writing problems in students with learning disabilities. Since 1980, they have been actively engaged in such research, which is characterized by rich theoretical conceptualization and methodological rigor. They have woven into their research the distinct and important component of self-regulation, which befits the passivity in learning among students with learning disabilities. Their research is multifaceted, ranging from basic research into the nature of the composing problems of these students (their knowledge of the writing process and how they write), to the design of various writing strategies in which self-regulation plays a cardinal role. To do justice to this talented and productive team's accomplishments in writing strategies interventions, I would need to write a full chapter, but it cannot fit appropriately into the scheme of this textbook. I cannot detail all the validated writing strategies designed by them and their research associates. Rather, I shall refer readers to the original sources: Harris and Graham (1992a, b) and Graham, Harris, MacArthur, and Schwartz (1991). Moreover, of their many writing strategies, I shall only describe one that greatly profits intermediate students. Readers interested in other writing strategies designed by Harris and Graham should read Harris and Graham (1992b).

According to Harris (1995, personal communication), a representative piece of their current instructional research in writing is their 1993 study (Danoff, Harris, & Graham, 1993). This study ensued from their Self-Regulated Strategy Development Model (SRSD) (Harris & Graham, 1992b). The SRSD focuses on students' active learning, interactions between students and teachers, and gradual ceding of responsibility in strategy use to students. Instructions conceptualized from this model give equal attention to strategy and self-regulation training.

In Danoff et al. (1993), a multicomponent instructional program was implemented in whole classes: two fifth-grade and one fourth-grade. Students whose stories were used as data comprised three students with learning disabilities and three average peers. The instructional procedures reflect those seen in current interventions, such as informed training (students are informed on the rationale of training), modeling of strategy by teacher, with much use of thinking aloud, scaffolding student learning, guided practice, collaborative work with peers and teachers, and independent work. In Danoff et al., care was taken to ensure students memorize the strategy steps. This instructional procedure is also common to strategy training procedures used by researchers at the Kansas Institute for Research in Learning Disabilities. Embedded in these instructional procedures was the writing strategy originally designed by Harris and Graham for the purpose of enhancing the quality and completeness (inclusion of all story parts) of story writing. The strategy consists of the following steps (see Danoff et al., 1993, p. 303):

1. Think of a story you would like to share with others.
2. Let your mind be free.
3. Write down the story part reminder (mnemonic):
   W-W-W
   What=2
   How=2
4. Write down story part ideas for each part.
5. Write your story—use good parts and make sense.

The mnemonic:

Who is the main character: who else is in the story?
When does the story take place?
Where does the story take place?
What does the main character want to do?
What happens when the main character tries to do it?
How does the story end?
How does the main character feel?

Englert has designed a writing strategy for use by elementary school students with the acronym of POWER (see Figure 3). Power stands for Plan, Organize, Write, Edit, and Revise/Rewrite. In the Plan stage, students learn to ascertain for themselves their purposes in writing, and to search their long-term memories for ideas or topics to write about. In Organize, students learn to cluster related ideas into various groups and then to prioritize the clusters in writing (i.e., which cluster they should begin with in their compositions and so on). Write stands for students generating their essays or stories. In Edit, students peruse their first drafts, identify parts they are satisfied with and parts they are dissatisfied with. Regarding the latter, they self-question on the clarity aspect of those sentences, and revise accordingly. Englert provides clues to help students in their revisions, such as, Did the student stray from the topic of composition? Did they have sufficient numbers of idea-clusters? Did they elaborate on the ideas sufficiently? Did they remember to use key words? Were their stories or essays interesting? Using these clues, and with help from conferencing with teachers, students revise their compositions.

The POWER strategy has widespread use both in the United States and Canada. Englert has used it in research to good effect with both normally achieving students and those with learning disabilities in elementary schools. More recently,

Power Questions

Plan
    WHY am I writing this?
    WHO am I writing for?
    WHAT do I know? (brainstorm)
Organize
    How can I organize my ideas into categories?
    How can I order my categories?
Write rough draft.
Edit
    Reread & Think
    Which parts do I like best?
    Which parts are not clear?
    Did I: • stick to the topic?
           • use 2–3 categories?
           • talk about each category clearly?
           • give details in each category?
           • use key words?
           • make it interesting?

Figure 3   The POWER Writing Strategy (designed by C.-S. Englert, reproduced with permission).

Thomas (1993) used the POWER strategy successfully to enhance the quality and quantity of writing in students with learning disabilities in grades 5–7.

Writing Strategies for High School Students

Turning to high school students with and without learning disabilities, the researchers at the Institute of Research in Learning Disabilities at the University of Kansas, under the creative and able leadership of Don Deshler and Jean Schumaker, have systematically designed and validated various teaching strategies to enhance the learning, studying, and performance of adolescents with learning disabilities. Many of these strategies are used in the United States and Canada, in particular, the error monitoring strategy in writing with the acronym of COPS (Schumaker, Nolan, and Deshler, 1985). COPS stands for Capitalization, Overall appearance, Punctuation, Spelling. Teaching students with learning disabilities to check for capitalization errors in their writing is necessary because many of them do not realize when they should use it. For example, they would often not begin with a capital letter at the start of a sentence. Equally important is the need to teach them to attend to the appearance of their writing. Schumaker et al. (1985) categorized four kinds of errors in a student's written work with elicit unfavorable reactions from readers. The first kind involves errors in handwriting, which range from illegible letters to letters not adhering to the lines on the paper. The second involves spacing errors: Either words are not sufficiently spaced from one another or they are spaced too far apart. The third kind of error involves margin errors, in which words that begin sentences next to the margin are not consistently next to it. The result is a peculiar lack of alignment of words next to the margin, so that the entire paragraph or all the paragraphs on a page have a peculiar zigzagging effect on the eyes of the reader! The last kind of errors are messy errors, which include crossing out words with the replacements over them, leaving messy traces of eraser marks. Messy errors also refer to additional writings on the sides of pages, and rip-outs or folded parts of the paper. The remaining two kinds of errors in punctuation and spelling are indeed those that most need addressing in the writings of adolescents with learning disabilities. On this point, I believe teachers of such adolescents would support me. These teachers should know!

I turn now to writing strategies that my research associates and I have validated for the past 5 years. The generous support from the Social Sciences and Humanities Research Council of Canada (SSHRCC) is gratefully acknowledged. A 3-year (1991–1994) research grant from SSHRCC supported my writing intervention research, which produced three genre-specific strategies: reportive, opinion, and compare and contrast essays. The target students were adolescents with learning disabilities and low achieving students in junior and senior high. For more details, see Wong et al. (1994; 1996; in press).

Prior Training

All students must have prerequisite skills in operating a microcomputer, for example, Apple Writer GS, or the Macintosh, an accompanying word-processing program, and adequate keyboard skills. These skills are necessary because we teach the students to write using a word-processing program on a microcomputer. We capitalize on educational technology to alleviate students' physical labor in revising essays during training. Teachers insistent on using paper and pen in writing and revising in high school risk eroding student motivation to learn. How many revision drafts do you think high school students would produce if they had to write them out with paper and pen?

Instructional Foci

Table 15 summarizes the instructional foci according to type of genre in the writing interventions conducted by Wong and associates (Wong et al., 1994; 1996; in press). As shown in the table, for all three kinds of essays, a common instructional focus is clarity of writing. Additionally, there are genre-specific instructional foci pertaining to each type of essay. Specifically, for reportive essay, the genre-specific instructional focus is thematic salience. We teach students that the theme of a reportive essay must be prominent both at the start and the end of the essay. Thus, if the student is writing about "The Most Embarrassing Event" in his life, then he

Table 15   Summary of Instructional Foci per Genre

	Genres		
	Reportive essays	Opinion essays	Compare and contrast essays
Instructional Foci			
General (applies to all genres)	Clarity	Clarity	Clarity
Genre-Specific	Thematic Salience	Cogency of arguments presented	Appropriateness of ideas that target either a comparison or contrast
		Organization of arguments presented	Organization of ideas

must state it (his theme) forcefully at the start of his essay. As well, he must repeat it at the end of the essay. Thus, as his theme sentence, he might write: "The most embarrassing event of my life was my first date." The bulk of his essay serves to elaborate and embellish his theme.

For opinion essays, additional genre-specific instructional foci include cogency and organization of arguments. Cogency of arguments refers to the persuasive logic or strength in the student's arguments proffered in support of both the pro and con sides of his or her opinion essay. Organization of arguments refers to the sequencing of them. For compare and contrast essays, additional genre-specific instructional foci include appropriateness and organization of ideas. Appropriateness refers to the ideas being relevant to comparisons or contrasts of topics in the student's essay. Because adolescents with learning disabilities and low achievers tend to be rather unthinking and put down ideas in their plan sheets that do not hone in on either a comparison or contrast of the topics in their compare and contrast essays, it is necessary for teachers to target appropriateness of ideas as an instructional focus. Lastly, it should be self-explanatory why organization of ideas is an instructional focus for this genre of compare and contrast essays.

Training

Training comprised three phases: (a) Collaborative planning, (b) independent writing, and (c) collaborative revising. In collaborative planning, the trainer demonstrated planning for writing through thinking aloud her thought processes. As an illustration, for reportive essay, she thinks aloud the sequence of events in her episode of "The Most Scary Event of My Life"; for opinion essay, she thinks aloud the ideas contained in two opposing views in "Why high school students should not have a dress code"; and for a compare and contrast essay on rock versus school concerts, she thinks aloud ideas that flesh out subthemes of goals, content, and demeanor. Subsequently, trainees are randomly divided into pairs or dyads and instructed to use thinking aloud to coconstruct a writing plan for an essay (reportive or opinion or compare and contrast). They are aided by a plan sheet (see respective plan sheets in Figures 5 and 7). Students choose topics provided by trainers. If they wish to generate their own topics, they are permitted with the condition that topics match genre demands.

When trainees have produced satisfactory writing plans, they write their essays *individually* on the Apple Writer GS, with the appropriate word-processing program (e.g., Clarisworks). Teachers must be on hand to assist them in their difficulties with word finding, sentence generation, and spelling. Subsequently, trainees print three copies of their first draft for the purpose of conferencing with a teacher and their dyadic partner in planning.

Collaborative revising occurs in conferencing. The trainer models for the dyadic trainees, questions to seek clarification, elaboration, and specification over ambiguities in each other's essay. Using such questioning or *interactive dialogues,* trainees identify ambiguities in each other's written essays. In conferencing, one student assumes the role of critic, and seeks clarification from the other, the student-writer, over the latter's ambiguities in writing. When she or he has finished questioning the student-writer, the teacher points out ambiguities missed by the student-critic. Subsequently, both teacher and student-critic help the student-writer to revise. The process of collaborative revising is repeated with the other trainee in the dyad.

When trainees' essays satisfy the teacher on the instructional foci of each genre, using COPS strategy (Schumaker et al., 1985), they check for and redress with the teacher's help errors in spelling, punctuation, and grammar. Subsequently, the teacher checks their essays on the computer screen. If satisfied, she instructs trainees to print copies of their perfect (final) drafts, to be kept in their individual files. (See Figure 4.)

To facilitate student learning, we use plan sheets and writing prompts (see Figures 5–9). The writing prompts are typed on 8 × 11-in. paper, laminated to increase durability. Each student with learning disabilities and low achiever has one for his or her own use, with his or her own name on it, kept in his or her own student file. Students are constantly reminded to use their own writing prompts, because our goal is to make them autonomous, self-monitoring, and self-regulating learners.

To motivate trainees' learning and performance, teachers should consider letting students' training essays contribute a certain percentage (e.g., 30%) to their grade in Modified English. Moreover, individual graphs should be kept on their writing progress that students could view daily. For example, a graph showing improvement on clarity of writing. The teacher can give a score on clarity per essay written. These

---

Prewriting
- Do I have my completed plan in front of me?
- Do I have my name, date, and title on my essay?

Rough Copy
- Does my first paragraph clearly present my opinion with supporting ideas?
- Does my second paragraph clearly express an opposing viewpoint to mine?
- Does my last paragraph include a summary statement and give reasons for my conclusions?
- Have I read my completed essay to make sure all ideas are clear?
- Have I printed three copies?

Editing
- Have I imputed all necessary changes?
- Have I reread my essay to make sure my ideas are clear?
- Have I printed one copy of my revised essay?

Revising
- Have I proofread my essay using COPS?
- Have I conferenced with a teacher?
- Have I imputed all necessary changes?
- Have I read my final draft to make sure all ideas are clear?
- Have I asked a teacher to proofread my screen?
- Have I printed two perfect copies?

Figure 4   Writing checklist for opinion essays.

graphs motivate student learning. Also, let students share their best essays in designated classes.

Instructional Steps in Planning for Reportive Essays

1. Memory access. Students are instructed to search their individual memories for the event they wish to write about in the following manner. For example, if they wish to write about the most embarrassing event in their lives, then they must recall all the embarrassing events that they have lived through. From this recollection of embarrassing events, they are to select the one event that they seriously consider the most embarrassing one.

2. Relive the event in one's visual and auditory images like seeing a videotape of that segment in one's life. After selecting the event that they wish to write about from their long-term memory, students are to relive it in their mind's eye, so to speak. Because adolescents are very familiar with video rentals, use the analogy to good vantage. Instruct them to relive the selected event like watching a rented video, only it is of a certain segment of their own lives. They should see and hear "it."

3. Activate all the emotions associated with that event. Simultaneous to reliving the particular segment of their lives, students must rekindle all the emotions asso-

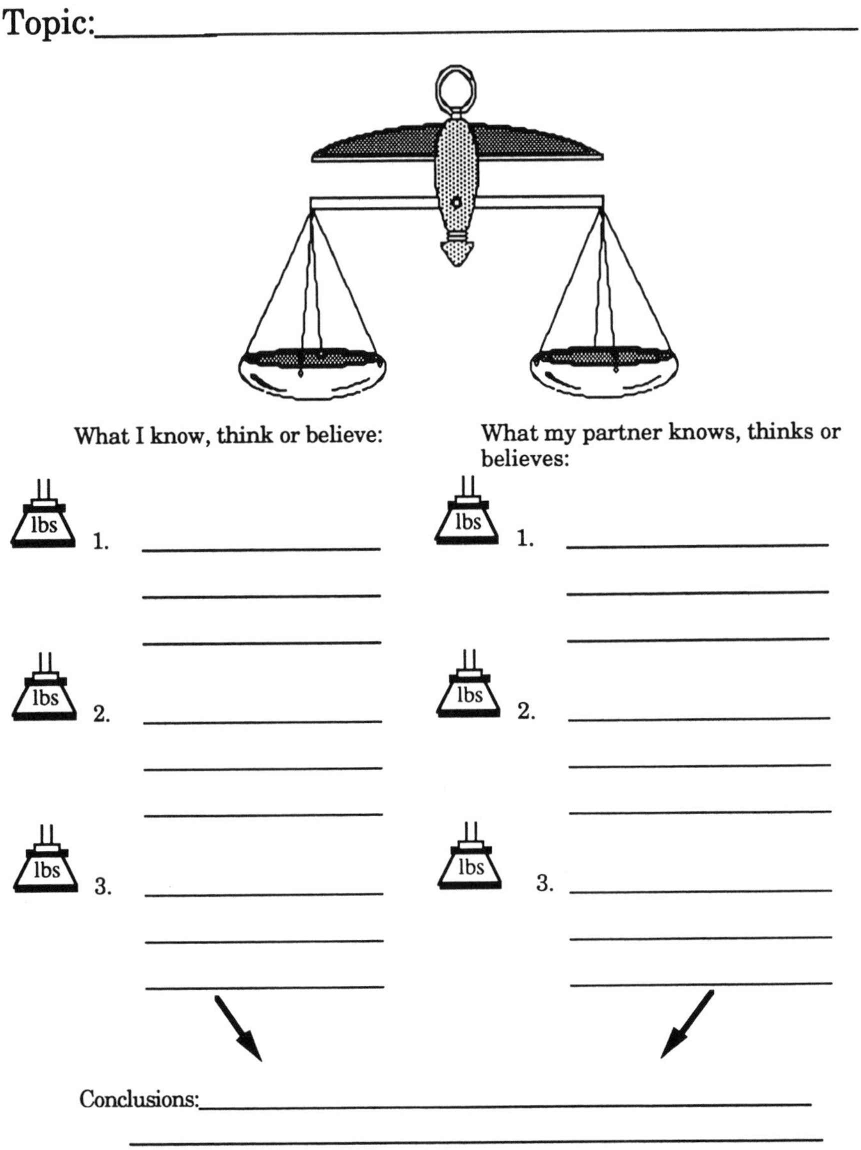

Topic:_____

What I know, think or believe:

lbs 1. _____

_____

_____

lbs 2. _____

_____

_____

lbs 3. _____

_____

_____

What my partner knows, thinks or believes:

lbs 1. _____

_____

_____

lbs 2. _____

_____

_____

lbs 3. _____

_____

_____

Conclusions:_____

_____

Figure 5   Plan sheet for opinion essay. (Designed by M. Cordon for use in Wong et al., 1996. Copyright © 1996 by Pro-Ed, Inc. Reprinted by permission.)

OPINION ESSAY: SIGNAL WORDS

Introductory Phrases
In my opinion,
I (dis)agree with
From my point of view,
I believe

Countering Phrases
Although
On the other hand,
On the contrary
However, someone who disagreed with my
opinion might argue

Concluding Phrases
After considering both sides,
Even though
To sum up,
In conclusion

Supporting Words & Phrases
First, Second, Finally,
Equally important
For instance,
As well

Figure 6   Opinion essay writing prompt card. Prompt is typewritten on 8 × 11-in. paper and laminated to increase durability. (Designed by S. Ficzere and M. Cordon for use in Wong et al., 1996. Copyright © 1996 by Pro-Ed, Inc. Reprinted by permission.)

ciated with the event that they are to write about. Thus, for the student who wants to write about his first date being "The Most Embarrassing Event of His Life," he should feel his face flushed, his ears should burn, and his neck should tingle. Last but not least, he should feel tongue-tied!

Reminders for Writing Strategy for Opinion Essays

1. Make sure adolescents with learning disabilities and underachieving high school students think aloud their planning. Have them put down on their plan sheets ideas that are logical (i.e., for the pro argument, they should marshall ideas that support it. Similarly, for the con argument, they should gather ideas that counter it).

Name _____   Date _____

COMPARE / CONTRAST PLAN

Topic:

Categories

Brainstorming for features

Introduction (refer to prompt card)

Features	Details	Sim	Dif
1. _____	a. _____		
	b. _____		
	c. _____		
2. _____	a. _____		
	b. _____		
	c. _____		
3. _____	a. _____		
	b. _____		
	c. _____		

Conclusion: (refer to prompt card)
After comparing and contrasting _____ **and**
_____ **, I think I prefer** _____ **because**

Figure 7   Plan sheet for compare and contrast essay.

2. Make sure that they use their plans and writing checklist (see Figure 4) in writing.

3. Monitor closely the interactive dialogues in collaborative revision between student and student, ask for elaborations, and help students to articulate their thoughts.

4. Remember to help students with learning disabilities in their revisions. For example, they would need your help finding the right words to express their communicative intent, structuring sentences, and with spelling.

Reminders for Writing Strategy for Compare and Contrast Essays

1. Be sure to explain the following to the adolescents with learning disabilities:
"features"
topic sentence
clincher sentence

2. If your adolescent with learning disabilities says he or she does not know how to write a topic sentence, try this:
Get the adolescent with learning disabilities to look at the ideas that she or he has put down in his or her plan sheet for the compare and contrast essay, then have him or her summarize those ideas. When she or he has finished summarizing his or her ideas, say, "That is your topic sentence. It tells the reader what you will be writing about. In the remaining sentences in this paragraph, you just simply flesh out what you said in your topic sentence."

3. Make sure the adolescents with learning disabilities use the writing prompt card and helpers in writing (see Figures 8 and 9).

Applications to Inclusive Classrooms

All the writing strategies described in this chapter are fully applicable to inclusive classrooms in which high-incidence special needs students, such as those with learning disabilities, are integrated. Indeed, Englert's POWER writing strategy is designed for use with all students, both normally achieving and learning-disabled. The COPS strategy has been effectively and rather routinely used by normally achieving upper intermediate and high school students. Similarly, the writing strategies designed by Graham and Harris have been effectively taught to normally achieving intermediate students. Finally, those designed by my associates and me have been taught to inclusive classes in grades 8 and 10.

Structure of Essay	Signal Words
Introduction (Paragraph 1)	*Introductory phrases* When comparing and contrasting in the novel/poem/short story
Purpose: Introduces the topic to the reader. Includes a thesis statement and outlines the features to be discussed	*Phrases for differences* On the other hand, However, In contrast to Although Whereas While But Even though
Body of the Essay	

1. First feature (Paragraph 2)
  a) Topic sentence
  b) Supporting details with examples
	Phrases for similarities
	In common,
	In the same way,
	At the same time,
	Similarly,

2. Second feature (Paragraph 3)
  a) topic sentence
  b) Supporting details with examples
	Supporting phrases
	Furthermore,
	As well,
	Also,
	Likewise,
	For instance,
	For example,

3. Third feature (Paragraph 4)
  a) Topic sentence
  b) Supporting details with examples	

Conclusion (Paragraph 5)	*Concluding phrases* To sum up, Thus, Therefore, In conclusion, After comparing & contrasting
Purpose: To summarize the features and/or express your opinion on the topic.	

Figure 8 Compare and contrast essay writing prompt card. Prompt is typewritten on 8 × 11-in. paper and laminated to increase durability.

REFLECTIONS

Researchers and teachers agree on the nature of writing problems in students with learning disabilities. These students have a production problem (i.e., they write pitifully little in the face of the amount of time given in writing). Constrained by a poor vocabulary, they experience much difficulties in finding felicitous words to express their communicative intents. As well, they have difficulties in structuring

---

Introduction (Thesis Statement)

In this essay, I am going to compare and contrast _____ and _____. I have chosen to write on three features: _____. _____, and _____.

I am writing this compare and contrast essay on _____ and _____. I will focus on the following three features: _____, _____, and _____.

Examples: In this essay, I am going to compare and contrast rock concerts and school concerts. I have chosen to write on three features: goals, content, and behavior.

Marijuana and LSD are both illegal drugs. Three important features of each that can be compared and contrasted are effects, usage, and appearance.

Conclusion

After comparing and contrasting _____ and _____ I think _____ because _____.

To conclude, it seems that _____ and _____ differ in their _____, but are similar in their _____.

Examples: School concerts and rock concerts both provide entertainment. I like school concerts better because they are free, they have my kind of music, and they let me wear what I want. However, they don't allow rowdy behavior!

After comparing and contrasting Christmas and summer holidays, I think I like summer holidays better because I really enjoy sunbathing!

Although marijuana and LSD differ in their appearance, they are similar in their effects and usage. Let's hope the usage is not too high.

Figure 9   Helpers in writing for compare and contrast essay. Prompt is typewritten on 8 × 11-in. paper and laminated to increase durability.

sentences. Their written products are replete with errors in spelling, punctuation, and grammar. More importantly, they lack both declarative and procedural knowledge of the writing process (i.e., they need to learn about the writing process, that it involves planning, sentence generation, and revising, and to implement these recursive processes in writing).

In designing and validating various writing strategies, intervention researchers in learning disabilities have benefitted both teachers of and students with learning disabilities. We have indeed gained much ground in writing interventions regarding enhancement of the quality and quantity of writing in students with learning disabilities. But there remains much to be attempted in intervention research on writing in students with learning disabilities. For future research, I name only issues of concern from my perspective. Hence, they are by no means exhaustive of potential areas for research.

There are at least four areas that need research in writing intervention in learning disabilities. (a) Graham and Harris (1993) call for more intervention research involving genre-specific strategies. They have indeed pinpointed a priority in writing intervention research. (b) Research on writing strategies that students with and without learning disabilities can use across curricular areas would be timely. However, we must attend to inherent differences between elementary and secondary schools that may well render such research much harder to conduct in the latter. (c) How should we address (physical) handwriting problems in primary and lower intermediate grades? Handwriting problems do impede composing. Steve Graham is addressing this issue in his current research. (d) How should we address spelling problems in the writings of high school students with learning disabilities? You may think that for those trained in keyboard skills, in using a microcomputer and word-processing program, we can teach them to redress spelling problems through spell-check. Alas, there is a constraint in using spell-check. It is that the spelling error itself must approximate sufficiently the correct spelling! Otherwise, spell-check cannot detect and correct it! Now those of you who teach high school students with learning disabilities know how horrendous and occasionally even bizarre the spelling errors of those students can be. In short, the usefulness of spell-check for them is moot! You can see then, why I raise this issue as a concern for researchers to redress.

Although much remains to be resolved concerning writing problems in students with learning disabilities, we have amassed much information on the nature of their problems, and a sufficiently rich store of writing strategies for use with them. Building on our empirical base here, we should venture forth in new research endeavors with cautious optimism that this area of writing research in learning disabilities will continue to excite and expand.

References

Danoff, B., Harris, K. R., & Graham, S. (1993). Incorporating strategy instruction within the writing process in the regular classroom: Effects on the writing of students with and without learning disabilities. *Journal of Reading Behavior, 25*(3), 295–322.

Englert, C.-S., Raphael, T. E., & Mariage, T. V. (1994). Developing a school-based discourse for literacy learning: A principled search for understanding. *Learning Disability Quarterly, 17*(1), 2–32.

Englert, C.-S. (1992). Writing instruction from a sociocultural perspective: The holistic, dialogic, and social enterprise of writing. In B. Y. L. Wong (Ed.), Cognitive process-based instruction. *Journal of Learning Disabilities, 25*(3), 153–172.

Englert, C.-S., & Thomas, C. C. (1987). Sensitivity to text structure in reading and writing: A comparison between learning-disabled and non-learning-disabled students. *Learning Disability Quarterly, 19*(2), 93–105.

Graham, S., & Harris, K. R. (1993). Teaching writing strategies to students with learning disabilities: Issues and recommendations. In Lynn J. Meltzer (Ed.), *Strategy assessment and instruction for students with learning disabilities: From theory to practice* (pp. 271–292). Austin, TX: Pro-Ed.

Graham, S., Harris, K. R., MacArthur, C., & Schwartz, S. (1991). Writing instruction. In B. Y. L. Wong (Ed.), *Learning about learning disabilities* (pp. 310–345). San Diego: Academic Press.

Graham, S., Schwartz, S. S., & MacArthur, C. A. (1993). Knowledge of writing and the composing process, attitude toward writing, and self-efficacy for students with and without learning disabilities. *Journal of Learning Disabilities, 26*(4), 237–249.

Hammill, D. D., & Larsen, S. C. (1988). *The Test of Written Language-2* (TOWL-2). Austin, TX: Pro-Ed.

Hammill, D. D., Brown, V. L., Larsen, S. C., & Wiederholt, J. L. (1987). *The Test of Adolescent Language* (TOAL). Austin, TX: Pro-Ed.

Harris, K. R., & Graham, S. (1992a). *Helping young writers master the craft: Strategy instruction and self-regulation in the writing process.* Cambridge, MA: Brookline Books.

Harris, K. R., & Graham, S. (1992b). Self-regulated strategy development: A part of the writing process. In M. Pressley, K. R. Harris, & J. T. Guthrie (Eds.), *Promoting academic competence and literacy in school* (pp. 277–309). San Diego: Academic Press.

Harris, K., & Graham, S. (1985). Improving learning-disabled students' composition skills: Self-control strategy training. *Learning Disability Quarterly, 8,* 27–36.

Houck, C. K., & Billingsley, G. S. (1989). Written expression of students with and without learning disabilities: Differences across the grades. *Journal of Learning Disabilities, 22*(9), 561–567, 572.

Newcomer, P. L., & Barenbaum, E. M. (1991). The written composing ability of children with learning disabilities: A review of the literature from 1980 to 1990. *Journal of Learning Disabilities, 24*(10), 578–593.

Poteet, J. A. (1978). Characteristics of written expression of learning-disabled and non-learning-disabled elementary school students. *Diagnostique, 4,* 60–74.

Schumaker, J. B., Nolan, S. M., & Deshler, D. D. (1985). *The error monitoring strategy. Learning Strategies Curriculum.* Lawrence, KS: The University of Kansas.

Thomas, K. M. (1993). *The effects of the cognitive strategy instruction in writing curriculum (CSIW) on expository writing skills and metacognitive knowledge of the writing process in learning-disabled students.* Unpublished Masters thesis, Faculty of Education, Simon Fraser University, Burnaby, B.C., Canada.

Wong, B. Y. L., Wong, R., & Blenkinsop, J. (1989). Cognitive and metacognitive aspects of learning-disabled adolescents' composing problems. *Learning Disability Quarterly, 12*(4), 300–322.

Wong, B. Y. L., Butler, D. L., Ficzere, S. A., & Kuperis, S. (1996). Teaching adolescents with learning disabilities and low achievers to plan, write and revise opinion essays. *Journal of Learning Disabilities, 29*(2), 197–212.

Wong, B. Y. L., Butler, D. L., Ficzere, S. A., Kuperis, S. (in press). Teaching adolescents with learning disabilities and low achievers to plan, write, and revise compare and contrast essays. *Learning Disabilities Research & Practice.*

Wong, B. Y. L., Butler, D. L., Ficzere, S. A., Kuperis, S., Corden, M., & Zelmer, J. (1994). Teaching problem learners revision skills and sensitivity to audience through two instructional modes: Student-teacher versus student-student interactive dialogues. *Learning Disability Research & Practice, 9*(2), 78–90.

10

Ab

Epilogue

In this last chapter, it seems fitting to write about principles in remediation, monitoring remedial progress of students with learning disabilities, and the rather hot topic of inclusion.

Principles in Remediation

When student teachers think of academic remediation of students with learning disabilities, they tend to envision specific instructional methods that they must learn, without considering what general principles underlie the effectiveness of remediation. In this chapter, I attempt to gently restrain their overwhelming urge to seize practical knowledge and curricular materials, and show them what principles in remediation they must understand in order to be effective in whatever remedial methods they may use. I proffer eight such principles for consideration by student teaches and other readers.

Remedial Principle (1)

Use a unified and comprehensive approach in remedial instruction. Effective remediation does not come from focusing exclusively on one isolated area (e.g., spelling).

216

Rather, it comes from a broad-based, unified front in the learning-disabled student's deficient academic area.

To illustrate, let me use reading rate. Suppose Adam, a fourth-grade boy with learning disabilities is found through formal and informal reading assessments to be reading at half the rate of his two average peers from the same class. Reading rate then becomes part of his individualized educational plan (IEP). The remedial tutor decides to use the reading rate strategy that has been presented in Chapter 7, "Informal Assessment of Reading Problems."

In that reading rate strategy, as the remedial tutor works with Adam on his reading rate, she also focuses simultaneously on building his vocabulary. His homework is vocabulary words learned that day in the session on reading rate. He is tested on them the next day, and the results are immediately graphed or charted for his own feedback and pinned in clear view in front of him on a corkboard. He is praised for the words learned. Any word not mastered automatically gets piggybacked onto the next day's list of vocabulary homework and so on. Meanwhile, because Adam has to copy from his reading text or story a sentence that contains a new vocabulary word, he learns proper usage of it, as well as increasing his repertoire of good sentence construction. After 2 weeks, Adam's vocabulary should be quite sizable. Now the remedial tutor heightens the task demands. She tells Adam she wants him to learn to spell some words of which he has mastered the meanings. She keeps the number down to avoid overloading him with excessive homework, because he still has to continue learning new vocabulary words. She asks him to pick the words he'd like to learn to spell. Because he is in fourth grade, she asks him to pick five words. The same testing procedure used with vocabulary words applies to spelling. After a month or so, Adam has to generate sentences with those words he's learned, whose sentential application he has studied, and which he can spell correctly.

Clearly, the above shows that remediation of learning-disabled student's reading rate includes equal focus on vocabulary building, spelling, and writing. Notice, each additional cognitive demand is given only after a necessary prerequisite store of knowledge has been in place. Specifically, Adam learns to spell words that he has already understood and the meanings of which he could readily recall. This is important because it is very difficult for students and ourselves to learn the spelling of a list of words that we do not find meaningful. We can learn to spell them through sheer brute force of rote memorization. But we all know how fast we forget when we learn like that! Because many students with learning disabilities have memory problems, it is sheer torture to make them learn by rote, and absolutely counterproductive when they forget it fast!

Similarly, it is unwise to ask students with learning disabilities to keep a journal without first increasing their vocabulary and repertoire of good sentences. Because students with learning disabilities who are reading disabled rarely read, they have a very poor vocabulary and equally poor knowledge of good sentences and their construction. If you ask them to write a journal without first spending time building their vocabulary and knowledge of good sentences and their construction, you will be wasting time on a futile activity and boring them to death! Do you honestly think you will see progress in their journal without prior work on vocabulary and repertoire of good sentences?

Lastly, observe the powerful motivational effects of your graphs and charts on the learning-disabled student's remedial progress. The students with learning disabilities are fueled by the upward curves of their graphs, which indicate progress or improvement. They spontaneously want to do well, to see the curves continue in their upward swing. And they will amaze you with their eagerness to work hard!

Remedial Principle (2)

Set up a priority list in your remedial plan (IEP). It is natural and perfectly understandable that your assessment data would show you that each of your students with learning disabilities has a host of academic needs. Despite your good intentions, you cannot attend to all of them at once. Hence, control or contain your missionary zeal and take a strong dose of that nasty medicine called realism! You must set up a priority list for remedial attention. To do so, ask yourself this question: "What is the concept or skill that is most important for learning and mastery by this student with learning disabilities when I consider his or her grade level and its attendant curricular demands?" Let me illustrate with some examples. For a second-grade child with learning disabilities who only knows two short vowels, I would suggest focusing on teaching him or her to master the rest of the short vowels as the first priority. For a fourth-grade learning-disabled child with math problems who still lacks mastery of the multiplication tables, I would put this as the priority in remediation of his math problems. For a seventh-grade learning-disabled student with reading disability, I would put reading comprehension and vocabulary building over phonics deficiency as remedial priority because he or she would soon be in junior high school where the curricula demand thorough comprehension of materials read. The student would be expected to draw appropriate inferences from novels, understand metaphors and analogies in poems, and understand expository texts in science and social studies. For this student then, learning comprehension and reading strategies and increasing vocabulary knowledge should take precedence over remediating phonics deficiency. However, do not neglect his deficiency in phonics. Tackle it in the context of his vocabulary learning in the following way. The teacher breaks each vocabulary word into its constituent syllables. Then she teaches the phonics contained in the syllables. For example, hamburger gets broken into: *ham/bur/ger.* The teacher then teaches the sound of the short vowel *a* and the *r*-controlled vowels of *ur* and *er;* the sound of the consonant *b;* and the hard *g* sound.

Failure to prioritize instruction needs in remediation of students with learning disabilities results in needless frustration in remedial teachers. Remember to curb your messianic impulse. Academic problems in students with learning disabilities take time to resolve, the effective remediation involves specific factors (see section below).

Remedial Principle (3)

Make success accessible to students with learning disabilities in your remediation. By the time they come to you, the special needs teacher, students with learning disabilities have experienced much academic failure, much assessment and testing, and perhaps erratic, haphazard, or unskilled remediation. You are dealing with a child or adolescent with a very low frustration tolerance for failure. To help this student with learning disabilities to invest effort in your remediation, you must make success accessible by setting realistic goals for him or her, and ensuring that you have done a good cognitive task analysis on the target concept or skills so that each subtask does not exceed the student's cognitive resources. For example, in reading rate, if the student with learning disabilities is found in assessment baseline, to read at 34 words per minute (wpm), a realistic initial goal for the first week of remediation would be 50 wpm. This goal makes success readily accessible to the student with learning disabilities. Thereafter, depending on his or her learning rate, you can increase the goal in subsequent weeks by 15 words or more per minute. In contrast, if you set the *initial* goal in reading rate to be that of the learning-disabled student's normally achieving average peer, you would be highly unrealistic, and setting him or her up for inescapable failure and frustration. You would reap the fruits of your own thoughtlessness: the student with learning disabilities will evidence instantaneous loss of motivation to learn; chances are he or she would not attend any more remedial sessions with you. In his or her eyes, you are associated with aversive experiences, your presence signals an unpleasant time and place! Putting yourself in their shoes, wouldn't you do what they'd do and generate ingenious excuses to avoid going to the Learning Assistance Center?

Remedial Principle (4)

Be flexible in your teaching. This means cultivate instructional sensitivity to your students with learning disabilities, and stretch and adapt instructional methods and/or materials for their benefit. Let me illustrate my point with the following examples:

Example (a)   The strategy of repeated reading can be used to increase either reading rate or to decrease/control error rate per page read.

1. The emphasis differs in "criterion" attained before tutee is allowed to proceed to a new page.
2. The emphasis in recording differs for reading rate and error rate.

Example (b)   Expand sources for vocabulary building.

If materials for repeated reading do not provide enough new or difficult vocabulary for the tutee to learn, draw vocabulary from materials used for other remedial areas (e.g., reading comprehension).

Example (c)   Focus on spelling vocabulary words.

If reading materials for reading comprehension enhancement are suitable, but the tutee does not have much difficulty with vocabulary, then work on having tutee focus on spelling accuracy of the vocabulary.

Example (d)   Change strategy

If tutee is plateauing, or not achieving progress (downward curve), change strategy.

Often young, at-risk children in grades 1 and 2 cannot endure seat-work or phonics games for more than 15–20 minutes. For them, it is useful to have strategies that allow them to physically move about. Activities described below achieve the purpose of teaching them phonics (short vowels, long vowels) while letting them exert their energy.

1. Ball in a sock and waste paper basket (this ingenious idea came from one of my students!)
   Tutor has phonic drill words on cards, put faced down at bottom of a clean waste paper basket (or have a clean garbage bag over the basket).

   Child stands about 3–4 feet from the basket, throws ball in sock into it. When ball in sock falls into basket, child picks up first card and says the CVC word. If CVC word is correctly pronounced, s/he keeps the word. Otherwise it goes back into the pile. (Tutor inserts it in pile.)

2. Variations of (1), just throw ball into a bucket (ball not contained in sock). Putting ball in a sock reduces noise when ball bounces into bucket.

3. Footprints. Using color paper, draw and cut out big footprints and then laminate them to increase durability in use. Then print on small index cards short CVC words containing specific phonic skills that are your instructional targets, such as short vowels of *a* and *i*. (So you may have words like cat, bit, etc.) Shuffle the pile of CVC words to that you have a randomized order of words with *a* and *i*! Place each index card on a footprint cutout. Tell child with learning disabilities these are footprints of the Sasquatch. His or her task is to step on each footprint cutout one at a time, pick up the small index card, and say the CVC word to you. If she or he pronounces the word accurately, she or he gets to keep the card. If not, you give corrective feedback, child repeats word after you and the card remains on the footprint cutout for another prac-

tice trial. The focus initially should be on accurate decoding of these CVC words. When that is attained consistently, say, on 2 consecutive days, then you move to focus on speed AND accuracy in decoding these CVC words. Those CVC words that the LD child can decode fast and accurately on two consecutive days will then be removed and substituted by new CVC words containing short vowels that now constitute the instructional targets.

Remedial Principle (5)

Instructional prompts. The purpose of using prompts is to alleviate memory load in the students with learning disabilities as they are learning a new concept or skill or procedure. For example, a student with learning disabilities is learning the procedure of long division from you. Having explained it to him or her in a demonstration example, worked through a problem together, then you want to ascertain his or her thorough understanding by asking him or her to do a sum for you independently. To facilitate the student, you provide a prompt. Basically it is a large index card, on which you have listed on one side the steps in long division with the same example you have just used in your instructional demonstration. On the other side, parallel to each illustrative numerical step, are verbal statements of the long division procedure. The student with learning disabilities can readily see the progressive steps in the long division procedure outlined in the example on the prompt, and obtain further clarification from the accompanying verbal statements. You see then that the prompt cuts down on memory load for the student with learning disabilities, freeing his or her cognitive resources to be devoted entirely to applying the long division procedure. In this way, acquisition is expedited. As well, the prompt reduces chances for errors, making success accessible for the student with learning disabilities!

Prompts however, must be carefully designed. An example of a bad prompt is

Why is this a bad prompt? It is bad because it fails to help the student with learning disabilities to learn the target word. The picture and the target word must appear together on the same side of the prompt card. Only thus can the student with learning disabilities using the picture–word association to learn the word, and overcome his or her retrieval problem. The picture helps anchor the word in his or her memory. To ensure teachers construct good prompts in aid of learning in students with learning disabilities, they should also attend to two additional points. First, is the prompt suitable for the age level of the student with learning disabilities? Does it consist of a cognitive overload as in a lengthy, wordy prompt? Second, which steps in a prompt may be redundant to the student with learning disabilities?

Prompts must be used in a tutor's teaching; they are not for display purposes! They must be prominently displayed in front of the child during the lesson, and at the right eye level! The tutee must be taught to use prompts to promote acquisition and retention! The tutor should also watch and ascertain which steps in the prompt (e.g., reading comprehension prompt) have been internalized by the tutee; then encourage the tutee to modify steps in prompt to suit himself or herself. Fading of prompts should occur after mastery of strategy (e.g., fade out comprehension prompts when tutee masters the "Before," "During," and "After" strategy and can automatically without prompting generate appropriate questions).

Remedial Principle (6)

Be analytical of your own remedial teaching! Use a 3-day interval as a rough rule of thumb to gauge your student's remedial progress. This interval forces you to make an instructional decision. You either stay on course in your remedial teaching (strategy + materials) or you may need to consider changing strategy or material or both.

To make an astute instructional decision, you need to pinpoint reasons for the learning-disabled student's quantum leap in progress, or unexpected regression, or erratic performance (i.e., a zigzag line across three points in your graph: Down Monday, up Wednesday, and down again on Friday!). Learn to pinpoint reasons for what you see in the learning-disabled student's learning progress as evidenced in their graphs or charts. This way, you learn to analyze your own teaching skills. You want to be able to take credit for instructional success with your students with learning disabilities. Similarly, especially with young, neophyte teachers of learning-disabled students, you do not want to blame yourselves needlessly for lack of instructional success and wail prematurely that you are not destined for teaching students with learning disabilities!

Remedial Principle (7)

The importance of training yourself to justify what you do. Very often, special needs teachers (and classroom teachers too), make instructional displays, prompts, and so on, and use particular teaching approaches and materials without sufficient forethought or foresight. It's a case of "Teacher knows best!" The problem is, we don't!

Effective special needs and classroom teachers do not lose sight of asking important self-questions such as, "Why do I need to change my instructional materials? My instructional strategies?" For special needs teachers, a self-question of particular importance is, "Why do I change the remedial goal line for this student with learning disabilities by that amount?"

Experienced teachers may feel miffed at my insistence that teachers justify their changing instructional strategies and materials. Let me plead my case for I have a good reason. Such disciplined self-questioning ensures that these decisions are data based, and focuses teachers on the key to effective remedial teaching: Matching instructional strategy and materials to the real instructional needs and characteristics of specific students with learning disabilities under one's charge! When we move away from ascertaining the rationale or raison d'être for the change in our teaching strategy and/or materials, we increasingly operate on a subjective rather than an objective base. And subjective hunches, even in fine teachers, are subject to error when they are devoid of objective vindication. An analogy comes from weight watchers. Having shed all their excessive pounds, those who think they no longer need to be vigilant about weight watching gradually eat a little bit more, and a little bit more. In no time, they find their excessive weight has stealthily crept back. The same moral applies to teachers who blithely change instructional strategies and/or materials with their students with learning disabilities without ascertaining the need for such change. They'll find at the end of the rainbow of changes in strategy and/or material, that instead of the promised pot of gold (quantum leaps of remedial progress), there is no substantive improvement in their students with learning disabilities!

Remedial Principle (8)

Communicate with classroom teachers. As special needs teachers, you must communicate regularly with classroom teachers of your learning-disabled charges if you are providing pull-out services. Remember, both of you share the same goal for the student with learning disabilities. You both want him or her to improve academically, and focus on the eventual goal of mainstreaming him or her in the area in which she or he currently has marked deficiency. You must yoke your remediation with the classroom teacher's curricular foci so that the student with learning disabilities does not receive fragmented instruction. If you co-teach with the classroom teacher in an inclusive school, this principal applies equally.

Three Factors of Effective Remediation

1. Skilled instruction results from understanding the instructional needs of a particular student with learning disabilities, the need to pinpoint an appropriate learning strategy for use with him or her, as well as choosing the appropriate instructional materials for him or her. In sum, skilled instruction is simply *matching* appropriate *strategy* and *materials* with the specific *characteristics* and *instructional needs* of a student with learning disabilities.

2. Intensity significantly impacts on effectiveness of remediation for the following reason. Without exception, all students with learning disabilities show academic retardation that ranges from a minimum of 1 year to a maximum of 3 or more years. Consequently, to help narrow the gap in their academic retardation vis-à-vis

class or grade level, we need to provide intensive remediation. Put more colloquially, we need to go full steam in remediation because there is no time to waste! Unless skilled remediation is done with intensity, both special needs teacher and the student with learning disabilities lose out. The latter will make neither substantial nor consistent progress.

3. Similarly, sustained remediation is a necessary condition for effective remediation to occur for the following reason. In order to reach mastery in any conceptual or procedural learning, students with learning disabilities need practice once they show understanding or initial acquisition of the target concept or procedure. Moreover, because of memory problems, many of them need much practice and review to reach mastery. Consequently, they must be given remedial sessions at least thrice a week, for at least a halfhour, to provide sufficient coverage of target remedial area. Hence, remedial help that occurs infrequently, or once or twice a week, is futile for attainment of mastery in the target area.

Clearly, effective remediation involves three factors: skilled instruction, intensity, and sustained remediation. All three must occur in tandem if the special needs teacher genuinely wants to achieve success with his or her charges of students with learning disabilities. For reasons given above, implementation of any of these factors singly is self-defeating.

Recording of Remedial Progress: The Relevance of Graphing and Charting

Why do we need to record systematically remedial progress in students with learning disabilities? Why does it not suffice for special needs teachers to just know that their individual charges "have come a long way" since they have started to teach them? I'd like you to pause and think about the answer to my questions, whether you are a student teacher or not, and especially if you are a teacher of students with learning disabilities.

There are four reasons for teachers of learning-disabled students to keep systematic records of their students' remedial progress.

First, it is of paramount importance to keep some form of record systematically on each student with learning disabilities because it gives crucial feedback on the student's remedial progress. Every special needs teacher needs constant feedback on his or her own learning-disabled student's remedial progress because it is a yardstick for instructional efficacy. If the student with learning disabilities shows remedial progress, it means the special needs teacher is using appropriate instructional strategy and materials. She or he can justly take credit for the learning-disabled student's progress. In contrast, if remedial progress in the student with learning disabilities is not evident or forthcoming, she or he must modify either instructional strategy or materials or both. She or he would seek explanations for the lack of remedial progress because it reflects lack of instructional efficacy.

Clearly, it is of cardinal importance that special needs teachers keep systematic records on remedial progress in students with learning disabilities. For any such teacher to rely solely on his or her own mental gauge of student progress indicates irresponsibility and unwarranted arrogance in his or her own instructional efficacy. Matching instructional strategies and materials to particular students with learning disabilities needs constant, vigilant monitoring.

Second, motivating students with learning disabilities is vital. When students with learning disabilities see daily records of their learning progress in areas targeted for remediation, they are very happy, especially when they see that they have reached their respective goal lines on the graphs. Elated with success in learning, and realizing that they have achieved learning success by themselves, they develop a nascent sense of positive self-efficacy. These two factors motivate them to continue to work hard in the remedial area. They become impatient to learn and achieve more!

Third, credibility with people is important. Visual displays of daily or weekly remedial progress of students with learning disabilities in the resource room speak to the instructional efficacy of the special needs teacher. She or he can explain the peaks and troughs of each graph, as well as the continual upward swings and curves in the graphs. Any visitor can readily see goal lines for various students with learning disabilities, and the frequencies with which they are met. Consequently, whoever steps in the resource room comes away duly impressed, be it the principal, the vice-principal, regular classroom teachers, parents, or students! Such a special needs teacher has the most enviable commodity in any school: credibility with peers, principal, vice-principal, parents, and students. She would be sought for advice on inclusion, for pull-out services for certain students with learning disabilities, and above all, students with learning disabilities wouldn't mind coming to see her!

Fourth, for teachers of students with learning disabilities, the sooner you adopt ways of record keeping, the better it is for you. In fact, in my undergraduate class, I teach student teachers certain ways of record keeping as they learn to teach children and adolescents with learning disabilities, because I want them to establish a good habit. Once you understand the cardinal relevance of systematic record keeping with learning-disabled students whom you teach, you must right away learn to do so, and get used to doing it. As we all know, good habits are worth cultivating, especially in the case of remedial teaching. After all, the presence or absence of remedial progress in your students with learning disabilities reflects directly your very own instructional efficacy!

There are many ways to record remedial progress in students with learning disabilities. I have always maintained that practicing teachers should use methods with which they are comfortable or that they have found to be useful. The following methods are ones that I find easy to use. Before elaborating on them, let me explain the interval that I use to gauge remedial progress of any student with learning disabilities. I call it the 3-days rule or 3 data points rule. Basically, for any student with learning disabilities who is seen by the special needs teacher in pull-out services, I check his or her daily progress within blocks of 3 days. If within 3 days, the graph continually plummets (i.e., went down on each of the 3 days), I would examine the instructional strategy to see if it is too complex for the student with learning disabilities, and if it needs modifying or should be abandoned altogether. The decision depends on a thorough discussion with the student's special needs teacher, and observing the learning-disabled student's application of it in learning, as well as questioning him or her on how she or he finds its usage. Simultaneously I would examine the instructional materials to see if they explain the learning-disabled students' lack of remedial progress. Of course, when we watch the student with learning disabilities apply the cognitive and/or metacognitive strategy to the materials, we can observe right away if the materials are appropriate or not.

If the graph zigzags within the 3-days block, I would continue with both instructional strategy and materials for another 3 days before deciding on changing strategy or materials or both.

For students with learning disabilities whom special needs teachers see for example, only thrice per week, say, Monday, Wednesday, and Friday, you can graph remedial progress of individual students across each week. In this case, you will be gauging progress weekly, and that is fine. The critical point to remember is that you need at least three data points per week to make any sense in gauging remedial progress. Two data points per week provide insufficient data to be of use in gauging remedial progress of the student with learning disabilities.

Graphing Student Progress in Reading Rate

Figure 10 presents a graph of a fictitious, very bright, learning-disabled student's remedial progress in reading rate. At assessment, his base rate was 50 words per minute (wpm). Making success accessible to him, we set 100 wpm as the initial goal in remediation. (Assuming a fast learning rate for this fictitious, bright learning-disabled boy, I set the initial goal line at 100 wpm. Otherwise, it would have been 70 wpm.) The strategy of repeated reading was subsequently applied, and his tests taken at the end of each daily remedial reading session indicated consistent (steady) progress towards the goal line. When he reached it on two consecutive days, we changed it to 150 wpm. This second goal was conservative because his remedial progress in the first week was steady but not dramatic. The third goal line, however, indicated more risk taking with the student.

In the above example, the remedial focus was on improving reading rate. If a student with learning disabilities cannot attain a goal line after 1 week, we automatically lower it because when instructional strategy and materials are appropriate and the student evidences sufficient motivation to learn, lack of progress points to inappropriateness of goal line.

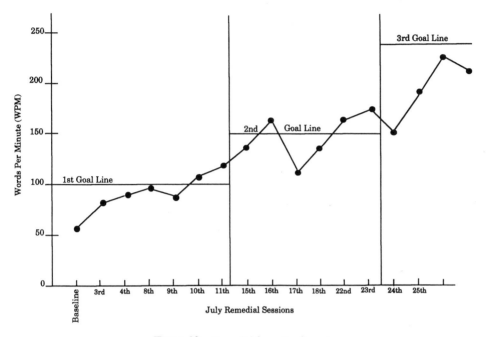

Figure 10. Remedial focus: Reading rate.

Let us now turn to remedial focus of reducing error rate in reading. Here the student with learning disabilities reads with sufficient speed but makes a tremendous amount of errors. He has to learn to read with care, and that excessive reading errors are unacceptable.

Figure 11 shows that he reads at 150 wpm at baseline (assessment), with 20 errors. The initial goal line for acceptable error rate per page in the first week is set at 10 per page. Don't gasp, remember we must make success accessible?! When this goal line is met in the first week of remediation, we change it to five errors per page for the second week, then three errors per page in the third week, and two errors per page in the fourth week of remediation. Making the student with learning disabilities stay with the same page in reading until goal of error rate is met ensures that each goal line set per week will be met. Hence, special needs teachers must apply this strategy firmly and rigorously. Avoid the weak-kneed syndrome in being flustered and beguiled by learning-disabled students' boredom with repeating the same page in reading. Inform them that they can readily escape boredom and continue to the next page by reading with more care and making fewer errors! Always remind them that the ball is in their park!

Figure 11 also shows goal lines for reading rate. Basically, this figure shows you

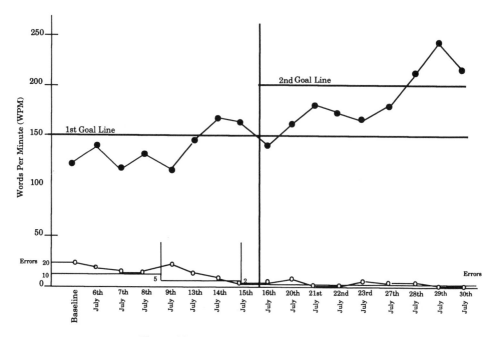

Figure 11. Remedial focus: Error control and rate.

how to graph rate and errors if your remedial foci cover both targets. If you choose to use it mainly for errors, you could simply set one goal line in reading rate that continues in place across the weeks as you focus on error rate (see Figure 12).

Graphing Vocabulary Building

To record students' growth in vocabulary, a bar graph is useful. It is very easy to make, and students with learning disabilities delight in helping teachers make and fill in their own bar graphs.

The bar graph in Figure 13 shows you the vocabulary growth of one student with learning disabilities. For a seventh-grade student with learning disabilities, we ask him to take home eight words a day to learn. These vocabulary words are from materials used in repeated reading or from materials used in increasing his reading comprehension. The amount of words he can define the next day corresponds to his score on the bar graph. On subsequent tests (days), the scores are cumulatively added to the bar graph. You should expect that sometimes this student would get five out of seven words right, sometimes all seven right, and so on. Hence the amount added to the bar graph each day may not stay constant. However, the mo-

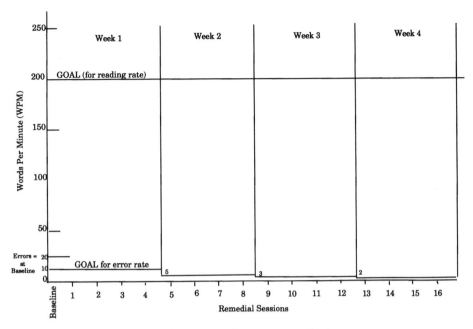

Figure 12.   Remedial focus: Error rate reduction.

tivating effect of the bar graph usually sustains the learning-disabled student's efforts at learning. They get very elated at the growth spurts of their bar graphs and are eager to sustain them. They love making the teacher make new bar graphs because they've outgrown the first ones! Bar graphs can also be used to record learning-disabled students' progress in learning to spell vocabulary words.

Graphing Students' Mastery of Phonics

In the section on remedial strategies we have covered the instruction of short vowels and double vowels (diphthongs, diagraphs). Because testing consists of five CVC words of each pair of vowels (*a* and *i* for example), for visual presentation purposes it is best to graph the results in percentages. Figure 14 shows you how to do it. Notice the goal line is permanently set at 100%. You want the child with learning disabilities to reach this on two consecutive days, for you to have the assurance that she or he has learned to discriminate the pair of vowels being taught. Thereafter, you want to maintain that goal line to help the child with learning disabilities to overlearn the discrimination and hence consolidate his or her new learning. The same logic in plotting the goal lines applies to teaching of other vowels.

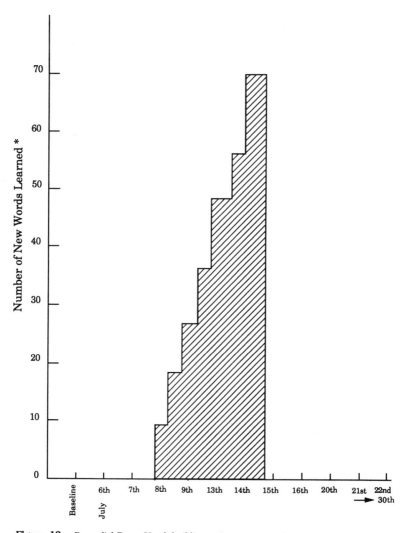

Figure 13.   Remedial Focus: Vocab building or increasing word recognition (sight vocab).

Graphing Arithmetic and Mathematics Remediation or the Learning of Main Idea Concepts in Reading Comprehension

In arithmetic or mathematics, sometimes students with learning disabilities need to learn and master multiplication tables, two-digit (addition or subtraction) problems with regrouping, multiplication, and long division problems. After explicit explanation and modeling of the computational procedures, and the use of guided

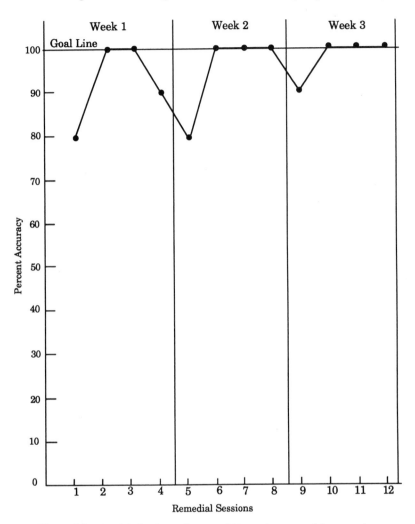

Figure 14.   Graph indicating students acquisition and mastery of short vowel *a*.

practice of a couple of problems, you are satisfied that the students with learning disabilities are ready for some independent seat work. You assign either two sets of 5 or one set of 10 problems, and instruct the students with learning disabilities to proceed with the aid of their individual prompt cards. Subsequently, you chart their scores and give praise and corrective feedback.

Your goal line is always set at 100% accuracy during the stage of student skill acquisition and mastery (overlearning to consolidate new learning). When students have indeed consolidated their new learning by consistent errorless performance, you move to focus on increasing speed in their computations. Here, you may lower your goal line to 80 or 90% accuracy. You want to communicate to the students with learning disabilities that they are allowed one error (one wrong answer out of 10 problems = 90% accuracy) as they focus on increasing their speed in performance (see Figure 15).

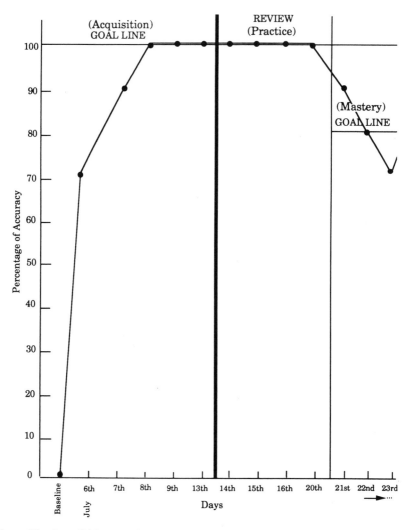

Figure 15.   Remedial focus: Arithmetic (e.g., multiplication and division).

The same graphing procedure can be applied to students' progress in learning the concept of a main idea. Here, keep your goal line at 100%. When the student with learning disabilities has reached the criterion or goal line in acquisition and then at mastery, you move to using two paragraphs in which the student with learning disabilities has to identify the main ideas, then on to longer and more complex single or two paragraphs and so on. You must match difficulty of instructional materials with the learning progress of the student with learning disabilities. Begin with the task demand of identifying main ideas in single paragraphs, then upon demonstrated mastery on the part of the student, move on to double paragraphs or more complex, longer single paragraphs that, like double paragraphs, contain more than one main idea sentence. Subsequently, as the student also reaches goal lines here, move onto using multiple paragraphs.

Inclusion

Readers, I cannot conclude the last chapter in my book without mentioning the term *inclusion*. I would be indeed remiss towards those of you who are student teachers or practicing teachers because this term is used by many school administrators, principals, and teachers.

Definition of Inclusion

The term inclusion refers to teaching all students in the same classroom, normally achieving students side-by-side with those with special needs. The putative merits of inclusion are (a) it fosters in normally achieving students acceptance and positive attitudes towards students with special needs; (b) inclusion ensures that special needs students receive instruction in higher-order cognitive skills instead of exclusively lower-order ones, such as drills in phonics or letter copying. Such exclusive focus on drill work has been found in resource room instruction (Allington, 1983; Palincsar, Brown, & Campione, 1993). (c) Inclusion profits both regular classroom and specialist teachers. Specifically, in coteaching within the same classroom in an inclusive school, the regular classroom teacher learns from the specialist teacher various cognitive and metacognitive strategies in promoting student learning. The specialist teacher learns about content instruction and management of the whole class. Thus, inclusion should bring about mutual professional growth in the two teachers.

Returning to the definition of inclusion, there are degrees of its implementation: Full inclusion and moderate inclusion. Full inclusion means including in the same classroom, children with low-incidence special needs. These would be students with severe handicaps such as severe mental retardation (Stainback & Stainback, 1992). Supporters of full inclusion are members of the Association of Persons with Severe Handicaps (TASH), and they seek radical changes that would see the elimination of special education (Fuchs & Fuchs, 1994). They also advocate changes to the academic curriculum, to give more weight to social skills training and evaluation. Readers, you must realize that low-incidence special needs students would not profit from the more typical academic instructions and evaluations of normally achieving students. They would more likely profit from training in social and life skills. It is fair to say that prominent professionals in learning disabilities (Kaufmann, 1994; Fuchs & Fuchs, 1994) who have analyzed astutely the concept, substance, and ramifications of inclusion do not agree with the goals and motives of TASH. Readers interested in how TASH threatens closer ties between special and regular education should read Kaufmann (1994) and Fuchs and Fuchs (1994). Moderate inclusion is inclusion of high-incidence special needs students, such as students with learning disabilities.

One last but important detail concludes the definition of inclusion. It concerns the fact that exclusive remedial services that we are familiar with, the resource rooms in the United States and the learning assistance centers in Canada, will no longer exist in an inclusive school. Inclusion means educating all students, normally achieving and special needs students in the same classroom! Where would the extant learning assistance teachers go? Before conjuring in your mind the gloomy picture of all those learning assistance teachers stampeding to collect UI (unemployment insurance), let me comfort you with this information: They are simply relocated from their resource rooms or learning assistance centers to various classrooms. Under inclusion or when their school becomes an inclusive school, they beget a new role, that of a coteacher with the regular classroom teacher in the latter's classroom. Yes, readers, they team teach with the latter. Implementing such teaching partnership involves much planning and prerequisite rapport between the regular classroom and specialist teachers. Here is one version of team teaching: The regular classroom teacher teaches content while the specialist teacher teaches cognitive and metacognitive strategies to enhance student learning. Both teachers attend to the instructional needs of all the students, but when necessary, the specialist teacher gives more help to high-incidence special needs students (e.g., those with learning disabilities). But she or he insures that students do not perceive him or her to be the teacher of special needs students exclusively. Sharp readers would have realized that I am illustrating coteaching basically in moderate inclusion. You are right! And you have shrewdly perceived or anticipated my position on inclusion.

Necessary Premises for Coteachers in an Inclusive School

The implementation of inclusion pivots around the coteachers in the classroom: the regular classroom and specialist teachers. They essentially hold the key to success in inclusion. But for them to produce this success, several conditions must be met. First, the partnership needs to be voluntary (Wade, Welch, & Jensen, 1990;

Meyers, Gelzheiser, & Yelich, in press). To this voluntary partnership they must add compatibility on at least four fronts: cognitive, philosophical, instructional, and affective compatibility.

To elaborate, on cognitive compatibility, coteachers must complement each other in their knowledge repertoires. Otherwise, they cannot capitalize on each other's cognitive strengths. For example, would a regular classroom teacher benefit from team teaching with a specialist teacher who is uninformed in cognitive and metacognitive strategies in reading comprehension and writing? On philosophical compatibility: They must share similar beliefs about and positive attitudes towards inclusion. On instructional compatibility, they would both be committed to the same instructional goals on enabling all learners to learn well in the classroom; and tacitly committed to mutual accommodation and trust. On affective compatibility, both teachers must have compatible personalities and working styles (Wong, in press).

Other conditions are in-service on team teaching, constant availability of consultant help in implementing inclusion, and time for planning and discussion of instructional responsibilities for the coteachers. Because teachers have not been trained to team-teach or consult with one another, continuous inservice on team-teaching is important (Robinson, 1991). Moreover, because inclusion is a new concept and procedure, teachers attempting it need ready access to help from school district consultants to resolve both expected and unexpected problems. This would mean regular rather than brief and episodic visits from the consultant, who has expertise on collaborative teaching and consultation. Last but not least, the school district must provide necessary funds to enable effective implementation of moderate inclusion, for example, coteachers need release time from teaching for planning moderate inclusion, and for reflections, discussions, and evaluations of their efforts in implementing inclusion.

Current Scene

Currently in British Columbia, Canada, there are some schools that have turned inclusive overnight without prior preparations and training of the school staff. We shall know in due time how students and staff fare in those schools.

What do teachers in general view and feel towards inclusion? Regular classroom teachers apparently desire a continuum of services for students; that means they would prefer to retain some form of pull-out services for special needs students (Patterson, 1994). Moreover, they tend to support moderate rather than full inclusion. They feel confused and somewhat alarmed at the prospect of being asked to implement inclusion in the absence of explicit procedural guidelines, preparations, and support (as delineated above).

Regarding research on inclusion, to date there are sufficient papers, in particular, papers in which authors argue, at times quite vehemently, either in support of or against full inclusion. Empirical research on inclusion that evaluates its impact on student achievement and social adjustments has just begun (see Zigmond & Baker, 1990; see special issue on inclusion in the *Journal of Special Education,* 1995, *29*(2)). We would need to wait for at least several years to see more published evaluative studies on the impact of inclusion on student achievement, especially that on special needs students. Apart from nascent attempts at evaluation of inclusion, there are some survey studies on teacher perceptions of inclusion (for example, Patterson, 1994), and actual detailed portrayals of specialist teachers assuming the new role of coteacher with the regular classroom teacher.

Future Needs

In this section, I raise issues that seek research or practical attention. First and foremost is the question on how to implement moderate inclusion effectively? I focus on moderate inclusion because it seems regular classroom teachers are uneasy about implementing full inclusion. In addressing this cardinal question, we must research *instructional variables* that promote effective and efficient dovetailing in teaching between regular classroom and specialist teachers. As well, we need to consider *logistics* such as the suitable number of specialist teachers in an inclusive elementary school of a particular size in order to render moderate inclusion possible and successful. Remember, these specialist teachers must simultaneously carry some responsibilities for a *parallel* pull-out system, because regular classroom teaches favor a continuum of services for special needs students.

Other issues that draw our attention include: The structural and systemic differences between elementary and secondary schools that make implementation of moderate inclusion in the latter much more difficult. Moreover, it bears emphasizing that high-incidence special needs students such as those with learning disabilities are typically 3 years behind in grade levels in basic skills in reading comprehension and writing when they reach high school. Their cumulative academic deficiencies pose serious barriers to their learning in a regular classroom. To integrate them into moderate inclusion needs much preparation and work (at least 2 years) by the specialist teacher (see Wong, in press).

Then we need to investigate the effects of moderate inclusion on the academic learning and performance and social attitudes towards the integrated special needs students among the normally achieving students. We should conduct observational studies and videotape their in-class interactions with the latter as they jointly participate in assignments and projects, and during recess. These investigations would provide data on whether or not in moderate inclusion, normally achieving students interact more and positively with integrated special needs students under constraints of assignments or projects and without constraint (free play during recess). Such behavioral data complement data on self-perceptions of social tolerance in normally achieving students toward integrated special needs students. Finally, evaluation studies are needed to address the effectiveness of moderate inclusion as an environment for optimal academic and social learning for all the students in the same classrooms.

REFLECTIONS

I view inclusion as a fragile ideal. And as an ideal, we should think of approximations of it in our attempts to implement it. It would be delusional to think we can attain it successfully overnight! Moreover, during these successive approximating attempts, the shape of the ideal may change (i.e., as we increase in knowledge about the parameters that govern its effective implementation, and the effects on student academic and social learning, we may refine the concept of moderate inclusion). But we remain clear and firm on our focus: Promoting and maximizing student academic and social learning on the one hand, and professional growth of the coteachers in the classroom on the other hand.

References

Allington, R. L. (1983). The reading instruction provided readers of differing reading abilities. *Elementary School Journal, 83,* 548–559.

Fuchs, D., & Fuchs, L. S. (1994). Inclusive school movement and the radicalization of special education reform. In J. M. Kauffman & D. P. Hallahan (Eds.), *The illusion of inclusion* (pp. 213–242. Austin, TX: Pro-Ed.

Kauffman, J. M. (1994). How we might achieve the radical reform of special education. In J. M. Kauffman & D. P. Hallahan (Eds.), *The illusion of inclusion* (pp. 193–211). Austin, TX: Pro-Ed.

Meyers, J., Gelzheiser, L. M., & Yelich, G. (in press). Do pull-in programs foster teacher collaboration? *Remedial and Special Education.*

Palincsar, A. S., Brown, A. L., & Campione, J. C. (1993). First-grade dialogues for knowledge acquisition and use. In E. A. Forman, N. Minick & C. A. Stone (Eds.), *Contexts for learning: Sociocultural dynamics in children's development* (pp. 43–57). New York: Oxford University Press.

Patterson, C. L. (1994). *Program evaluation of a collaborative consultative service delivery model for students with learning disabilities.* Unpublished master's thesis, Simon Fraser University, Burnaby, B.C., Canada.

Robinson, S. M. (1991). Collaborative consultation. In B. Y. L. Wong (Ed.), *Learning about learning disabilities* (pp. 441–463). San Diego: Academic Press.

Stainback, S., & Stainback, W. (1992). Schools as inclusive communities. In W. Stainback & W. Stainback (Eds.), *Controversial issues confronting special education* (pp. 29–43). Boston: Allyn & Bacon.

Wade, S. E., Welch, M., Jensen, J. B. (1990). *Alternatives to remedial and special education: The possibilities of collaboration.* Unpublished paper, University of Utah.

Wong, B. Y. L. (in press). The TEAM model: A potential model for merging special education with regular (general) education. In J. Lupart & A. McKeogh (Eds.), *Schools in transition: Rethinking regular and special education.* Scarborough, ON: Nelson, Canada.

Zigmond, N., & Baker, J. (1990). Mainstream experiences for learning disabled students (Project MELD): Preliminary report. *Exceptional Children, 57*(2), 176–185.

Author Index

Numbers in italic indicate page on which the complete reference is listed.

Subject Index

A

AAMR, *see* American Association on Mental Retardation

Academic learning disabilities, *see also* Academic subtypes
  as basis for Siegel's subtype classification scheme, 54–56
  as primary characteristic of learning disabilities, 41–42

Academic performance
  attributions made by learning disabled students for success in, 97–98
  discrepancy between measured intelligence and, 28
  failures in
    attributional patterns, 96–97
    characteristics arising from prolonged, 42–43
    effect on self-concept, 95, 126
    emotional and behavioral problems arising from, 45, 46
    eroding motivation to learn, 126
    metacognitive problems versus processing problems, 137
    requiring setting accessible goals in remediation, 219

knowledge of criterial task in enhancing, 122–123
  learning disability subtypes based on, 51
  of low achievers versus learning-disabled students, 46
  in metacognition, attributional patterns in, 126
  strategy instruction for adolescents for improving, 18

Academic subtypes, 51; see also Academic learning disabilities

ACLD, *see* Association of Children with Learning Disabilities

Acoustic confusability, 57–58

Acquisition, *see* Reading acquisition

AD, *see* Arithmetic-Disabled subtype

Adaptive skills, mental retardation diagnosis and, 44

ADD, *see* Attention deficit disorder; Attention disorders

ADHD, *see* Attention deficit–hyperactivity disorder; Attention disorders

Adolescents, learning disabled, *see also* High school students
  mathematics instruction of, 177–192
  metacognitive research in writing with, 136
  self-esteem ratings, 95
  social skills in, 111
  social skills training of, 115–116

C

S